LIGHTREADINGS

FILM CRITICISM AND SCREEN ARTS

CHRISDARKE

WALLFLOWER

LONDON

This book is dedicated, in memoriam, to Hrvoje Horvatic (1958–1997) and Marc Karlin (1943–1999): film-makers, elders and teachers.

CONTENTS

ACKNOWLEDGEMENTS

Thanks to the following who commissioned, edited and, in some cases, talked through with the author the material collected here: Leslie Felperin, Nick James, Philip Dodd and Pam Cook at *Sight and Sound*; Nick Coleman, Richard Hollidge, Mark Pappenheim and Chris Maume at *The Independent*; Gavin Smith at *Film Comment*; Amanda Sharp and Matthew Slotover at *Frieze*; Daniel Etherington at *Artists Newsletter*; Gareth Evans and Ben Slater at *Entropy*; Giles Lane at *Coil*; Steven Bode and Mike Jones at *Film And Video Umbrella*. Thanks also to the staff at the British Film Institute Library.

For inspiration, support and example above and beyond the call of film-going, special thanks to Jonathan Romney, Breda Beban, Keith Griffiths, Simon Field, Sandra Hebron, Helen De Witt, Karen Alexander, Deborah Salter, Sarah Turner, Peter Playdon and Dominique Hoff at L'Institut Francais. For scholastic guidance, Ginette Vincendeau and V. F. Perkins at the University of Warwick. For the Super-8 days, Pat Magnolo and Nigel Karikari. To a fellow hooligan for meaning, Jonathan Derbyshire. Also, to Jean, Sarah and Nathalie. And Nina.

21st CENTURY CINEMA:
CONFESSIONS OF A FREELANCE FILM CRITIC

When I was a schoolboy in the mid-1970s, I had a friend called Dan who's father worked as an art director at Pinewood Film Studios. One day, he took us both to Pinewood and we were allowed to ramble around the site. Dan and I gawped at the vast submarine bay stage-set constructed for the Bond film *The Spy Who Loved Me*. We played in a derelict Western landscape of clapboard-fronted saloons where we chucked rocks at each other that could be swatted with a stick and reduced to a mangled rubble of *papier-mâché* and chicken-wire. Dan's father showed us the models he was working on for a scene in the psychological thriller *The Medusa Touch*, in which an airliner would hurtle into a high-rise building. There were at least three different scale models, one each of the airliner and the building and all constructed with an incredible attention to detail. The largest, which was to be shot for the scene, had the airliner hung on a thread-thin system of strings and pulleys to allow it to swoop into the mocked-up skyscraper. All that care and small-scale artistry to go up in flames. Later that day, Dan and I were allowed onto the set of the first *Superman* film. The scenes being shot were interiors in the offices of 'The Daily Planet' where the mild-mannered, off-duty super-hero did his day-job as reporter Clark Kent. The set was a series of stacked portakabins giving on to an open lot where the city exteriors would be visible through the office windows. We were introduced to some of the cast and politely shook hands with the producer. Desks, coffee cups, people in shirt sleeves; to a kid it was dull enough to be a convincing office. What was outside was a lot more interesting. We were taken to a window and shown what the metropolis beyond the newspaper bureau was made from. Huge cardboard cut-outs of skyscrapers whose windows were lit from within by bulbs loomed behind thin sheets of muslin to diffuse the light from the arc lamps. On film, it would be all city-haze and distance. Looking onto the streets below, there was traffic and pedestrians. When we stepped down from the office we saw, close-up, that this vista was made up of tiny model cars running on tracks. The magic was intact even as the wizard was revealed to be made of cardboard and string, toys and paint, smoke and mirrors.

More than twenty years later, and during months spent in preview theatres trying to make out my own scrawled screening-notes from the glow of someone else's light-pen, I have found these memories have returned from time to time. But it only struck me in compiling this collection that, as a schoolboy, I was witness to a dying art, that of the model-maker and art-director, the artisan who labours over the background minutaie of a film. And if I think now about how one might film such reminiscences, they would have to start with the image of that derelict western-set leaching up from black-and-white. Then the image should hold on a sepia tone to match the ersatz desert of the tumbleweed back-lot onto which two young, late-twentieth-century boys would wander. Then flood it with colour as they crash their paper rocks through the thin walls of a saloon. Pre-digital days, the frontier yet to be breached. To make this scene today would require neither the labour to build the rocks, nor the lighting assistants to balance the colour tones. This backdrop of anecdote is hung with the dust and slight sorrow of childhood games played in movie-set rubble. But what games can kids play against a bluescreen? I am aware that there is a kind of unearned nostalgia at work in this vignette that comes of conflating my childhood with cinema's old age. In retrospect, visiting Pinewood was like a trip to a museum or an antiques shop, the Studios were a theme-park to cinema's past before I was even aware of its passing. There is also the temptation to retroactively cast these moments as the harbinger of a future as a writer on film and, to avoid yielding completely to *Cinema Paradiso*-style anecdotage, I should say that to claim a sense of memory – not matter how personal – is a way of getting to grips with the history of the medium that one writes about. Short-term cultural memory is both a symptom and a cause of cinema's impoverishment in the UK as well as further afield, and of much else beside. The cool consensus of cultural futurology that happily dispenses with so much of value from the past needs to be combatted. As a vast repository of history – its own and of the twentieth century – cinema is a good way of keeping one eye on the past's receding horizon as we are thrown headlong into the digital future.

In some respects, these are a dilettante's notes, the work of a freelance film critic. Which means that one writes without institutional affiliations, free of any responsibility other than hitting the deadline. Being freelance can mean the freedom to range as widely within the world of cinema as one wants. That's the kindest interpretation of the term; not entirely false but still a slightly starry-eyed account. But then, being 'freelance' is a quality of the modern condition, especially if one works in the media. So, there are 'up' months and 'down'; weeks when the workload appears inexhaustible and weeks when there's nothing on the desk and little in the bank. The freelance film critic has to be a journalistic scavenger snuffling about for the next assignment, an information-broker for cultural consumers, a content-provider on a short-term contract. The only full-time commitment is to thinking and writing about the moving image. Inevitably, the freelance film critic is both a bit of a generalist and something of a specialist. Someone with the right combination of knowledge and journalistic skill to turn a feature piece around in an afternoon – to think and work at speed, risking it at the borderline of glibness. I've written like this and there's no way round it; there's a satisfaction, a dispassionate pleasure, in knocking out a piece, washing one's hands of it and moving on to the next. The only sense of continuity that comes from this type of journalistic writing about cinema is in the process itself and the minimal professionalism it requires; the ability to find the spin, the angle, the hook with which to convince an editor to run with a piece. There's no shortage of full-time cultural commentators, many of whom are active across the media. So active, in fact, that one wonders whether they don't have their immediate families chained to the word-processor, churning out the throwaway scripts and knocking up the instant opinions. This form of commentary is the dominant way in which all cultural products gets processed for discussion and is entirely in keeping with a cultural economy in which everything with a high enough profile is seen as worthy of comment, if not analysis, and where the question of value is to be avoided. Such commentary almost always has the alibi of the 'now' and, being of the moment, it is date-tied, event-bound and frequently personality-led. The same opinions end up being espoused by different people about the same things. It's not hard for a film critic to be cynical about this economy of ideas around cinema as a game of metropolitan whispers, pre-digested *idées reçus* for the dinner-party circuit. 'Did you see so-and-so's piece in The Indy, today? Apparently, Spielberg's the new video-art.' To which, for some time now, I've found myself wanting to shout 'Sod so-and-so! Did you see the piece in this underground journal, eh? Apparently Spielberg's the new McDonalds.' I've found that one of the dangers of freelance film-criticism is the occasional lapse into cantankerousness. And slowly the invitations to the dinner parties disappear.

The material collected here represents seven years of writing about film and video and covers a fair swathe of the 1990s and, by way of introduction, it makes sense to describe the context from which it has emerged. The account is bound to be partial. Better to plot the coordinates and come clean than pretend to an impossible impartiality. The trajectory behind my writing hasn't been exclusively journalistic but has taken in a set of engagements with academic Film Studies and television filmmaking, curatorial work as well as scattershot involvements with screenwriting and production. So, it's been a matter of doing more than only write about film – often for the sake of earning a living – and being sporadically involved in the hinterlands around film and video. The result of these various engagements has been a desire to write about images beyond cinema 'proper', hence the inclusion of the writing in the section entitled 'Cinema Exploded' in which I've bought together some thoughts on video-in-film, art-video and the way in which cinema can be seen to play a major part in the contemporary art gallery. This material came out of 1990s Britain and is bound to be symptomatic of a moment in film culture. Except there's no such thing. Not in the sense of a culture than values cinema in the way that it's valued in France where various different perspectives can co-exist in a kind of antagonistic harmony and where the mainstream is defined by its oppositional voices and vice-versa. But to look to France from Britain when it comes to cinema can be counter-productive and induce the peevish sense that, as regards film, we're just not very interested. There's plenty of evidence to back this claim other than reprising the time-honoured laments about British philistinism versus French sophistication. The general acknowledgement in the UK is that film is business first and art later, if at all. So what is there for a film critic to do in such a climate? The answer is – write about it. So with this in mind, I've also attempted to provide a context for the coverage of French cinema in the second section here, 'Cinema *sans papiers*'.

One might reasonably expect that a critic has gained some formal knowledge of the art-form that they write about, that a literary critic has studied literature, an art critic has studied art history, and so forth. Not, it seems, when it comes to cinema. In fact, with journalistic criticism it seems wise to conceal such knowledge. There are precious few places in the UK where it's possible to write about cinema as though it were a medium that has a history – several, in fact – let alone to broach it as an art. It's not a gross mischaracterisation to assert that much of the criticism that's written in the UK is led chiefly by a film's content or by plot and character psychology. That's not to say that these aspects are negligible but rather that they are the orthodoxies of journalistic film criticism and I'm aware that many of the *Sight and Sound* reviews collected here are guilty of just such an approach. But this raises interesting questions. Perhaps there is something inherent and incommensurable in the task of *writing* to convey the experience of the moving image. That, in its very nature, film criticism is always several steps behind the fact of experiencing a film, marked by the need to try and catch up with the memory of its initial impact, what the American critic Manny Farber described as the 'struggle to remain faithful to the transitory, multisuggestive complication of a movie image'.[1] Whether one is writing a journalistic review or a critical essay just such incommensurability is at the heart of the act; it's still about the moment of an encounter between the writer and the film, between the screen and the notebook. Hence the time-honoured critical strategy whereby the writer extracts a moment from a film as representative of the whole. On one hand this can be a necessary editorialising, a pragmatic metonymy. After all, in film (as Victor Perkins, one of my former tutors, never failed to remind me) the relationship of the part to the whole forms the fabric of the aesthetic object just as it instructs the process of aesthetic understanding. On the other hand, unless it's interestingly developed, this strategy can become an easy way out of dealing with the greater complications of the film, a writer's set-up for a punchline or put-down. But it can also be a way of delivering to the reader a sense of the writer's encounter with the film and I have come to understand film criticism in terms of such encounters and with the sense that develops of what cinema is and has been, what it can and could be.

Looked at another way, of course, the critical faculty is a defence mechanism in such encounters – the critic is the observer of his or her own pleasure or offence, the voyeur of their own implication in the film's processes. But the film critic is also formed by the films they see (or, as the French critic Serge Daney put it with arch precision, 'the films that see us'). When confronted by week after week of unimaginative film-making, that same defence mechanism starts to find redeeming features in single elements: the quality of the cinematography, say (never mind the story), the presence of a favourite actress (never mind the direction). In other words, the critical faculty becomes a defence against fully accepting that the film is of indifferent quality. If one works as a regular reviewer this reflex is understandable. For the hardy breed of hack who has to sit, month in, month out, through the most lacklustre movies, the option of emerging from each press screening muttering to a colleague 'Well, hardly Bresson, was it?' rapidly fades. Back at the word processor one finds that it's easier either to turn out savage knocking-copy or to fall back on the 'favourite actress' routine than to do criticism. In this respect, I've been fortunate enough not to have had to do the grind of weekly reviewing. I have, more or less, chosen to write about films that are, let's say, hardly multiplex material. But that covers a huge range of cinema that might just as well not exist for most cinemagoers.

The critic can't do much to affect the state of distribution and exhibition in the UK which overwhelmingly favours the American cinema but he or she can, if so inclined, track a fraction of the 'world cinema' that makes it onto our screens. So, the material gathered here inclines to what used to be called 'art cinema', a now almost useless term that means 'non-Hollywood' product, while it also attempts to follow the mutation of the moving-image via video across cinema into the gallery and beyond.

The curious thing about the 'lack' of a film culture in the UK is that it exists, or fails to exist, alongside two other significant phenomena. The increasingly unforgiving market-led consensus as to what is and isn't worthy of attention and whose power equation can be broken down, not entirely cynically, as follows: marketing spend equals column inches. So the idea of the critic going out of their way to either find interesting work or heading up their weekly review with a low-profile European movie comes across, in such a culture, as plainly perverse. Allied to this is the explosion of academic courses in Film Studies with the attendant professionalisation (one might even call it the Taylorisation) of such specialised study. But does qualifying with a degree in Film Studies make one a film critic? It's a question that I've asked myself in assembling this collection because I'd hesitate to describe it as 'film criticism' in any academic sense but rather as the chronicle of a set of encounters between the screen and the writer, the image and the page. Perhaps this is itself a working definition of journalistic film criticism as an act that comes into being with the encounter and is continually shaped by it. I may arrive at the press screening thinking I'm a film critic but I always hope to leave with those instincts sharpened and challenged. I have to admit to what feels like an almost nostalgic idea of the value of criticism which comes in part from having emerged from a background in academic Film Studies but that also has as much to do with the value of the object of that criticism. After all, you only really critique the thing you love. I studied film theory and history in the late 1980s and early 1990s at two institutions, what was then The Polytechnic of North London between 1988 and 1991 and at the University of Warwick between 1991 and 1992. I then lectured at a number of institutions, including Warwick, for another three years in an increasingly part-time capacity as I began to publish more regularly. So there was an overlap between the period of my academic engagement with film and my journalistic criticism. Some of the pieces in this collection are definitely marked by Film Studies, both in the pragmatic sense of the discipline having enabled me to research and absorb material free from the short-term deadline pressures that come with journalism but also in the sense of being able to develop the interests that inform this collection and that remain with me. Hence my belief that there is some continuity across the academic and journalistic influences that inform this collection and that manifests itself most clearly in the concentration on French cinema and on video.

Cinema can open your mind – to painting, music, photography, literature. Engaged with openly, cinema inevitably leads one on to the other arts. My experience of academic Film Studies certainly had an element of this about it, but ultimately academia felt suffocating. I came up against what were either the limits of my intellectual stamina or the limits of the discipline. Possibly a bit of both. Teaching and studying film as an academic pursuit I found that, after a while, all roads led back to basic questions of aesthetics and philosophy, questions to do with art and judgement. I discovered that Film Studies, in the forms that I encountered it, could not fully accommodate the basic issues and principles that might be presented on a course called 'Aesthetics 101'. It's a truism to say that, in Film Studies, one is generally taught to 'read' a film rather than 'see' it. And the discipline has incorporated intellectual positions without their origins being acknowledged. As a student you're not generally given an idea of how the critical equipment you work with was developed. Certainly, you'll go back as far as Bazin. But talk about what it means to refer to Bazin as having a 'theological' view of art and you're sailing out of the waters chartered by Film Studies. To me this is a sign of its limitations. As a relatively young discipline, the turf wars that have been fought over academic legitimacy have made Film Studies vulnerable to intellectual fashion in ways that don't do the subject justice or deliver the academic rigour that a 'young' subject requires. To which charges any of my former colleagues in Film Studies could justifiably respond 'Sure, you were so concerned about the lack of academic rigour you became a journalist!' I can only offer the reasons for my going AWOL as being down to a combination of being temperamentally unsuited for it, the desire to see if I could actually hack it as a hack, and to write for a constituency beyond that of other academics.

One can, somewhat unkindly but not without justification, interpret much of Film Studies as a major displacement activity around the vexed question of value. In training critics of the visual, Film Studies has a responsibility to deal with questions of value, just as much as it has to provide students with the ability to read 'across' films. All of which boils down to an unwillingness to subscribe to the cliché that the young are supposed to be so much more visually 'sophisticated' than their elders. The logic of this frequently made assertion barely bears investigating. How can one be visually sophisticated without the knowledge of where such images come from? Without the ability to stand back from them, critique the values they embody, understand the history and technologies that enable them? So, it's less sophistication to my mind than saturation and surely this is a state that requires the armoury of criticism more than ever before? What's been developed instead is the passive and deeply consumerist reflex of irony. We know, for example, that advertising imagery is out to con us but we absorb its aesthetic values, as well as its far more insidious ideological values, and we do so with the defeatist world view of ironic detachment, only to discover that we embody the ultimate in patrician postmodernism.

All of the material collected here was written after the 'death' of cinema. Which is nothing more than a way of thinking about cinema's transformations and not the first time that the form's mortality has been announced. The transition from 'silence' to sound in cinema was the first such moment when the technological transformation of the medium saw the 'death' of a certain idea of cinema that, at the time, was encapsulated in the fluidity and expressiveness of a visual abstraction sacrificed to the demands of narrative. This time round, the idea of cinema's death has been one that's had plenty of time to develop. Ever since the advent of television, cinema has been in the process of being absorbed into a circuit of media that has inevitably transformed our relationship to the moving image. And while the language of cinema has been adopted by all the other moving-image media, the sense of what might be specifically cinematic about cinema is now hard to be precise about. Since TV, there's been video and now the digital image will further transform not only what is meant by the term 'cinematic' but also the access to cinema and the possibility of working with the moving image. It's hardly surprising, then, that a discourse of cinema's death should have built up around the anxieties concerning the technological, aesthetic and ontological nature of the medium. But such anxieties tend to be based around ideas of the 'specificity' of a medium - the way in which it differentiates itself from other media, a quality that the Soviets would have located in montage, for example. So there's more at work in the idea of cinema's 'death' than a form of pessimistic rhetoric which can either serve to mobilise a set of laments for the lost purity of the cinematic image or as a form of jubilant post-cinematic technological fervour. In fact, what we mean when we talk about the 'death of cinema' is actually the death of a certain vision of cinema, one in which the medium was accorded a degree of cultural authority and entertainment supremacy.

From its origins, cinema was described as 'an invention without a future'. Louis Lumière's statement is dosed with an enigmatic fatalism. Does its emphasis on a future in the singular now lend itself to being interpreted as accurate? That cinema, the bastard hybrid of other forms, could only have multiple futures in multiple forms made possible through its encounter with other technologies? What I'm trying to argue is that 'cinema' can provide a way of looking at the moving-image as it mutates across media. That, in approaching forms and styles as diverse as art-cinema and video and digitally-enabled films, it can still provide the perspective from which such transformations can be understood. So, 'cinema' becomes a way of interpreting these changes, a way of reading across film, video and other forms. By which I mean, to look within these forms for their residual cinematic qualities, what they've taken from cinema, how they relate back to cinema, what they might tell us about twenty-first-century cinema.

NOTES

1.   Farber, Manny (1998) *Negative Space: Manny Farber on the Movies.* Da Capo Press: New York, 9

WITTGENSTEIN
DIR: DEREK JARMAN UK 1993
ORIGINALLY PUBLISHED IN *SIGHT AND SOUND* APRIL 1993

SYNOPSIS

The young Ludwig Wittgenstein, announcing himself as 'a prodigy', introduces us to his Viennese family, describes the rigours of his Austrian education, and debates philosophical questions with a Martian. His intellectual talents take him initially to England where, at Manchester University, he studies Engineering. He quickly transfers to Philosophy at Cambridge, where he is befriended and encouraged in his radically original philosophical ideas by Bertrand Russell who, writing to his mistress Lady Ottoline Morrell, proclaims him the most gifted philosopher of his generation.

Wittgenstein leaves Cambridge to journey first to Norway where, in seclusion, he begins to write his 'Notes on Logic', then back to Austria where he informs his family he intends to volunteer for the army. His sister Hermione regards the decision as stupid; his brother Paul is encouraged to join up with him. During World War I, Paul loses an arm and Ludwig begins work on what will become the 'Tractatus Logico-Philosophicus'. On returning home he decides to delay his return to Cambridge by taking up a provincial teaching post, further angering Hermione who insists he is wasting his talents. Ludwig experiences the elementary school as deeply frustrating and is forced to leave after being accused of bruality towards his students.

His return to Cambridge is facilitated by the offer of a teaching post and the offer of a grant arranged by the Professor of Economics, John Maynard Keynes. Wittgenstein, however, finds it frustratingly difficult to relate his ideas to his students, and seeks solace in daily visits to his local cinema. He is accompanied by his friend Johnny, a young philosophy student who is also Maynard Keynes' lover. Wittgestein and Johnny begin a relationship, during which the philosopher attempts to persuade the student to relinquish his studies in favour of the more 'honest' world of manual labour. Russell and Keynes reprimand him for influencing a young man whose working-class background meant that his parents underwent great sacrifices to educate their son at Cambridge. Wittgenstein attempts to leave Cambridge to work as a factory labourer in Soviet Russia, but the Soviet authorities offer him instead a choice of two University posts. He returns to Cambridge in 1951 where he is diagnosed as suffering from cancer of the prostate. After a last voyage, this time to Ireland, he returns to Cambridge to die, where he is attended at his deathbed by Maynard Keynes and the Martian.

REVIEW

Originally conceived as part of a Channel Four series on philosophers to include films on Spinoza and Locke, *Wittgenstein* – shot in two weeks and for less than £300,000 – takes Jarman's trademark exquisite minimalism to a new extreme. The already reduced *mise-en-scène* of *Edward II* is here further contracted to a series of lush colour tableaux on a depthless pitch-black background.

This refusal of depth and, by consequence, of any realist visual perspective, while making a telling virtue of economic necessity, is a visual strategy in keeping with the film's agenda. For it becomes increasingly clear that at one prominent level *Wittgenstein* is a disquisition on the futlility of dramatasing the life behind the work, an extended Brechtian parody of biopic conventions.

The insistent dedramatisation comes across particularly in the film's use of spare sets and anti-realistic costumes, a single prop becoming the motif of a particular period or place. Vienna becomes a group portrait around a grand piano, and Cambridge a group of students seated in deckchairs around a blackboard – English gentleman-philosophers sunning themselves in the light of the imported mittel European eccentric. This latter-day Brechtianism might also derive from the fact that the film's first draft was the work of Marxist academic Terry Eagleton. In studiedly distancing itself from the Minelli/Van Gogh paradigm of the biopic (attempting at all costs to avoid becoming 'Lust for Logic'), *Wittgenstein* toys with the standard characterisation of the Genius as Romantic Outsider, personally and professionally misunderstood, and identifies melancholia and torment as the wellsprings of creativity.

Actors 'quote' their parts: Bertrand Russell played as an amiable lounge-lizard academic, Maynard Keynes as a stiff-spined manipulator of the Old Boys Network and Lady Ottoline Morrell as a brittle, charming bitch aristo – ciphers all. But the holding of the biopic tendencies at arm's length results in a curious lack of conviction. This conflict of formal strategy and latent content is particularly emphasised by moments when the starkness works towards either a visually expressive effect – the retreat to Norway given with beautiful economy, a single lamp and a dappling light on the boatside; or to accentuate a character trait – Ludwig's disastrous spell as a teacher at a provincial Austrian primary school, when the camera closes in on the faces of the impotently raging teacher and his terrified pupil. The fact that this sequence returns as the single flashback in the film, to accompany the philosopher's repeated, agonised refrain of 'Do you understand me?', is an internal recognition that it packs the film's only powerful dramatic punch.

Wittgenstein also represents a continuation of Jarman's highly personal Grand Tour through the mausoleum of European High Culture. But whether the cultural model is literary (Shakespeare, Marlowe), painterly (Caravaggio) or philosophical, Jarman's fascination remains in isolating and interpreting the marginal inscriptions of class and sexuality in culture. *Wittgenstein* is a further development of this sustained cinematic reading of cultural history 'against the grain'. The film's central thesis concerns the philosopher's masochistic faith in material reality, in the 'everyday' as superior to 'the poison of the mind' that his philosophical vocation represents and this is investigated partly through his sexuality, but largely through class.

Surprisingly, Jarman never really exploits the visual possibilities of the engineer-turned-philosopher's artisanal activities, which included building two houses. These adventures, as well as his Tolstoyesque communions with nature, his mistaken attempt to defect to Soviet Russia and his enlistment in World War I, are presented as acts of classic bourgeois bad faith, arising from a sense of class shame. He is accused of such by both Maynard Keynes and Russell, who are presented as comfortably socially integrated. This complex of issues cystallises around the character of Johnny, a rough trade cipher and the lover of both Maynard Keynes and Wittgenstein. The philosopher's repeated attempts to dissuade Johnny from continuing his studies in favour of the more 'authentic' life of manual work provokes both Keynes and Russell, who justify their angry disagreement in the name of the sacrifices of Johnny's working-class family. That the philosopher is simply unable to comprehend this argument demonstrates the extent to which each of the three characters regard Johnny as a *tabula rasa*: Keynes and Russell projecting onto him their own feelings and attitudes of, respectively, desire and paternalist patronage; Wittgenstein affectionately incorporating the young man into his own schema of self-hate and self-delusion.

The irony that the film constantly points up is that Wittgenstein's philosophical brilliance (the maxims here are deliberately tossed about like so many after-dinner *bon mots*) is less a condition of his acceptance in Cambridge than the tacit understanding that he is – however much he kicks against it – of the same class as Russell and Keynes. At the philosopher's deathbed, Keynes offers a poetic homily that collapses the contradictions of his character into two elemental images; Wittgenstein as constantly pulled between 'the ice world' of logic and 'the earth' of material reality. Abetted by its own icy formalism, the film never really touches the earth of its character.

SLIVER
DIR: PHILIP NOYCE USA 1993
ORIGINALLY PUBLISHED IN *SIGHT AND SOUND* SEPTEMBER 1993

SYNOPSIS

Book editor Carly Norris, recently divorced and looking to change her life, takes an apartment in a Manhattan 'sliver' block. Her apartment's former tenant, Naomi Singer, plunged to her death in mysterious circumstances. As Carly moves in, a young man offers to help her; he introduces himself as Zeke Hawkins, a tenant living on the top floor. Carly also encounters her neighbour, a friendly young English woman, Vida Jordan. At a business lunch, Carly's boss introduces her to Jack Lansford, a successful true-crime author who has apparently lost the will to write and who also lives in Carly's building. When she has returned home she finds she has received a gift of a telescope from a mysterious admirer.

Out jogging one morning, Carly is startled by Jack, and although she is irritated by his lecherous bad manners, they discuss the fate of Naomi Singer. On her return, an older tenant, university professor Gus Hale, introduces himself and tells Carly that she bears a startling resemblance to the dead woman. Shortly afterwards he is found dead in the shower of his apartment. At Carly's flat-warming party, Jack and Zeke arrive uninvited. Both men ask Carly out and she has difficulty in getting Jack to leave. Later she accompanies Zeke to his gym and learns that he writes video games for a living. They return to his apartment where they make love; he tells her that he owns the building and that he gave her the telescope.

At work, Carly receives Zeke's declaration of love by email, while her workmate tells her of an uneventful weekend spent with Jack at his ranch. Shortly after, Vida is brutally murdered in the building and Carly discovers Jack beside the body. Although arrested, he is released on bail and Carly finds him in her apartment where he attempts to persuade her that Zeke is the killer. Zeke arrives and diffuses the situation. He then shows Carly the control room of his video surveillance system, which allows him to watch everything that takes place in the building. Initially horrified, Carly becomes fascinated until she witnesses a young girl telling her mother of her father's sexual abuse of her. Zeke calls Carly at work to say that he has spoken anonymously to the father, hoping to end the abuse. Carly leaves work to rejoin him, and when he goes out to get food, she discovers old videotapes detailing Zeke's sexual relationships with the murdered woman. On his return, and terrified that he is the killer, she defends herself with a pistol as a tape of Naomi's murder unwinds before them. When the murderer's face is revealed as Jack's, Carly begins systematically to shoot out the video monitors and finally admonishes Jack to 'Get a life!'

REVIEW

It is tempting to imagine an early draft of *Sliver* having the working title of 'sex, high-rise and videotape'. The video voyeurism crucial to Steven Soderbergh's film, together with its seemingly inescapable corollary of sexual impotence, is relocated in *Sliver* geographically, to a Manhattan tower block, and generically, into the frame of an erotic thriller. And while this must be attributed partly to the twin presences of Sharon Stone as star and Joe Eszterhas as screenwriter and executive producer,

Sliver succeeds in being neither particularly erotic nor thrilling.

Where *Basic Instinct* was take-it-or-leave-it pulp, making a virtue of its bravura tackiness, Philip Noyce's film opts to play Stone in reverse, switching her former persona of polymorphously perverse hatchet-woman to that of a recently divorced 35-year-old book editor. But this casting against type goes no further than replacing the ice-pick under the bed with surveillance cameras concealed in the walls, and putting them in the hands of William Baldwin's creepily super-capable landlord.

The premise of Stone's character thus established (we know next to nothing of her former marriage except that it was unhappy), cliché follows cliché, from her emotional state being coded through her clothing – muted colours, soft fabrics buttoned up to the neck – to the sex games in a restaurant, complete with the regulation reaction shots of incredulous middle-aged diners. The dress that Zeke gives her is a metonymic echo of the totemic cocktail dress of *Basic Instinct*, bringing that film's Catherine Trammell firmly into the frame. But when it comes to portraying a woman-in-peril, Stone doesn't fit the bill; to adopt the Hitchcockian frame of reference, she's closer to Kim Novack's glacial unfathomability than to Tippi Hedren's tousled panic.

But the real star of the film is its video technology. From his state-of-the-art control room, Zeke, unknown to them, surveys the lives of the apartments' occupants, transforming his building into a high-tech, high-rent panopticon. Or, more accurately for Zeke, an interminable soap opera with as many vying narratives as there are inhabitants. Noyce's use of video flits between being palmcorder-pornography and everyday surveillance. The 'secondary soaps' that are the other lives of the block appear far more fascinating than Zeke's, but they are evoked only to be dropped or dealt with in the narrative equivalent of a channel-hopping flourish.

The four-act mini-drama of child abuse that takes place within the film via its video is the starkest expression of this tendency and signals one of *Sliver*'s major missed opportunities. Carly's growing fascination with Zeke's voyeuristic intervention into other lives is prevented from being developed by the increasingly irrelevant murder mystery. Ultimately the film becomes an unsatisfying Stone-Baldwin two-hander played out under the eye of the ubiquitous surveillance camera, with the video-soap back-stories proving potentially far more interesting than the formulaic thriller that houses them.

Sliver has a couple of interesting minor characters in Polly Walker's West End girl uttering profanities with perfect SW1 diction, out of her depth and up to her neck in Manhattan coke; and Keene Curtis' NYU professor teaching an option in 'The Psychology of the Lens'. A pity that he doesn't last through the first reel – *Sliver* would have benefited from a more equal ratio of old-fashioned psychology to balance out its high-tech lens fixation.

BLUE

DIR: DEREK JARMAN UK 1993
ORIGINALLY PUBLISHED IN *SIGHT AND SOUND* OCTOBER 1993

SYNOPSIS

A group of voices, Derek Jarman's among them, accompanies an unchanging image, a blue that fills the screen completely. These voices, supplemented and punctuated by sound effects and music relate fragmentary details of the director's treatment for symptoms of the HIV virus, the experience of slowly losing his sight, of meeting others undergoing similar treatment, of living with the virus. The voices also mourn the deaths of friends, consider the plight of those caught up in the war in Sarajevo and relate anecdotes of the travels in mythical lands of a character called Blue. Throughout the film the voices meditate on the colour itself, its place in nature and its spiritual qualities as well as bursting into bawdy song.

REVIEW

Blue is, quite simply, blue, and over the duration of Jarman's film the single colour makes of the frame a combination of canvas, mindscreen and eye. Blue is the colour of silence, subjectivity and suffering.

To talk of a film that has such a carefully worked and impressionistic sound-track as 'silent' may seem perverse, but it is a silence that is installed at the level of the image, a strategic silence that Jarman has chosen in response to what he calls 'the pandemonium of the image'. It is suitably ironic, then, that *Blue* should have been premiered at the 1993 Venice Bienale where it shared exhibition space with work by Oliviero Toscani, the photographer responsible for the shock-tactic images of the imfamous Benetton advertising campaign. Toscani and Benetton, and more specifi-cally the notorious campaign image that depicted a dying HIV patient surrounded by his grieving family, are perhaps only the most notorious examples of clamorous 'event-images' that serve ultimately to publicise only themselves, losing sight utterly of the specific realities from which they generate their self-serving controversy.

In the face of such images and their heavily mediated profligacy *Blue* retains the 'silence' of abstract painting – influenced notably by the monochrome work of the French painter Yves Klein, who himself died an early death at the age of thirty-four. But its silence is one pregnant with the subjective responses of artist and spectators alike. For the form of the work provokes an active viewing which the soundtrack has been designed to elicit – its combination of monologue and prose-poem, sound and music occasionally coalescing to lyrical, almost song-like effect. This property will be most fully accommodated by the simultaneous broadcast of *Blue* on Channel Four and Radio Three, the old Brechtian idea of 'separation of the ele-ments' receiving here a novel multi-media twist. The soundtrack works to spark the spectator's own images off the silent blue canvas; this is a film that takes place as much in the spectator's head as it does onscreen – 'an infinite possibility becoming tangible', as Jarman puts it in one of the monologues.

The asceticism of *Blue* appears to be a refusal of fictional melodrama and the auto-censorship inherent in demands for 'positive' images, at the same time as constituting a less-is-more *volte face* when confronted with the Benetton imagery.

But the film resists being reduced solely to the strategic dimensions of its form. This is because, abstract in conception as it might sound, *Blue* is also a resolutely personal meditation on life with, and approaching death from, HIV. Incorporating excerpts from the diary Jarman kept while undergoing therapy at St Bartholomew's Hospital, the commentaries return repeatedly to his treatment for encroaching blindness. *Blue*, then, is the colour of creeping sightlessness ('the shattering bright light of the eye specialist's camera [that] leaves an empty sky-blue after-image ... darkness made visible'); the artist's response to the infection's terrifying robbery of his faculties ('If I lose half my sight, will my vision be halved?'); and of suffering borne with remarkable humour ('The Gautama Buddha instructs me to walk away from illness. But he wasn't attached to a drip' – one of the several painful punchlines in the soundtrack's sombre comedy of infection).

The humorous sense of absurdity co-exists with stark anger, particularly directed at government-induced dependency on the work of AIDS charities, and tender laments for dead friends. The range of emotional responses emerges as a refusal to be consumed by horror and despair, a defiant gesture of freedom in the teeth of death. Likewise, *Blue* itself seeks to refuse the already clotted repertoire of images and scenarios resorted to in representing the unrepresentable. For eyes immune to images of agony, *Blue* fulfils the imperative to sometimes turn the gaze away and within, towards an image as 'silent' as that proposed here. But it is an image whose richness and beauty nevertheless make it impossible to forget that *Blue* is also the colour of a shroud.

MANUFACTURING CONSENT:
NOAM CHOMSKY AND THE MEDIA
DIRS: PETER WINTONICK & MARK ACHBAR USA 1992
ORIGINALLY PUBLISHED IN *SIGHT AND SOUND* NOVEMBER 1993

SYNOPSIS
Part One: 'Thought Control in a Democratic Society'
The work of radical US intellectual Noam Chomsky on the organisational structures and hidden agendas of the American news media, in particular their coverage of US foreign policy, is set in the context of brief biographical details: Chomsky's years as a revolutionary linguistic philosopher, his politicisation as a child of working-class Brooklyn Jewish parents during the Depression and his involvement in anti-war activism in the 1960s. These details are interspersed with Chomsky in debate with Michel Foucault, William Buckley Jnr, Bill Boyers, and with comments by Tom Wolfe. Chomsky's analysis of the American media is approached through his theoretical 'propaganda models', concentrating on their applicability to *The New York Times* and in particular to US coverage of the Indonesian invasion of East Timor; and on the relationship between the media and the state during the Gulf Crisis, at which time Chomsky asserts that the media were instrumental in going to war 'in the manner of a totalitarian society'.

Part Two: 'Activating Dissent'
Chomsky is shown in debate with the hostile Dutch defence minister Fritz Bolkestein, and his involvement in the defence of the civil rights of controversial French historian Robert Faurisson is examined. The activist-intellectual's role is explored in relation to the growth of independent media networks in the US, as are his thoughts on the role of the media in the election and inauguration of George Bush. Finally, Chomsky discusses his deep-seated libertarian socialist convictions.

REVIEW
In one of his 1993 Reith Lectures, 'Representations of the Intellectual', Edward Said devoted much attention to the linguist, political activist and media analyst Noam Chomsky as a model of the committed modern American intellectual. Listening between the lines, however, one would not have been hard pressed to detect the tones of pretender-to-the-throne of chief dissident. While this may be unfair to Said, Chomsky has undoubtedly become characterised, over the past twenty-five years, as the most turbulent priest in the American academy. Such a cult of personality is one way in which the power of ideas can either be transmitted or diminished, depending on whether they are deemed germane or detrimental to society. It is the media that create such personalities and that simultaneously encourage and restrict the flow of information and ideas. Peter Wintonick and Mark Achbar's *Manufacturing Consent* is about this process – exploring not only what information gets through and why, but equally what happens to those, like Chomsky, who attempt to use the media in order to condemn their power to create the 'necessary illusions' that maintain the political dominance of particular elite groups.

Five years in production, and a distillation of more than 120 hours of material, *Manufacturing Consent* is an ambitious *mise-en-scène* of ideas that, while aiming to explore something of Chomsky's life, is committed above all to his thoughts on the political economy of the media. Hence it avoids the conventional documentary features – 'Voice of God' narration, chronological exposition – and makes its *modus operandi* dialectical both in form and content. Chomsky is presented largely in debate and interviews, and the juxtaposition of those against whom he is pitted is judicious, telling and often entertaining. In an interview with the arch-conservative William Buckley Jnr he admits that he is wont to lose his temper on such occasions. The sleek Buckley imperiously warns him not to, adding 'If you did, I'd smash your face in' – Ivy League arrogance and casual WASP brutality mobilised to put the upstart Jewish subversive in his place.

Across numerous interviews it becomes apparent that Chomsky's strength as a TV performer is itself the paradoxical corollary to his intellectual status: marginalised but an agent provocateur by his very presence. In drawing the fire of Buckley and his ilk, he exposes the enemy's position and deals with it amiably; then he returns a fusillade of facts in a voice that sometimes approximates a James Stewart tremor, but that either puts his opponents on the defensive or sees them falling back on to weak institutional rationalisations (the latter tactic being particularly favoured by *New York Times* journalists, it appears).

However, Chomsky's fondness for facts and die-hard research-based empiricism sometimes appears as a refuge rather than a strength. This tendency surfaces most clearly in the film's second part, which broaches his defence of the French revisionist historian Robert Faurisson, impeached in France for declaring that there was no evidence to prove the existence of the Nazi death camps. In defending Faurisson's right to freedom of speech, Chomsky was accused of tacitly supporting his thesis and it is a credit that the complexities of Chomsky's position are explored in a film which, on the whole, accepts his media analysis at face value. But then it is hard, at times, not to – particularly when the case of the American media's silence over the genocidal invasion of East Timor by Indonesia is set against the clamorous outcry against the Khmer Rouge in Cambodia. These two examples of American news priorities are used to illustrate what Chomsky calls his 'institutional' analysis of the media, and what others – here, the Dutch defence minister and the writer Tom Wolfe – have predictably dismissed as conspiracy theory.

If the first part of *Manufacturing Consent* imaginatively illustrates selected Chomskyan ideas on American media, the second part looks for alternative media networks and finds a host of print media, local radio and TV stations that are resisting the *New York Times* and CNN hegemony. It also features an absolutely hypnotic sequence filmed at George Bush's Presidential inauguration ceremony. To the twin accompaniments of Laurie Anderson's 'O Superman' and the Presidential address, the camera threads through the crowds and away across the rooftops – Bush's voice never fading in its amplified metallic drone – until it comes across the backstreet cluster of satellite vans, as if to show us where the real power lies.

This is an unmissable and heartening film, if only for the wonderful spectacle of Chomsky live in a Laramie shopping mall on 'the world's largest point-of-purchase video-wall installation' and informing a radio presenter who insists on styling herself 'Jane USA' that: 'It's true that the emperor doesn't have any clothes, but the emperor doesn't like to be told it.'

KALIFORNIA
DIR: DOMINIC SENA USA 1993
ORIGINALLY PUBLISHED IN *SIGHT AND SOUND* APRIL 1994

SYNOPSIS

Writer Brian Kessler needs to honour a book contract and decides to undertake a voyage through several southern states of the USA, visiting infamous murder sites along the way. Accompanied by his girlfriend Carrie Laughlan, an unsuccessful art photographer, he intends to compile his written impressions with her images to produce the manuscript. In this way they hope to break out of their unfulfilling lifestyle and head for California. To subsidise the journey they advertise for a ride-share and pick up Early Grayce and his girlfriend Adele Corners. Unknown to the other three, Early, on parole for other crimes, is an amoral killer fleeing after the recent murder of his landlord.

At the first of the murder sites, the new tenants of the house that Brian wants to visit refuse him entry, while Early steals a bag from the house. Carrie's misgivings about Early mount after Adele tells her that he beats her, when he savagely cuts Adele's hair in a messy approximation of Carrie's own bob, and when he begins to express a sexual interest in Carrie. At the next gas station, short of money, Early stabs a customer to death out of view of the others. Stopping at a motel, Early and Brian go out to play pool while Carrie stays in with Adele to fix her haircut. At the pool hall, Brian is harassed by an aggressive customer, whom Early sees off with a brutal beating. Back at the motel, Adele tells Carrie how she was gang-raped at the age of thirteen and that her relationship with Early now makes her feel secure.

At the next murder site, Early gives Brian a lesson in gunmanship, much to Carrie's disgust. At another site, while exploring inside, Carrie and Brian argue. Storming out, Carrie observes Early and Adele in the car having sex and photographs them from a distance; Early notices her, smiles and carries on. At the next service station, Carrie sees a TV broadcast declaring Early to be a wanted criminal; when Early realises this he threatens her, intimidating her by torturing, then killing the attendant. Stopping at the next site, a disused mine-shaft, they are disturbed by the police. Early kills one of the officers, injures the other and attempts to make Brian kill the injured officer. Brian refuses, so Early finishes him off himself.

Early imprisons Carrie and Brian at the next house they stop at, and kills the elderly husband of the house. When Adele helps his widow escape, he kills her. With Adele dead, Early takes off with Carrie. Brian tracks them to an abandoned house on a former nuclear test-site and after a battle with Early, kills him and escapes with Carrie. They make it to California and move into a beachfront house.

REVIEW

In the light of *Kalifornia*, Jean-Luc Godard's recipe for film-making as being 'a girl, a car and a gun' now calls for one crucial extra ingredient: a primer in Cultural Studies. Dominic Sena loads up his road movie star vehicle so visibly with all the extra baggage that the genre is these days expected to deal with – identity politics, issues of sexuality and class – that its narrative motor can only splutter along under the weight. Not that Brad Pitt doesn't put in a show-stopping performance as Early

Grayce, the killbilly hick from hell, with an accent as thick as a mouthful of chewing tobacco and body language straight from *A Streetcar Named Desire* Brando.

But that is precisely one of the film's major problems. It's such an over-the-top performance that Early simply dominates the film and its other characters, making them little more than fellow passengers caught in his murderous tail-spin. At least in *Wild at Heart*, one of *Kalifornia*'s generic cousins, David Lynch gave his characters a kind of cartoon equality and dialogue that could have been sitting in bubbles above their heads. And, in *Reservoir Dogs*, Quentin Tarantino delivered dialogues whose geeky insistence on repetition and detail took them straight back to a sense of the everyday absurd. In *Kalifornia*, however, the dialogues and by extension the characters – except for Early, who doesn't so much speak as slobber eloquently – do not really go in either direction. Instead, a voice-over appears to serve the numerous functions of being simultaneously a homage to Terrence Malick, adding a writerly textual density and most nauseating of all, providing an Olympian moral perspective on matters of Good and Evil.

One of the reasons that *Reservoir Dogs* was dragged so often through the talk-show mud was because of its refusal to go for this easy option on violence, moral responsibility and point-of-view in film; it preferred to provide multiple points-of-view and hence a complex perspective. Not so *Kalifornia*, which culminates in Brian's sanctimonious 'them and us' discriminations by the time he and Carrie have reached their Californian hideaway. So much for the socially-conscious baggage; the film travels from liberal bad faith to Darwinian natural law with precious little pathos en route.

Stylistically, Sena can handle two registers of images, both of which he employs to the fullest extent – the insouciance of lifestyle-chic ads, where the camera prowls low through loft apartments just to make sure that none of that gorgeous diffused lighting goes missing in the shot; and the kinetic enthusiasm of the rock video register that shows up, predictably, during sequences involving speeding cars and fighting.

These approaches provide a sheen that serves to distract from the emptiness of the characters. But Brian and Carrie, Early and Adele go no further than being unsuccesful second-degree embodiments of ideas about the *recto* and *verso* of the serial killer: the real thing and its victim (Pitt and Lewis), and the rapacious media-voyeurism that pursues it, taking shape in word (Duchovny) and image (Forbes). Readers of *The Modern Review* will love this movie.

THE SHAPE OF PAIN: INTERVIEW WITH ATOM EGOYAN
ORIGINALLY PUBLISHED IN *FRIEZE* JANUARY/FEBRUARY 1995

'You have to ask yourself – what brought this person to this place?'

The opening words of Atom Egoyan's *Exotica* are a refrain that echoes across all his work with its cast of characters in professional, emotional and psychological extremes. The place in question in *Exotica* is the eponymous strip club at which Francis, the person in question, an auditor, is a regular client. To the accompaniment of the increasingly edgy patter of Eric, the resident DJ-cum-Greek chorus for the club's male habitués, Francis comes to watch one performer in particular, Christina, whose stage persona is that of schoolgirl jailbait. 'Five dollars is all it takes to have one of our beautiful foxes come to your table and show the mysteries of their world,' Eric drools over the microphone. Francis pays his five dollars, regularly. blank-faced, permanently rigid with shock, Francis watches Christina's table-dancing routine. Leaning towards her he whispers, aghast, 'What would I do if someone hurt you?'

The scene is archetypal Egoyan – sexuality, ritual, repression and the ever present threat of a transgression that borders on perversion and derangement. The setting of the club is central to the film, a literal *mise-en-scène* of voyeurism and deferred desire, as well as being the arena in which Francis's and Christina's private arrangements and the personal agony of Eric over the loss of Christina, his former lover, are played out. Within and around this setting are woven the other strands of the story that involves Thomas – a pet-shop owner who cruises the ballet for gay pick ups, operates a highly lucrative egg-smuggling scam and whose store is being audited by Francis – and Tracey, the daughter of Harold, Francis's brother, who pays Francis to 'baby-sit' at his house which is no longer a family home, his daughter having been murdered some years previously and his wife dead in a car crash.

The French have a pretty phrase for the condition of which Egoyan is cinema's foremost poet – *la déformation professionelle*. Which translated literally means 'job conditioning', the way in which the careers we pursue, the professional circles in which we move can warp and inflect our personalities. When applied to Egoyan's universe this phrase takes on another dimension that the director has consistently used as a dramatic principle – what happens when the *déformation* is also personal? What results in the collision of the two spheres of the social and the emotional, the personal and the professional, under psychological duress?

Egoyan's films often take place in strictly demarcated professional environments where this drama unfolds. In *Family Viewing* (1987) the action develops across a nursing home, a condominium and a telephone sex establishment; in *Speaking Parts* (1989), a hotel and a video mausoleum, in *The Adjuster* (1991) a censor's screening room and a motel supply the principal social locales. *Calendar* (1993) differs slightly, but only to the extent that the camcorder location footage of the Armenian countryside could well be interpreted as being screened in the apartment of the emotionally paralysed photographer (played by Egoyan), from which he is never seen to move. Defined in part by their jobs, Egoyan's characters seek to accommodate their secret lives and the frequently overwhelming weight of their emotional baggage within these contexts, but their equilibrium is shown to be fragile and breakdown is an implicit possible consequence of the strategies they choose.

AE: It's to do with boundaries and parameters and social codes. What types of behaviour are accepted in the context of a society? So you have people behaving in a way that if they exhibited or manifested those characteristics outside of their professions would be classified as pathological. But because some aspect of their job allows them to indulge or curb their impulses, their madness is somehow controlled or accepted. What you're seeing in all the films are the limits of that. You are seeing people who have been harbouring certain tendencies over a period of time in the guise of their profession and having these forces and pressures somehow building up beyond what those titles and positions can contain, and the crisis of that. So, in *The Adjuster*, you have Hera, a censor, who has been secretly taping pornography to show her sister for presumably what she believes are altruistic reasons and her being caught by another censor who has his own agenda and there's this strange, barbed conversation where they're both trying to explain each other's motivations and impulses and they're on completely different tracks. Or, in the same film, you have Noah, an insurance director, who is so lacking in self-esteem that he can only understand or feel a sense of personality when other people are projecting their need onto him. In *Exotica*, you have Eric, a DJ, who is so traumatised by the loss of his love that he has to deconstruct it, he has to break it down in the crudest, most obvious way and he's sanctioned to do that to an extent. But we see the result, as the club owner says, 'the customers are feeling uncomfortable'. So he's not doing his job properly, and at a certain point the characters' jobs are not enhanced by their neuroses and that sends them into a state of panic. The fact is that these people go out of their way to distort themselves into an unrecognisable form because they can't really address who they are.

For ten years Egoyan has been an auteur director in the fullest sense of the term – writing, directing and producing his films and working with a virtual stock company of performers that includes Arsinée Khanjian who, in *Exotica*, plays Zoe the club owner who is pregnant with Eric's child and Elias Koteas, Noah in *The Adjuster* and who plays Eric like a loping riff on De Niro's Max Cady, the same sense of grungy menace but here used to conceal a terrible emotional desolation. If the themes through which Egoyan approaches characterisation and milieu are clearly constant across his work, it is the issue of his filmic style and the orthodox conception of him as cinema's video *wunderkind* that has consistently marked him down as occupying a place at the experimental end of contemporary art cinema. The irony is that, with *Exotica*, the film that deserves to push Egoyan through to a seriously mainstream art-house audience, this feature has been refined down to a minimal but nonetheless telling place. Now that mainstream cinema has cottoned on to only the most limited of all the formal possibilities made available by video-in-film – 'You want voyeurism? You've got it. Just shove in a bit of footage shot off a surveillance monitor. You want first-person confessional? No problem. Give the second assistant director a camcorder' – Egoyan must at least have the satisfaction of knowing that, along with modernist supremos such as Godard and Wenders, he has been able to use video, that most anonymously corporate and quotidian of technologies, in a way that has been developed to personal, expressive ends in his films. Perhaps it was time for a change, time to confound expectations of him as a camcorder fetishist. *Exotica* connotes its thematic strand of voyeurism in ways other than the now conventional tropes of video. Two-way mirrors proliferate, as a motif established at the film's beginning in a customs hall through which Thomas is smuggling his eggs, and through-out the club sequences where Eric broadcasts on a radio microphone while observ-ing Christina and Francis's anguished therapeutic transactions of solace and guilty desire. After *Calendar*, in which camcorder imagery was deployed extensively and accrued a density that had as much to do with the film's use of off-screen space as it has with video imagery *per se*, *Exotica* uses one repeated camcorder image, that of Francis's wife and child playing at the family's piano, the mother with her hand raised to shield them from the lens that Francis brandishes.

AE: The value of that sequence is that it allows us some kind of entry into Francis' dilemma, which is that he has put himself in a situation where he's conducting a therapeutic relationship with Christina based on a need to deal with his grief at the loss of his daughter. He has projected the image of his daughter onto Christina and he plays out dark fantasies with her that are not even sexual. But it's because they are surrounded by a sexual context that he has inadvertently sexualised the image or memory of his daughter and is dealing with a tremendous amount of guilt as a result of that. The repeated image of the mother protecting the daughter takes on a very ominous tone and we associate this image with a sense of threat and menace. What we see at the end of the film is that its a very innocent and playful moment. So the technology allows us to reformat our own history to serve an emotional imperative and that's what interested me in this film and it's quite a different use of video from the other films where video becomes a way of filtering experience. The problem with film, as opposed to other art forms, is that you're not allowed to use devices that are closest to you for fear of self-parody. If you look at the work of artists like Cindy Sherman or Jenny Holzer, these are artists that have been able to repeat the central devices that have distinguished their careers without fear of it in any way hampering their developments. The themes that I'm interested in are pretty obvious but the devices that I use to explore these themes had to be modified. So, instead of a video image in the film you have a uniform, a schoolgirl's costume, and that becomes the filter, the image that you have to understand. Someone has transformed themselves into this myth, this object. Why? What is the nature and the history of that decision? What is being dealt with in that relationship? How is it being worked through? What is being seen ultimately? These questions are still being invited but not in so obvious a way as in *Calendar* or *Family Viewing*.

Perhaps because of their appearance of being overwhelmingly formalistic in concern, Egoyan's films have rarely been acknowledged for the powerful emotional pull they exert, and never so forcefully as in *Exotica*. It's a difficult issue to address because the emotional landscapes in Egoyan's films are not pretty and often, especially in the case of the character of Francis, come close to broaching taboos – in this case, incest and sexual abuse, as well as the run-of-the-mill darkness of male sexuality – that cinema generally prefers to render through manichean polarities. There are no such easy options here – although we are not dealing with the self-flagellating machismo evident in a very different but equally uncompromising director such as Abel Fer-rara. Egoyan seems less interested in the moral orthodoxies that coalesce around subjects such as pornography than he does in the personal and ethical trials of characters living in the thick of it and – God forbid – finding a therapeutic value in the perverse. But once caught in their circuits of solipsism and deadening self-pleasure, his characters are scrutinised with an understanding that it would not be amiss to call a sort of humanism. For, if it's a matter of catharsis – for characters and spectators alike, and most of Egoyan's characters are themselves spectators, often of their own lives – the moment of emotional pay-off in his films never acts as closure in the conventional narrative sense; the cases may well have been opened and examined but we know when we leave the cinema that the emotional baggage has still to be packed away somewhere. In *Exotica* there is a moment of such partial catharsis when Francis, lurking outside the club, is prepared to kill Eric. It transpires that it was Eric who, with Christina, first happens upon the body of Lisa, Francis's daughter. The two men embrace. As Egoyan observes, 'It's a simple gesture. But why was it so long in coming? The reason, when you think of it, is odd. At one point Eric says to Christina – "It used to be comforting watching you dance for him. It soothed me." Which is to say that, while they were in a relationship, to see Christina with Francis was a way of proving to him, Eric, how generous she was with her emotions. Watching her give a gift to him was satisfying to Eric and, in a way, he found that more compelling than breaking this wall and making contact with Francis directly.'

Intimately linked with these issues of character and motive, and certainly responsible for generating the emotional force of the film, is the question of structure. Of *Exotica*, Egoyan has written that 'I wanted to structure the film like a striptease, gradually revealing an emotionally loaded history'. But there's another, equally applicable analogy that springs to mind. The shapes of his films, particularly *Exotica*, is the shape of a pathological condition, with its rituals and compulsions to repeat, seen from without and steadily inhabited – the enigmatic and bizarre details are exhibited, developed, deepened and their underlying causes are revealed. Revealed perhaps, but resolution remains a long way off. *Exotica* closes with a version of the same image that ends *The Adjuster*, the family home. In *The Adjuster* the family home is a masquerade, a mirage in a wilderness, a show-home that at the end of the film, goes up in flames. *Exotica* ends on an extended flashback sequence of Francis and Christina before Lisa was killed. Driving her home after she has visited their house, he mentions that Lisa has told him that she, Christina, 'is not happy at home', the inference is one of domestic abuse. Like many a successful 'open' ending, it works – as Christina walks up the driveway, closes the front door, the camera rests on the facade of the house – because it gathers into itself the cumulative force of all that has gone before. But, as a flashback, it is part of an approach to structure that, whilst present in his previous films, is brilliantly worked through in *Exotica*. The closing sequence is a flashback apart, as it were, the main body of the film has a parallel structure that brings the past firmly into the present by gradually developing the scenes of the search for Lisa's body as the first meeting between Eric and Christina. Past and present are juxtaposed, contrasted and clarified cumulatively. Barely cued as flashbacks in the conventional sense, when the two tenses come together they do so with maximum impact and emotional force.

AE: In *Exotica*, we go into the flashback off of someone and we come out off of someone else. They're shared experiences. How do we experience and play back our memory? Do we see ourselves as a participant, or do we see it from our point of view? These are questions that I used to torture myself over. The formalistic concerns are something that if you indulge yourself in can become paralysing. I've been so self-conscious about the technique of the flashback that what has happened in the past has been characters playing flashbacks. Like in *Family Viewing*, the boy finds the videotapes, puts them in a monitor and we see these flashbacks. But they're cued, they're mechanical, they're in present time. Or, in *Speaking Parts*, watching the images of the boy in the mausoleum, we are aware of a process that is conjuring those images and a lot of that was largely because I never quite understood how to construct a flashback. The one time before that I used the technique, it was largely unsuccessful, the very important flashback at the end of *The Adjuster*, when you realise how Noah met these people he has installed in the motel. I found that so few people understood that as a flashback and most understood it as a state of mind. I thought that the reason so few people absorbed it as a flashback was because I was unsure of my use of this device. *Calendar* was so important for me, as a sketch really, because it taught me to be a lot less concerned and just to move and not to be so self-conscious about shifts in time. Based on that film, I was able to approach the flashbacks in *Exotica* with more confidence and not to worry about cueing them. I was so inspired by Tarkovsky's book *Sculpting in Time* – that's what cinema is about. There are two things that my generation is really suspicious about and they're both devices that are really important in cinema. One is the flashback and the other is the voice-over. The hair on my neck immediately bristles when I hear the words voice-over because I immediately think of it as a compromise, that somehow it's an attempt to explain what should be evident. The same goes for the flashback, it somehow suggests that the narrative structure hasn't conveyed enough. Yet it's absurd because both are devices that can be poetically employed.

If Egoyan's concerns with filmic structure as a means of conveying the working of the memory has been distilled away from the use of video towards a more fluid, less recognisably mediated form, another equally characteristic stylistic element that attains a level of extremely refined effect in *Exotica* is camera movement. I remember that the first time I saw *The Adjuster* being struck by the meditative pace that gives the film its slow-burning strength. Certainly, in *Exotica*, this has as much to do with editing and the overall structural conception but the movements have to match from shot to shot and across the sequences. Egoyan discussed the approach to the camera method he has consistently applied throughout his films with Paul Virilio in an exchange of videos transcribed in the only available monograph of his work (Carole Desbarats (ed.) *Atom Egoyan*, Editions Dis Voir, 1993), where he commented, 'In all my films there are very important characters, or even a central character, who is missing and I choose the camera as being the embodiment of that missing person'. In *Exotica*, the strategy has a clear application.

AE: The missing person is the daughter. In my earlier films it was explicit. There are actual moments when people confront the lens with the fear and anticipation with which they would regard someone they were avoiding or looking for, and it was a very self-conscious device. Now I think it's in my mind when I'm choreographing a scene. Someone is watching these people going through this process, the spirit of someone who has been removed yet who is intrinsic to their happiness. Lisa was someone Christina could talk to and the first witness to Christina's abuse. I was aware when choreographing these scenes that this is Lisa watching them. Now, Lisa has no place in Thomas's story, or even in Eric's story, but that idea of my position behind the lens is very important to me while I'm making a film as somehow being a means of accessing someone who is not in the central drama but who binds it all together. Because there is an overall attitude to the camera as an observing force contained to character this gives me more freedom in the cutting where I'm able to cut from one sequence to another and very often the camera is moving at the same pace and when you watch the finished result it seems extremely elegant and it's just the result of having this consistent attitude and not as in most films, going in for the attempt to cover the action from as many different angles as possible so that it can be moulded later on, which I find really distressing and quite savage as an approach.

The paradox that often occurs in a filmmaker's career is that by the time they produce the work that most ably condenses and displays their essential thematic and stylistic concerns, they already have a body of perhaps more marginal work behind them. *Exotica*, as Egoyan's 'breakthrough' film, should announce him to a wider audience even while the director himself is fully and perhaps uncomfortably aware of it marking a transitional moment in his career.

SUTURE
DIRS: SCOTT McGEHEE & DAVID SEIGEL USA 1993
ORIGINALLY PUBLISHED IN *SIGHT AND SOUND* FEBRUARY 1995

SYNOPSIS
Clay Arlington arrives in Phoenix to meet his half-brother Vincent Towers whom he encountered at the funeral of their wealthy and powerful father Arthur, who was murdered. Vincent is suspected of the crime. Inviting Clay to stay at his home, Vincent informs him that he has to leave overnight on business and asks him to drive him to the airport. The car is rigged to explode and, before departing, Vincent triggers the car bomb. Dressed in Vincent's clothes and carrying identification Vincent has planted on him, Clay survives the explosion but suffers from complete amnesia. Requiring extensive plastic surgery, Clay is remade as Vincent. Two specialists treat him; plastic surgeon Dr Renée Descartes and psychoanalyst Dr Max Shinoda. Shinoda begins to discover elements of a personality that do not tally with Vincent's cold and anti-social reputation.

The Phoenix police continue their murder investigation, questioning a witness who claims to remember clearly the killer's face. The opportunity to identify Vincent must wait for his plastic surgery to be completed. Meanwhile, Clay begins to recall details of his past in dreams and flashbacks which confirm Shinoda's suspicions that Vincent Towers is someone completely different. On leaving hospital, Clay moves into Vincent's house and remains haunted by dreams of an impoverished crane operator and visualises a dusty, rundown town. Under analysis, it transpires that the place he remembers is called Needles. Accompanied by Descartes, who is in no doubt that he is Vincent Towers, Clay visits Needles but finds it ugly, depressing and without memories. The two of them spend the night together in a motel.

The police call in Clay for the line-up but the witness cannot identify Vincent and the investigation is terminated. Clay is suspicious that he is still being tailed, but on telephoning the police, is assured that they no longer suspect him. The phone call triggers his memory of the call that Vincent made to him in the car before the explosion. It is Vincent who has returned to kill Clay, who stands to inherit their father's wealth. Vincent breaks into the house but is shot by Clay.

In their final session, Dr Shinoda attempts to persuade his patient to acknowledge his true identity as Clay Arlington: 'I am Vincent Towers' is his obstinate response.

REVIEW
Suture, the noun, comes with three definitions; one each from medicine, Lacanian psychoanalysis and 1970s French Film Theory. *Suture*, the film, deploys all three in a generic cocktail of paranoid thriller, film noir, and American avant-garde. The first definition simply means the stitching together of a wound. The second concerns the relationship between the individual subject and its place within language and derives from Lacan's celebrated dictum that 'the unconscious is structured like a language'.

The psychoanalytic idea of 'suture' refers to processes by which the subject is 'stitched' into language or a chain of discourse which defines and is defined by the work of the unconscious. In the late 1960s theorist Jean-Pierre Oudart applied this idea of suture to cinema contending that the psychic processes which constitute subjectivity are reiterated in film by operations such as shot/reverse shot which bind the spectator into the coherence of the filmic system. If the unconscious is structured like a language, then one such language that discloses this structuring is cinema.

While it is perfectly possible to appreciate McGehee and Seigel's film knowing nothing of psychoanalytic film theory, the filmmakers have clearly constructed their film to accommodate several layers of pleasure and interpretation. One such level is that of *Suture*'s genre and tone. Generically, the film sits somewhere between Hitchcock's *Spellbound* – which the filmmakers acknowledge as the source of the basic story of an amnesiac suspected of murder, and John Frankenheimer's *Seconds* in its concern with an identity transformed by plastic surgery. In tone, however, *Suture* veers dangerously close at times to *Twilight Zone* parody spookiness. This impression is reinforced by voice-over interjections at the film's beginning and end by Freudian analyst Dr Shinoda – whose office is emblazoned with two huge Rorschach inkblots. Presenting the psychoanalyst's attempt to delve into Vincent/Clay's authentic personality in semi-parodic terms makes it as doubtful a method of evaluating the truth as those represented by police officer Lt Weismann and plastic surgeon Dr. Renée Descartes. The police case against Vincent/Clay rests on the testimony of a partially blinded eye witness who must identify someone who has undergone extensive plastic surgery. The futility of such an investigation is ironically juxtaposed with the plastic surgeon's devotion to the pseudo-science of physiognomy which, resting on Renaissance ideals of beauty, declares that personality is legible through physical features. That the plastic surgeon should be called Descartes screams out that *Suture* has intentions beyond the capable remodelling of genre premises, it wants to deconstruct their underlying philosophical presuppositions.

Conceptual ambition is matched by formal audacity – Clay, Vincent's half-brother is played by Dennis Haysbert, a black actor whose blackness is never acknowledged. It acts as a distanciation effect; while the characters don't see Clay as a black man, we do. It's a nice idea but, in execution, a host of implied ideological problems remain unaddressed. It also returns us to the notion of suture because, as spectators, we are constantly aware of the illusory, incomplete nature of identification with screen characters. In this sense, it is a winning strategy, working with the film's conclusion that Clay, by denying his real identity, is living a lie with potentially disastrous psychological repercussions.

Suture also brings this formally disorientating approach to bear on the editing, where an apparently normal continuity cut within a scene will jarringly displace us from one space to another, and, in the use of overlapping sound where one scene intrudes aurally into another, each technique serving to disallow the easy 'suturing' of the spectator into the film. Vincent's pad, a plush modernist rotunda, is as half-unpacked and as yet unlived-in as the shifting personality of Clay/Vincent. Clay's memory returns in flashes and dreams, triggered by everyday events such as a phone call to the police after they have concluded their investigation. Vincent returns like a repressed memory, but armed with a gun, and he has to be denied by Clay, who kills him by shooting off his face. The call to the police that Clay makes revives his memory of the call that Vincent made to him on the car phone just before the explosion. Crucially, this moment has the cumulative effect of Clay's total remembrance of his past – from here on in, the implication is that Clay is fully conscious of his imposture.

In the light of this, the film's closing images – a series of still photos of Clay and Renée holidaying, socialising and playing the beautiful couple – take on the pathos of a life lived purely as social performance and surface appearance, but whose reality speaks of entrapment, imprisonment and psychic entropy.

DUMB & DUMBER
DIR: PETER FARRELLY USA 1994
ORIGINALLY PUBLISHED IN *SIGHT AND SOUND* APRIL 1995

SYNOPSIS

Lloyd Christmas, a hapless Rhode Island limousine driver, picks up Mary Swanson, an attractive fare. Taking her to the airport, from which she is en route to Aspen, Colorado, Lloyd tells her the story of his hopeless life. He notices that she has left her briefcase in the lobby and rushes to retrieve it for her, while his limo is towed away, for which he is sacked.

Harry Dunne, a dog groomer, has a van customised to resemble a giant dog. Having lost his job on the same day as Lloyd, Lloyd enlists Harry and his 'Mutt Cutts' van to drive the pair to Aspen with the intention of reuniting Mary with her brief-case and with the hope of following up his own romantic interest in her. Unknown to either Lloyd or his room-mate Harry, the briefcase is stuffed with dollar-bills, a ransom for Mary's husband who has been kidnapped by Nicholas André, a family friend of Mary and her extremely wealthy parents. Now, having had the ransom snatched from under their noses by Lloyd, André's thugs, Joe Mental and J. P. Shay, are in pursuit of Lloyd and Harry. On the road, Lloyd and Harry encounter numer-ous misadventures, including run-ins with a vicious gay trucker and a Pennsylvania State Trooper. Joe Mental is finally and accidentally despatched after a red hot chilli pepper-eating contest with the pair.

Finally arriving in Aspen, they fight over the briefcase, knocking it open and discovering the money. They go crazy with the money, renting a Presidential suite, buying tasteless new clothes and a Lamborghini Diabolo, dutifully replacing each dollar bill with an IOU note. They meet up with Mary at a gala for The Aspen Preser-vation Society to benefit the Icelandic Snow Owl, hosted by her parents and André. Romantic confusion ensues, in which Harry, rather than Lloyd, takes up with Mary. Lloyd, jealous, spikes Harry's drink with laxative in order to ruin his planned evening with Mary and arrives to tell her that the briefcase is in his hotel room. They go back to the hotel room together, only to be captured by André. Harry arrives in the nick of time, kitted out with a bullet-proof vest. He and the FBI save the day. Mary and her husband are reunited. Lloyd and Harry hit the road.

REVIEW

Dweeb, dork, geek, nerd: American English luxuriates in its vocabulary of the dumb, and judging from its recent output in the same register, so does the American cinema. So *Dumb & Dumber* arrives wearing its no-brow credentials on its sleeve and inherits from a rich, if hardly reputable, vein of dumb that stretches in various generic directions, including the *National Lampoon* series and the *Porky's* movies. Noticeably inherited from these particular motherlodes of low comedy is *Dumb & Dumber*'s taste for frat-house scatology, showcased in re-runs of ye olde piss-for-beer and laxa-tive micky-finn routines – the latter being played out with bowel-contorting insist-ence by Daniels.

But it is Carrey who is on show here, with markedly less success, however, than in either of his two previous outings. In *Ace Ventura* there was at least a certain brash and breezy novelty to the comedian's manic mugging, while *The Mask* took Carrey's contortions to an inspired yet logical extension with its computerised prostheses. However, in this vehicle, in the combination of his toothy gurning and pie-bowl hair-cut, Carrey seems stuck in atavistic Jerry Lewis mode. Interestingly, though, Carrey remains surrounded by animals; there has always been a slightly other-than-human quality to his gymnastic facility for shape-changing and conceptual free-forming. More evident in this film than the others is the lining of malevolence to Carrey's comedic persona, a feature hopefully to be more fully exploited in his forthcoming role as the Riddler in the upcoming *Batman* sequel. One wonders how soon it will be before someone tempts him along the Hollywood-seeks-cred path of a Shakespearean role – following Mel Gibson and Keanu Reaves, why not Carrey? – he might make a fascinating *Richard III*.

It seems that the genre of dumb has, like so much else, suffered from the Gump effect. The publicity material for *Dumb & Dumber* has Lloyd and Harry sitting, à la Forrest, on a bench, staring vacantly, expectantly, utterly gormlessly at something. So, while *Dumb & Dumber* promises a parodic take on the culture of dumb – as well as on the culture that seems increasingly inclined to face up to its internal horror and anomie only through dazed and confused slacker-chic or through a more perni-cious glorification of freedom-through-lobotomy – it doesn't deliver on the promise. What it does offer, in terms of the casualties of parody along its narrative arc, is an almost-comedy of confusion, road-movie and our boys at large in Aspen, Colorado, playground of the rich and famous. Laughs are, it has to be said, few and far between, although, at the packed preview screening, it was evident that Carrey has a sympa-thetic audience that laughs as much in sympathy with his character's misfortunes as at the performer's virtuosity.

Dumb & Dumber is not a step forward for Carrey, but it provides more depressing evidence that the Dumb Club is growing; with Wayne and Garth, Beavis and Butthead, Bill and Ted now being joined by Lloyd and Harry. Maybe the whole family could be united in some final carnival (and the comedy theorists will lose no time in making excuses for this movie by recruiting Bakhtin to its defence) of self-immolating cretinism.

INTIMATE WITH A STRANGER
DIR: MEL ROBERTS USA 1994
ORIGINALLY PUBLISHED IN *SIGHT AND SOUND* AUGUST 1995

SYNOPSIS
Los Angeles. Jack Hawkins, a former professor of philosophy, makes a living as 'femme-service' – he receives women at his home who pay him for sexual services. He successively encounters a variety of women but is doing the job as a way of escaping from the academic lifestyle he associates with his former girlfriend, Michelle, whose photograph he keeps in his bedside drawer along with the cash he earns from his clients. Their relationship having collapsed some time ago, Michelle unexpectedly calls on Jack and a row ensues. They part acrimoniously. While he continues in his work they nevertheless meet again, first sharing a happily intimate meal together. One day Michelle arrives unexpectedly while one of his clients is still in his bed. Michelle storms out. A first-time client, Ellen, calls and is very nervous. She relates her misgivings over coming to him which revolve around the tragically early death of her husband. Jack's misgivings about his profession harden and are further strengthened by an emotionally wearing and potentially dangerous encounter with a client named Vicki, who abuses him and threatens him with a gun. Jack resolves to make a fresh start. Packing up his possessions he tries to call Michelle, but discovers her line to be dead. He drives to the beach front where he locates her and explains his decision and informs her of his new teaching post. He tells her he loves her and they are reunited.

REVIEW
'You can be intimate with a stranger but a stranger to intimacy' runs one of the smug little formulae around which Mel Roberts' film weaves its story of an emotionally damaged ex-philosophy professor, his relationship in tatters, who sets up as 'femme-service', in other words as a gigolo who specialises in stay-at-home making-out. The promise the film holds of exploring philosophy in the bedroom, of linking the carnal and the cerebral, only provides a 'sensitive guy' veneer to the character of Jack Hawkins. Roderick Mangin Turner – who also co-wrote and produced the film – is helpfully built like a Chippendale (and has less emotional range than the eponymous furniture), his good looks being dredged up from the primordial soup of the rock-star gene pool – think Sting meets Michael Hutchence (plus ponytail). The film is really less concerned to offer insights into male vanity and the supposedly traditionally male ability to disengage emotion from sex than it is to provide Jack as a device for a variety of walk-through cameos of female desire.

As one would expect of a film that takes its cues for characterisation and tone from somewhere between an Oprah-style talking cure and a 'Cosmo'-confessional we have a parade of female 'types' rather than characters: Summer, the teenager wanting to lose her virginity with an experienced older man, rather than risking 'getting diaper rash from the boys I know'; Barbara, the slightly jaded woman-of-the-world with a healthy interest in sex toys; Carol, the Jewish housewife, who agonises about her husband, her kids and her cellulite, wanting to rediscover sex as 'an emotionally affirming experience'; Ellen, having lost her husband through a terminal disease, who craves companionship without emotional commitment; Vicki, the 1980s career woman, with neither the time nor the inclination to do anything other than pay for the attentions of someone like Jack. Then there's Michelle, the ex-girlfriend who returns to give their relationship a second chance, the breakdown of which Jack uses to justify his dropping-out of academia and turning-into Mr Stud-U-Like. That the film's narration does nothing to qualify or even complicate this simplistic piece of motivation indicates the ambitious level of character psychology at which it is happy to operate, but it also gives the preordained sense that the couple will be reunited. Jack's various women thus become little more than a series of cumulatively decisive encounters en route to inevitable reconciliation with Michelle and blessed narrative closure.

The film's major failing is the complacency at the level of its founding premise. It asks first that one accepts an ex-philosopher-turned-gigolo and then almost immediately sets out to tell why he took this bizarre career path. And that's it. Nothing else happens. A few women turn up, do their cameos, give Jack the impression that, hey, maybe he's in the wrong line of work after all and, what the heck, why not make it up with Michelle rather than having to make it with women like Ellen – whose tragic story softens even the self-involved heart of Jack the master-narcissist – and Vikki – 'one hard-boiled bitch ', as he charmingly describes her and who sets about wrecking his apartment before pulling a gun on him. The message being – all work and no play makes Vikki a man-hating psychopath. When not daubing its characters in such lurid cartoon-camp strokes, the film serves them up as TV talk-show portions of time-managed sexual hysteria. From its complacent premise comes the film's torpid sentimentality – everything works out fine for everyone and hence fails to engage at all. One gets the feeling that the slightly risqué element of Jack's sanctioned promiscuity – rendered respectable in the film's terms by the fact that it's just a job – works in a curiously puritanical way to try and mask the overridingly saccharine heart of the film. Jack's gigolo-act, the film infers, shouldn't be seen as an emotionally-scarred male taking a holiday in misogyny but, rather, as altruism: he's a one-man charity, a fucking therapist. Although, at times, the film clearly wishes to masquerade as an examination of the current state of sexual mores it has none of the hard-edged introspection that characterises more successful takes on the same subject such as *Carnal Knowledge*, *Looking For Mr Goodbar*, *American Gigolo* and, more recently, *Exotica*. *Intimate with a Stranger* is neither erotic nor is it really about sex; it's about sex as the consummation of talk-as-foreplay.

The static staging doesn't help matters – the action rarely leaves Jack's pokey boudoir except for some desultory motorbiking around the LA beach front shot in an airbrushed *Baywatch*-style heat haze sheen. Nor does the often fabulously risible dialogue: 'I don't recall sending you an invitation to come back into my life', hisses Jack to Michelle. Without any stand-out performances – the best here being Amy Tolsky's Bette Midler-ish vivacity as Carol – and lacking any sense of visual bravura or any agenda other than middlebrow sentimentality, *Intimate with a Stranger* is, well, a limp experience.

DEAD PRESIDENTS
DIRS: ALBERT & ALLEN HUGHES USA 1995
ORIGINALLY PUBLISHED IN *SIGHT AND SOUND* SEPTEMBER 1995

SYNOPSIS

North East Bronx, 1968. Anthony Curtis, an eighteen-year-old black man, does his milk-round with his friends Skippy and José. They debate their futures: go to college or serve in Vietnam? On his way home, Anthony calls at his girlfriend Jaunita's house.

Spring, 1969. Anthony is running numbers for Kirby, a pool hall owner. Cowboy, a hustler, challenges Anthony to a frame of pool. Kirby bets on Anthony, who wins. Cowboy scars Anthony's face with a knife. Anthony, his parents and his brother Edward, a graduate student, talk about his options. To his mother and brother's disappointment Anthony tells them he intends to serve in Vietnam.

Graduation night, 1969. At a party, the trio discuss their future: Skippy wants to be a pimp, José and Anthony have been called up. Jaunita tells Anthony that she has the house to herself for the night. They go back and make love. She asks him if he will marry her on his return from Vietnam. Jaunita's mother returns home in the early morning and Anthony has to hide in the back garden before fleeing across the neighbouring gardens.

Vietnam, April 1971. Anthony is serving with Skippy in a reconnaissance platoon pinned down under enemy fire. Dougan, the platoon leader, calls for a napalm strike to free their position. Dougan then commands them to investigate the enemy position for intelligence papers. One of their number, Cleon, hacks off the head of a dead Vietcong as a souvenir. At base camp, Anthony tells Skippy that Jaunita's had his daughter. On the next mission, Cleon is forced to bury the putrefying head and insists that he is burying their good-luck charm. Following one of their team into the bush they come across his disembowelled body and a Vietcong propaganda note targeting black servicemen. Anthony carries his wounded comrade, who insists that he put him out of his misery with a shot of morphine, which Anthony does. Dougan is killed in an ambush. Six months later, Skippy is sent home.

North East Bronx, 1973. Anthony returns home to find Skippy addicted to heroin. Visiting Kirby's poolhall he discovers José who has served in Demolitions. Anthony visits Jaunita's house where Delilah gives him a Black Power lecture. Jaunita returns home with his daughter, Sarah-Marie. Sitting in a car later that night, Jaunita chats to a local gangster, Cuddy. Jaunita and Sarah-Marie go back to Jaunita's new flat, which is infested with cockroaches. Back at Kirby's, Cowboy taunts Anthony, who beats him up. Five months later, Jaunita is pregnant, Anthony is drinking heavily and working in a poorly paid job. Anthony, Kirby and José plan a heist on a bank van carrying dollar bills to be burnt in Washington. On his way home, Anthony finds Cuddy leaving the flat and confronts him. Cuddy humiliates him and knocks him down the stairs. Anthony and Jaunita have a row and he walks out. Wandering the streets, Anthony visits a Black Power meeting where Delilah is speaking. They go for a drink and he tells her about the heist. The group, now including Delilah, plans the job and Anthony insists they need another man. He recruits Cleon, now a preacher.

Friday 6.27 am, Noble Street Federal Reserve Bank. Anthony and José wait for the lorry to load, Delilah hides in a bin opposite. Cleon and Skippy are look-outs, Kirby is the getaway. A passing policeman questions Cleon and overhears shots as the robbery begins. Cleon shoots the cop, José blows up the van and Delilah is shot dead. José is chased and killed by police. Christmas. Anthony distributes free toys to the local children. Cleon is giving away dollar bills at his church. Going to tell Cleon to stop drawing attention to himself, Anthony sees him being arrested. Cleon informs and police raids begin. Skippy is found dead from an overdose. Anthony and Kirby are about to flee to Mexico when they are pinned down by the police. Anthony is convicted to fifteen years to life.

REVIEW

In its own way, *Dead Presidents* is a heritage picture, a wannabe revisionist-historical epic, tooled in postmodern MTV-style following the gangster film templates of *Good-Fellas* and *Once Upon a Time in America*. Spanning the years between 1968 to 1973, the film takes in the Vietnam War, Black Power and the 'ghetto-ization' of the Bronx. Anthony's is a strictly generic trajectory through these moments, from naïve street kid through hardened soldier to desperate gangster. However, the ambition of the film's historical scope is not helped by its style. *Menace 2 Society*, the Hughes Brothers' first film, won Best Picture at the 1994 MTV Movie Awards and *Dead Presidents* is an example of how an MTV-influenced style can fail its subject matter. It's easy to be glibly dismissive of the MTV aesthetic without ever having to define what one means by it, but the film's treatment of Vietnam is illustrative. *Dead Presidents* wants to unpack the complexities of black urban Americans fighting in what Anthony's 'hood pals and the Vietcong both describe as 'a white man's war' while too often depicting it in a visual shorthand straight from *Apocalypse Now*. The Hughes Brothers know their audience's genre predilections and thus combine them – gangster film meets war film meets buddy movie – and couch them in the visual *lingua franca* of American youth culture. As a way of addressing an audience it's a low-risk option, but as a way of doing justice to story, characters and to the underlying themes of the ever-diminishing opportunities for African-Americans and a Black History perspective, this aesthetic option reveals itself as inadequate.

This impoverishment is revealed most clearly in the two levels of history the film deals with; the socio-political dimensions of the story and its attitude to film history. In the latter case, there is a straightforward lifting of moments and motifs from other films. While this is always part of the ritual of genre, visual quotation here is unmotivated, simply there. So we have a Lynchian cigarette end, shot in lovingly extreme close-up, smouldering like a fuse; a series of *Apocalypse Now*-style superimpositions during Anthony's dark combat-zone night of the soul and standard issue Scorsesian camera pirouettes through Kirby's pool hall. These borrowings sit on the film rather than feeling like they're embedded in it; they are flashy but by no means fundamental.

Likewise with the film's use of transitions. The opening sections – which feel like the most authentic, lived moments, shot in nostalgic autumnal hues – melt together through a series of slow fades-to-black. The transition to Vietnam is handled with what seems like a bravura cinematic solution: hiding out in Jaunita's back garden, Anthony flees across neighbouring fences and yards. All clambering limbs and hurtling headlong motion, the transition from Anthony's flight straight into the smoke and turmoil of a platoon mission is sudden, startling and meaningful on several levels. It sets up the pace for the rest of the film – from hereon in the pressure is on – and implicitly links home to war-zone, announcing the conditions of one as being analogous to the state of the other. At the same time, this transition tells us that Vietnam – in many respects the film's central sequence, in which Anthony becomes a decorated soldier with a clear-eyed survival strategy and 'becomes a man' in terms that the film later problematises – is to be swiftly galloped through, with sickeningly graphic violence en route, as a merely significant interlude in his life. But everything prior to and including Vietnam functions to lead up to the closure and narrative pay-off of the robbery of the 'Dead Presidents' (slang for dollar bills), which appears more as a generic contrivance than an absolute narrative necessity. The heist is too clearly signalled as doomed to fail when Delilah and Cleon are recruited, as well as being handled in a clumsy fumble of cutting that drains it of vital tension.

Revisionist genre films take on myth and history simultaneously; the iconic mythology of the cinematic tradition into which they insert themselves and the 'big history' of the periods in which they are set. So it is with *Dead Presidents* which, while pulling back from the conventional generic terrain of recent black gangster cinema, sets out to provide a history lesson from two generations before. Style again jeopardises the laudable intention. Films as disparate as *GoodFellas* and *Forrest Gump* both demonstrated that such an undertaking is an excellent excuse to parade period styles and exploit a 'Best of...' soundtrack. But whereas *GoodFellas* was inspired both in its choice and application of music, *Dead Presidents* falls more into what might be called the K-Tel/Clothes Show Theory of History: the music's great, the clothes accurate, but as applied here neither serve to thicken, complicate or counterpoint the plot.

The final image of Anthony being bussed to a life-sentence should feel tragic. It doesn't. He's too stolid, too straightforwardly straight-up to carry the full weight of the story. His circumstances trap him but the bright kid on his milk round doesn't become the reckless armed robber with anything near the degree of bitter opportunism that might make this transformation moving. In this respect, Anthony's progress might be read as a fable about the path of least resistance being the one most likely to lead to a dead end. We don't even discover what happens to his mentor Kirby, a major character well rounded by Keith David in tones of 'hood resourcefulness and surrogate fatherliness. This relationship alone could have made an entire film, but with its Ur-MTV stylistic leanings and its ambitious but problematic relationship to the history it wants to screen, *Dead Presidents* comes across as a perfect postmodern movie, which doesn't mean it's a good film.

L' AVENTURRA

DIR: MICHELANGELO ANTONIONI IT./FR. 1995
ORIGINALLY PUBLISHED IN *SIGHT AND SOUND* DECEMBER 1995

SYNOPSIS

Sandro, a jaded architect who has settled for easy success rather than professional fulfilment, joins a small cruising party along the north-east coast of Sicily given by Princess Patrizia on her yacht. Sandro accompanies his fiancée Anna, daughter of an ex-ambassador, who brings her friend Claudia, a young woman who is not of the same privileged class. The group swim and then go ashore to investigate a volcanic island. Anna is growing increasingly upset over the inadequacy of her relationship with Sandro. A storm rises and the group prepares to leave the island, but Anna is nowhere to be found. In the ensuing search, Sandro becomes attracted to Claudia who, in turn, is confused by his advances and rebuffs him.

Anna remains missing but Claudia and Sandro continue searching for her. Individually at first and then together, they visit places on the mainland where a woman fitting Anna's description has reportedly been seen. Struggling with her feelings of guilt and shame and with the thought that Anna is dead, Claudia eventually succumbs to Sandro's attentions and becomes his mistress. Their search effectively over, the couple attend a lavish party in a hotel where they encounter members of the original cruise. Claudia, fatigued, misses the party to rest. When Sandro fails to return to their room she searches the hotel for him and finds him in the arms of a prostitute. Nevertheless, she forgives the tearful Sandro. Anna is never found.

REVIEW

In the early 1960s, Michelangelo Antonioni visited Mark Rothko in his New York studio, having spotted a kindred sensibility in the painter's abstract expressionism. 'We both make work about nothing...' Antonioni explained, 'but with precision'. By that time Antonioni was established as the European director whose work demanded the sort of scrutiny normally accorded to painting. Although his style divided critics none denied his importance, alongside Godard's *A bout de Souffle* and Resnais's *Hiroshima, mon amour*, *L'Avventura* signalled a new departure in cinematic language – with these works film entered its modernist phase. Antonioni's sixth feature, *L'Avventura* was a cause célèbre in its day, scandalising the 1960 Cannes Festival with its long-take sequences and evanescent plot, it launched the director internationally, as well as being the first film in an enduring collaboration with Monica Vitti, his *actrice-fétiche*. This re-release, presaging the director's forthcoming Wenders collaboration *Beyond the Clouds*, will hopefully provoke a reassessment of this great modernist filmmaker, unjustly neglected by the British.

L'Avventura is often seen as the first of the 1960s quartet of films that includes *La Notte* (1961), *L'Eclisse* (1962) and *Il Deserto Rosso* (1964), in which Vitti is the female consciousness through which the director filters his 'psychoanalysis of the boom', as P. Adams Sitney has described the films' examination of the post-war Italian 'economic miracle'. It's a nicely weighted phrase that condenses within itself Antonioni's anatomising of social specifics through the scrutiny of his characters' sentiments. From which approach the following themes rapidly became prime Antonioni territory: alienation, the impermanence of relationships, the impossibility of communication between men and women, the fragility of moral certainties in a brute consumerist object-world, the director's expression of them being famously disparaged by Pauline Kael as 'Antoniennui'.

As in the sixties, so in the nineties. It's possible still to see in *L'Avventura* an appearance of solemnity, an insistent dedramatisation of events that epitomises the 1960s art-film. Nevertheless, one remains struck by Antonioni's sympathy towards his women. Vitti's Claudia, troubled and independently-minded, was as significant a portrait in 1960s European cinema's gallery of new female characters as Ainouk Aimée in *La Dolce Vita*, Jeanne Moreau in *Jules et Jim*, Emanuelle Riva in *Hiroshima, mon amour* and effectively set the mould for her forthcoming work with the director. While Vitti may well be the definitive sixties icon of sexualised anguish, she cannot be reduced to this alone. There is a questing element to Claudia that runs through her feelings of guilt over Anna's disappearance and the sense that she has betrayed her friend by embarking on the desultory affair with Sandro; her yearning for lucidity is accompanied by a readiness to face disillusionment, and then to move on. In the 1960s quartet it is Antonioni's men who are weak and it is only with *Blow Up* (1966) and *The Passenger* (1975) that he concentrates on driven, metaphysically-anguished male protagonists. Sandro, however, pursues Claudia more out of reflex than through active desire; his is one version of the testosterone-automatism that recurs throughout the film and of which Claudia uncomfortably finds herself the focus. Anna, present even in her absence, presides over the film like a ghost. Hers is a spectral subjectivity that comes to be ominously identified with the camera itself, as implied in the eerie travelling-shot that advances along a narrow street on Claudia and Sandro as they leave a deserted, De Chirico-like village.

L'Avventura's beauty is not fashion-spread glamour airbrushed with angst. It's altogether stranger. Writing about an Antonioni film can be like attempting a running commentary on clouds, there is shape and form yet the narrative contours are limit-cases of liminality which allow the films to be allusive, evocative, atmospheric ... and paradoxically exact. Antonioni proceeds tangentially, approaching the edges of his object of interest and finding central significance in fugitive undertow and repercussion. Antonioni's technique puts equal emphasis on length and depth. His sequences include moments before and after events that, in narrative convention, are usually considered *temps mort*. These moments show that Antonioni is as vigilantly observing landscape as character. The relationship between character and setting, between 'figure' and 'ground', is crucial to his films. Nothing happens but everything in the frame counts. Through the tunnelling perspectives of Antonioni's compositions or the bisected frames in which characters face away from one another, foreground is always intimately tied to background. The moment when Claudia, visible through the window of the room as a speck on the piazza, waits outside for Anna while she and Sandro make love gives a typical unnerving edge of isolation to the scene. The inhospitable volcanic island, the opulent sterility of the haut-bourgeois interiors and the backgrounds of brooding nature and classical architecture all combine phenomenological realism (Antonioni always remained a neo-realist in his taste for location shooting, even if he was tempted, with *Il Deserto Rosso* and *Blow Up*, to do a little colour retouching) with pathetic fallacy (the jaded surveyor Sandro and his encounter with the aspiring young architect for example, over which the buildings preside with almost oppressive authority) and symbolism. Antonioni's attention to such relationships between 'figure' and 'ground' is complex, multi-dimensional and his films are always dramas of fragile transitions between wavering states of presence and absence, visibility and invisibility, togetherness and isolation. It is not only Anna who disappears and yet remains present. The search for her itself fades imperceptibly as a plotline into another story of emotional aimlessness and bad faith. This moment of transition from one story to another may be the object of Antonioni's investigation. If *L'Avventura* is the perfect introduction to Antonioni's 'cinema of absence' – as well as to a style both unique and influential, Wenders' *Kings of the Road*, Scorsese's *Taxi Driver* and all of Egoyan are inconceivable without the possibilities that Antonioni announced – then *The Passenger* is its later, more political elaboration. Both films are remarkable and David Thomson best summed up their enduring relevance when he wrote 'I suspect that Antonioni's best films will continue to grow and shift; like dunes in the centuries of desert. In that process, if there are eyes left to look, he will become a standard for beauty'.

SMOKE

DIR: WAYNE WANG USA 1995
ORIGINALLY PUBLISHED IN *SIGHT AND SOUND* MARCH 1996

SYNOPSIS

Brooklyn, 1990. Auggie Wren is the proprietor of the Brooklyn Cigar Company, a neighbourhood tobacconists. Among his regular customers is Paul Benjamin, a novelist in his thirties suffering from writer's block. Several years before, Paul's pregnant wife was gunned down outside the shop. Every morning, Auggie takes a photograph of the corner outside his store, a ritual he has repeated every day for the last fourteen years. One evening, as Auggie is closing, Paul calls by for some cigars. Auggie shows Paul the photographs. Paul spots a shot of his wife Elaine and breaks down.

A few days later Paul is almost run down by a bus, but is saved by a young man, Rashid Cole. To show his gratitude Paul buys Rashid lunch. Learning that he is on the run, Paul offers him a place to stay. Meanwhile, Auggie is visited by an ex-girlfriend, Ruby McNutt, who he hasn't seen in eighteen years. She tells him he has a daughter, Felicity, who is living in Brooklyn, pregnant and addicted to crack. Auggie refuses to believe it, thinking that Ruby is trying to hustle him. Finding Rashid's presence distracting, Paul asks him to leave the flat. Soon after, Paul is visited by Rashid's aunt who is looking for him. She tells Paul that Rashid's real name is Thomas Jefferson Cole and that his mother was killed and his father, Cyrus, severely injured in a car accident when he was a boy. Cyrus abandoned him. Rashid has learned that Cyrus is working in a gas station just outside the city. Rashid goes there and discovers that Cyrus has built a new family life for himself. Unaware of Rashid's true identity Cyrus gives him a job.

Ruby convinces Auggie to visit Felicity, who is violently rude to them, triumphantly declaring that she has had an abortion. Rashid returns to Brooklyn and tells Paul the truth: he had witnessed a heist by a local gangster known as the Creeper, during which Rashid picked up a bag containing $5,800. Rashid has hidden it in Paul's appartment. Paul begs him to return it but Rashid refuses. Paul and Rashid celebrate Rashid's birthday with April, a young woman who works in the local bookstore. Paul and April find themselves mutually attracted. Auggie offers Rashid a job but the young man accidentally ruins a shipment of Cuban cigars. Having sunk $5,000 in the stock, Auggie is devestated. Paul orders Rashid to pay Auggie back with his own money. This he does, but the Creeper comes looking for him at Paul's appartment. Refusing to reveal anything, Paul gets badly beaten.

Paul and Auggie trace Rashid to Cyrus's gas station where an emotionally explosive father-and-son reunion occurs. The Creeper is killed mid-heist. Auggie gives the $5,000 to Ruby for Felicity's welfare. Paul, his block overcome and now involved with April, tells Auggie that he has been commissioned to write a Christmas story, but is out of ideas. The two men go for lunch, where Auggie tells Paul the following story. Shortly after starting working at the store he chased a young black boy who was stealing magazines. The boy escaped, dropping his wallet. At Christmas, Auggie found himself alone and decided to return the wallet. The young man's address was in the Projects. Arriving there Auggie was welcomed by the boy's elderly, blind aunt who mistook him for her nephew. Auggie played along and the two ate Christmas dinner together. Later, Auggie departed, leaving the wallet but taking an obviously stolen camera with him. Some months later, and feeling guilty, Auggie decided to return the camera but the aunt was no longer at the address.

REVIEW

It's not often that one can argue for the writer-as-auteur but *Smoke* demonstrates that a novelist's fictional world can make it to the screen without being compromised by approximation or a stolid fidelity to detail. Scripted by the novelist Paul Auster and directed with disarming selflessness by Wayne Wang, the idea for *Smoke* was initially conceived in 1990 when Wang read Auster's 'Auggie Wren's Christmas Story' in *The New York Times* and the story occurs at the end of the film, as told by Auggie to the novelist Paul Benjamin. *Smoke* expands on it by installing Auggie's Brooklyn Cigar Company at the film's core, while keeping the original story's ambiguous, fabulist tone. What is so pleasing about *Smoke* is that Auster's voice as well as his abiding preoccupations and motifs are recognisably intact and cinematically effective. One need not have read anything by Auster to enjoy *Smoke*, but should one read him after having seen the film it's a fair bet that the novelist's world will seem familiar.

A fabulist is a liar by defintion, one who concocts fictional ruses. While this aspect of Auster's fiction might put him in the company of other American fabulists like Don DeLillo, Robert Coover and Donald Barthelme, it's a tendency that has always existed alongside others in his work. From *The New York Trilogy* – metaphysical doubt sweated out in hard-boiled pulp idiom – through *The Invention of Solitude* – metafictional memoirs that call on Auster's early career as a translator of the high priests of French modernism, Stéphane Mallarmé and Maurice Blanchot – to the grander historical scope of *Moon Palace*, Auster has increasingly placed his fabulist's fascination with the self-as-fiction in specific milieux and peopled these with regular guys in crisis. The crisis privileged above all in his work is fatherhood; so it is with *Smoke*. The place is the Brooklyn-in-microcosm of Auggie's store; the guys – Auggie, Paul, Cyrus and Rashid – are each depicted as men still being born. Their identities forged by wrong turnings and everyday catastrophes, each is unable to throw off or come to terms with his past without the help and friendship of the other. In the absence of trustworthy blood fathers, a surrogate counts.

If *Smoke* is predominantly male in focus, its men are shown to have been cut loose, often against their will, from family and intimate relationships. Paul, the blocked novelist whose pregnant wife Elaine was accidentally shot dead in a robbery outside Auggie's store, is a man floating disorientated in the fluid of his own grief until he is inadvertently delivered back to the world by the incursion of Rashid. Auggie's friendship with Paul is also shadowed by the guilt Auggie feels at having served Elaine on the day of the robbery and at not having kept her in the store for a few seconds longer. Rashid, the boy from the Projects, played by Harold Perrineau in alternating registers of impudent street-savvy and baroque flights of the imagination, conceals a fear and isolation that comes from his mother having died in a car driven by his drunken father Cyrus who, disowned, he has not seen in twelve years. Cyrus, his grotesque cigar-shaped artificial arm a memento of his irresponsibility, is cultivating a new family life into which Rashid's arrival is a further unwelcome reminder of the past.

Auster has spoken of the characters in *Smoke* as representing 'an undogmatic view of human behaviour. No one is simply one thing or the other. They're all filled with contradictions, and they don't live in a world that breaks down neatly into good guys and bad guys'. It's an attitude to character that echoes the film's treatment of milieu. *Smoke* depicts Brooklyn as the New York borough *par excellence*, utterly mongrel in its mix of races and classes, with an emphasis on how lives can change when its different worlds overlap for an instant. How they come to overlap owes a lot to the author's other preoccupations – chance and coincidence. Auster's novels explore a veritable theology of coincidence in which he examines the many permutations of how a chance encounter or event can up-end a life. Coincidence is seen as the presence of the extraordinary in the everyday and is often the prelude to a character's slow-motion epiphany; Rashid's gradual path back to Cyrus by way of meeting Paul, for example. The concentration on coincidence in *Smoke* allows Auster to suggest lives that were, lives that might have been, as well as the life to come.

One of Auster's favourite methods of dramatising chance is through the use of money as a motif. In *Smoke* money arrives as a cause of upheaval. When Paul pulls Rashid's stashed bag of bills from the bookshelf we get a high-angle shot of the notes tumbling onto the aghast Rashid – *dollars ex machina*. Nevertheless, the money becomes the material symbol of the growing affinity between the characters, passing from Rashid to Paul then via Auggie to Ruby and Felicity. As bad money is made good and a theft is transformed into a gift, so life is transformed into art. Paul, Auggie and Rashid are each artists in their own way. Novelist, photographer and promising draughtsman respectively, each is able to transform the brute material of his life and surroundings into something other. In Auggie's case, his bizarre photographic 'record of my little spot... my life's work' indicates an almost Zen-like devotion to the contemplation of mundane detail through which the flux of life is revealed. It's a telling moment when Paul and Auggie bond over the photo-albums, a *mise-en-abyme* of the film's own project.

Weaving its intricate chain of characters and relationships together with great *legerdemain*, *Smoke* has an almost soap-like format – you might call it a smoke opera – with Auggie's shop as base, a feature further developed in the Auster/Wang companion piece, *Blue in the Face*. Wang's direction allows the ensemble great freedom, working gradually from a preponderance of master shots to the final tight close-up on Auggie's mouth as he delivers his Christmas story spiel. Keitel's rueful stogy-sucking moue frequently splits into a Brooklyn equivalent of a Cheshire Cat grin, delivering a combination of banter, braggadocio and bullshit that lifts the weighty themes of fatherhood and identity, chance and fabulation into its comic slipstream. David Thomson has asked of Wang: 'Can he make American pictures?' As well as being a remarkably faithful rendition of Auster's world and voice, *Smoke* is American cinema at its most humane and life-affirming.

BLUE IN THE FACE
DIRS: WAYNE WANG & PAUL AUSTER USA 1995
ORIGINALLY PUBLISHED IN SIGHT AND SOUND MAY 1996

SYNOPSIS

Brooklyn, 1994. Auggie Wren is standing outside his tobacconists, the Brooklyn Cigar Company, with his assistant Jimmy, the OTB men and his new girlfriend Violet, who is reminding him of the time and date of her brother's performance with his band. A young woman walks by and has her handbag snatched by a passing young black kid. Auggie gives chase, catches the boy and returns the bag. He is about to call the police when the woman decides she doesn't wish to press charges. She and Auggie begin to argue ferociously until Auggie takes her bag from her and hands it to the kid who eventually runs off with it. The woman is furious.

Auggie is visited in the store by numerous local characters, including Bob and The Man with Unusual Glasses, who relate their feelings about living in Brooklyn and their feelings about smoking. Dot, the wife of Vinnie the shop-owner, comes in to complain about her husband's unwillingness to take her on holiday to Las Vegas. A young hustler comes in and attempts to sell watches to Auggie and the OTB men. He delivers a rap and berates Tommy for being a black man who hangs out with white guys. Interspersed with these events are local residents relating statistics about life in Brooklyn, interviews with locals about their lives and documentary footage of the history of the Brooklyn Dodgers, the former baseball team.

Vinnie reveals to Auggie that he is considering selling the shop. Auggie is aghast and attempts to persuade Vinnie that the shop is important to the community. Vinnie is unconvinced but the ghost of Jackie Robinson visits him and makes him think again. Dot returns, even more frustrated than before, and she attempts to seduce Auggie into acccompanying her to Las Vegas. When he refuses, Dot takes money from the till for the journey. Vinnie appears and eventually the two are reconciled and take off together for Vegas. Auggie and Violet have an argument when he tells her he can't make her brother's band's performance. She has doubts about their relationship.

Auggie and the OTB men are visted again by a sharp-suited guy with a strong Spanish accent selling Cuban cigars. It quickly dawns on them that this is the same guy who previously attempted to sell them watches. He reveals he's a rapper on his way to sign a record deal. Auggie is visited by a singing telegram girl who delivers a raunchy message that tells him that Vinnie has decided that he will not sell the store. A crowd gather outside and an impromptu dance of locals starts up. Auggie and Violet have a baby, named Jackie, whose first solid food was a Belgian waffle.

REVIEW

Blue in the Face comes across like the handrolled companion to the luxury-length, filter-tipped pleasures of Smoke, a deliberately ramshackle assembly of sketches interspersed with musical and documentary interludes and celebrity cameos. Conceived in order to make the most of characters and performances that its companion piece could not incorporate, Blue takes the pseudo-soap format of Smoke and develops it into a kind of hip 'Cheers', the bar-room replaced by the over-the-counter culture of The Brooklyn Cigar Company. Filmed over six days, the shooting strategy dictated that each scene should last no longer than a ten minute reel of film, with one take for rehearsal and one with the camera rolling for real. The emphasis, then, is on improvised performance and dialogue, with Auggie Wren as the street-corner MC presiding over a festival of Brooklyn mouthiness and the OTB men brought to the fore as an earthy in-store Greek Chorus.

The film's cameos are one of its principal pleasures: Roseanne is shrewish with frustration as Dot, Vinnie's love-hungry, Vegas-aspiring wife; Michael J. Fox ingratiating and unsettling as Tommy's schoolfriend Pete, a former high-flier now plainly in a parallel universe, his low-key madness hinted at in the way Fox gnaws at the neck of his Snapple bottle; Lou Reed's to-camera drollery as The Man with the Unusual Glasses just about overcomes the comedy of his magnificently awful perm and Jim Jarmusch is charmingly witty as Bob, the wannabe ex-smoker delivering nice takes on cinematic smoking. The principle of the cameo – the famous face being all the more recognisably itself when popping up thinly disguised in a walk-on part – has a strange effect on the main performers. While the cameos range from straightforward to-camera recitation to unrecognisable masquerade – Lily Tomlin in shabby drag as The Belgian Waffle Man – the performers from Smoke here appear to be almost 'quoting' their previous roles, holding them at a distance from the development demanded by the more conventional narrative structure of Smoke.

If Blue in the Face appears a bit cameo-happy this has something to do with the improvised nature of many of the scenes but is in keeping with the more schematic nature of the film's celebration of 'Planet Brooklyn' in all its street-level, historical and mythical diversity. So we get archive footage both of the great days of the Brooklyn Dodgers and the sad day of the demolition of the Dodgers stadium, as well as the mythical presence of star-player and local hero Jackie Robinson. When the ghost of Jackie appears to Vinnie in the cigar store the scene is played both as whimsical fantasy and nostalgic remembrance, but the visitation bears heavily on Vinnie's later decision not to sell the store but to retain it in the name of community as a focus for a corner of Brooklyn. While Smoke treated the theme of community in terms of emotional kinship, a function of family and friends, Blue approaches it from the point-of-view of locality. Auggie's store is both an urban oasis where a sense of civic belonging is forged, but also an image of the endangered hangout, a reminder that the 'space' of the city has to be made up of smaller 'places', built to a human scale in order to be inhabitable. It would be interesting to compare Blue in this respect to a film like Clerks, another profane, logorrhoeic take on over-the-counter-culture, but based in the nowheresville of smalltown America.

Blue makes the most of its metropolitan setting, grounding itself in the statistics and precise map-locations of its situation, as well as providing video-reportage on 'real-life' locals. Anyone who lives in a city must have regularly noticed plastic bags caught in the branches of trees. Blue treats this tiny and fascinatingly troubling detail of city life in its video footage of a local white-collar guy's vendetta against what he prettily describes as these 'little flags of chaos'. While this might seem a bit cute in synopsis, the documentation of an eccentricity for its own sake, it ends up making perfect sense in terms of the film's own insistence on the place of local detail within the bigger urban picture. The 'tough love' sentimentality that somewhat blurred the rough edge that Smoke required is here replaced by a devotion to place and a clearer focus on racial politics. That this should take place in scenes that feature impromptu song routines gives a nicely distanced effect – the issues addressed at a melodic tangent – while the question of racial 'authenticity' in a city as hybrid as New York is handled with comic effectiveness. *Blue* is a good-natured baggy monster as a companion piece to *Smoke*. The question remains as to whether some enterprising TV producer will buy up the format for the first smoke-opera to be sponsored by Schimmelpenincks.

BEYOND THE CLOUDS
DIR: MICHELANGELO ANTONIONI FR./IT./GER. 1995
ORIGINALLY PUBLISHED IN *SIGHT AND SOUND* JULY 1996

SYNOPSIS

Chronicle of a love affair that never existed. Ferrara, Italy. A young man, Silvano, meets Carmen in a hotel and seems to fall in love with her. Although she offers herself to him, Silvano leaves the hotel alone. Three years later they encounter each other again. Silvano is still a bachelor, Carmen a divorcee. They go back to Carmen's room, where she willingly lets him undress her. But Silvano backs off. He gets up and before leaving asks her, 'Why spoil our desire?'

The Girl, the Crime... Portofino, Italy. A director in search of characters is entranced by a beautiful girl. In the shop where they meet, he hallucinates. He thinks he sees her acquiesce to his desires by showing him her legs. He goes out, his thoughts in turmoil and sits down on the terrace of a seaside cafe. The girl finds him there. She explains to him that she killed her father by stabbing him twelve times. They return to her room and make love.

Don't Look for Me. Paris. Three years before, Patricia's husband was seduced by a young woman, Olga. Their love affair became a passion which he could not live without, in spite of his strong desire to stay with Patricia. Patricia leaves him. In the empty apartment she has just rented there is a man, Carlo. The apartment is his and she has just discovered that his wife has left with all the furniture. The phone rings. It's Patricia's husband. She tells him 'Don't try to find me.' Carlo caresses her hand and she does nothing to stop him.

This Body of Dirt. Aix-en-Provence, France. A young man comes out of an apartment building. A girl brushes past him, hurrying out. He catches up with her and, without a word, walks alongside her, scrutinising her. 'Where are you going?' he asks. 'To Mass,' she replies. Conversing, they reach the church. The girl goes off to one side and kneels, well away from him. He stares at her, fascinated by her fervour which only sharpens his desire. He falls asleep and when he wakes up she is gone. He catches up with her and they walk side by side. He follows her into her apartment block. In front of her flat she stops and turns to him. 'Can I see you tomorrow?' he asks. She laughs and tells him 'Tomorrow I enter a convent.'

REVIEW

In the thirteen years since he directed his last feature film, *Identification of a Woman*, in 1982, much has happened to Antonioni. In 1985, illness left him barely able to move and talk. In 1995 he was honoured by the inauguration of a museum dedicated to his work in Ferrara, his birthplace, and by an Oscar for Lifetime Achievement. Shot in 1995 when he was 83-years-old, *Beyond the Clouds* arrives with the air of a prestige art-cinema event. Its cast is a combination of old and new European stars, and its production credits include Wim Wenders in the combined role of stand-by director, screenplay co-writer and director in his own right of the prologue, interludes and epilogue to Antonioni's sections of the film.

The film is made up of four episodes based on short stories collected in the anthology of the director's writings *That Bowling Alley on the Tiber*. These episodes are framed by the character of Malkovich's 'director' who links and narrates them and in the case of *The Girl, The Crime...*, one of the more successful episodes, appears as a protagonist. *Beyond the Clouds* is, in every respect, a film about couples: the couple that forms provisionally and in passing in *The Girl, the Crime...*, the ideal of a union stronger than its reality in *Chronicle of a love affair that never existed*, the married couple that split up in protracted agony in *Don't Look for Me* and the desire for the ideal union given a divine dimension in *This Body of Dirt*. A film about couples also shot by couples – Michelangelo and Enrica Antonioni; Wim and Donata Wenders. Then there is the question of the Antonioni/ Wenders couple.

Brought in partly for insurance purposes, Wenders here continues the cinephilic trajectory visible in his association with Nick Ray in *The American Friend* and *Lightning over Water - Nick's Film* and his homage to Ozu in *Tokyo-Ga*. One can't help wondering if all this genuflecting to elderly, dying and dead directors is healthy, if it's a case of Wenders the vampire in the guise of the ever-respectful amanuensis to the great filmmakers. As if to dispel this rather morbid profile, Wenders plays a light and modest skit on the problems of discipleship in a linking sketch with Mastroianni and Moreau, who both starred in Antonioni's *La Notte* (1961). Mastroianni, a painter, stands before the Mont Saint-Victoire in what appears to be a useless recreation of Cézanne. Moreau teases him and the landscape has changed, become ugly. With an edge of pomposity that plays off Moreau's quizzical mockery the painter admits that he recreates the scene only in the hope that he might recreate one of the original artist's gestures. A little parable about knowing one's place in the artistic scheme of things, in other words, where Wenders recognises that, while his own film style definitely owes to Antonioni's, it can only ever be a kind of mannerism, even if applied with absolute sincerity.

With the exception of *The Oberwald Mystery*, Antonioni has never made a film set in the past and *Beyond the Clouds* is both a recapitulation of past themes, ideas and characters as well as a statement of principles and ideas solidified over fifty years of filmmaking. This autobiographical dimension is fairly carefully constrained within the fictional frames of Malkovich's musings on the work of the director. While not detracting from Antonioni's formidable energy and the great beauty of many of the images, the stories are definitely uneven at different levels. *Chronicle of a love affair*, for example, is held back from being the ultra-refined fable of a kind of modern-day courtly love that it might have been by the curious sensation that its performers are just too ordinary – despite both Kim Rossi-Stuart and Ines Sastre being fashion-mag perfect to look at. One gets the sense here that the real object of fascination is Ferrara, that the director is paying homage to the birthplace whose particular ironic, aristocratic sensibility has so informed his work; as the story says of the couple's unconsummated relationship: 'Only a citizen of Ferrara can understand a relationship that lasted eleven years without ever existing'.

This Body of Dirt, the closing episode, is more successful in its telling of the same story from a different angle. Again, a town, this time Aix-en-Provence at night, is filmed with such careful attention that one has the sense of its silent stones and murmuring fountains turning gradually into a mineral landscape through which the ardent young man pursues the would-be convent girl. This sequence alone is magical, Jacob and Perez's performances are perfectly pitched, the punchline funny and slightly horrifying and the barely hidden meditation on death poignant, giving another dimension to a sketch which could have been slight and gag-like. Strangely enough, I was reminded here of Marcel Carné, with whom Antonioni worked as an assistant on *Les Visiteurs du Soir* in 1946, and of the tendency in French poetic realism (that probably owed to the contribution of screenwriter Jacques Prévert) to conceive characters as the walking embodiments of qualities. And, despite all that is said about the modernity of Antonioni's characters, in this case what might have come across as archaic attains the deceptively limpid clarity of a fable.

Despite a strong performance by Fanny Ardant, *Don't Look for Me* is less satisfying, its emotional violence too close to the surface of the story, too strained and melodramatic. This episode fares less well than the perverse attraction/repulsion dynamic between the director and the young murderess in *The Girl, the Crime...*, where simplicity again conceals layers of possibilities in the telling of the story by concentrating on communicating visually. *That Bowling Alley on the Tiber* provides clues to the success of this episode when Antonioni writes that he 'starts with an image and works back to a state of affairs'. This explains the director's pursuit of the woman who goes from being 'just' an image trapped behind the glass window of the shop she works in – a sequence whose framing and editing demonstrate that Antonioni's eye is as remarkable as it ever was – to a woman who confronts him with a fact so devastating that he is stunned and the tables are turned, a kind of equality established, an understanding reached, an ambiguous attraction expressed. While it is a little too stately at times, glimmers of Antonioni's genius come that have one wishing for a last film of the quality of *The Passenger*, say. *Beyond the Clouds* is an elegant resumé of a remarkable talent that illness, incapacity and old age have yet to eclipse.

THE LAST SUPPER

DIR: STACEY TITLE USA 1995
ORIGINALLY PUBLISHED IN *SIGHT AND SOUND* SEPTEMBER 1996

SYNOPSIS

Iowa, the present. One night during a rainstorm Pete, a graduate student, hitches a lift with a stranger, Zac, after his car breaks down. Pete invites Zac to join him and his four house-mates for their evening meal. Zac turns out to be a violent redneck who insults them all before threatening Marc with a knife. Pete retaliates and Zac breaks his arm. Marc stabs Zac and kills him. The group's initial panic subsides as they plan to bury Zac in the garden and Marc makes the suggestion that, having rid the world of one 'bad person', they should use the opportunity of their regular Sunday evening dinners to which they ritually invite a guest to continue their purging the world of reactionaries.

Their next guest is the Reverend Gerald Hutchins who Jude has interviewed for her graduate thesis. The group have poisoned a decanter of wine which, when the Reverend starts to make homophobic pronouncements, they pass him. Innocently, he drinks from it and dies. The group continue to invite likely candidates for poisoning, despatching, one after the other, a misogynist, a female pro-lifer, a young Militant Black Muslim and a chain-smoking slob. Each body is buried in the garden and disguised by a heavy, ripening crop of tomatoes. Meanwhile, a local policewoman is investigating the disappearance of a young girl, Jenny Tyler, and Zac is among the suspects. Pete is questioned by the police and he mentions that he was given a lift on the night of the girl's disappearance. The policewoman presses him for details of truck and driver but Pete plays dumb.

At the next dinner, their guest is a young conservative girl. As they talk with her, the doorbell rings. It is the policewoman, who asks Pete, Paulie and Marc and the others if they recognise any of the mugshots she shows them. They deny recognising any of the faces, but the policewoman's suspicion of the group increases when she observes them pause over Zac's shot. When they return to the dining-room the young girl has been stabbed. The next would-be victim is Heather, a priggish seventeen-year-old. Luke is infuriated by her and wants her to drink the poisoned wine, but Jade manages to prevent her from being killed. By now, the group is beginning to unravel. The policewoman starts to snoop around their garden after having overheard an argument between Luke and Jade. Luke discovers the policewoman and decapitates her.

Luke and Peter decide to get away for a while after the policewoman's disappearance is reported. Waiting at the airport they spot Norman Arbuthnot, a famous right-wing TV shock-jock. With the flights delayed, Luke and Pete invite him back for a meal. Arbuthnot turns out to be a surprisingly convivial guest who rationalises his public persona, inadvertently convincing all but Luke that he should be spared. The group retire to the kitchen, leaving Arbuthnot in the dining room, and a furious row ensues while a storm rages outside. Luke insists that Arbuthnot dies and pulls a gun on Jade when she picks up the phone and threatens to call the police. She won't back down and Luke crumples in tears. Back in the dining room, Arbuthnot notices the burial mounds in the garden and puts two and two together. Back around the table once more, the wine remains undrunk and Arbuthnot lives. The final image is of one of Marc's paintings featuring a table in a forest with five figures lying scattered around it and a single figure walking away from the scene. We hear Arbuthnot speaking at a public event admitting that he is considering a political career.

REVIEW

A dark comedy that lampoons the excesses of the American PC mentality has been a long time coming. The Last Supper, a mixture of black comedy and political satire in which a group of American liberal graduate students decides to bump off those whose opinions they find repellent, is not as savage as it could and should have been. Holding court at their regular Sunday evening meals they invite a reactionary of their choice. After the first murder, self-justification kicks in in the guise of Marc's hypothetical proposal. Suppose that one were in an Austrian bar in 1909 sharing a schnapps with a young art student named Adolf. With the benefit of hindsight 'Do you kill him? Do you poison his schnapps to save all those innocent people?' It's the question that spurs them into action after the killing of the Southern psycho Zac, tastily played with Swampland throwback relish by Bill Paxton, who taunts them that, as liberals, they 'talk and do nothing', whereas he is prepared to follow through on his white supremacist beliefs, to die and kill for them. The liberal worms turn and, with one target down in the shooting gallery of PC folk devils, they get the taste for bloody self-justification. But they're too well heeled to get down and dirty straight off. They insist on a civilised prelude to murder; fine food and wine — PC here also stands for poisoned Chablis — and conversation.

These are liberals shown as in love with their own sense of outrage. So we wait for the guests to deliver the required un-PC lines and seal their fate as tomato fertiliser. The group's incredulity at the gamut of reactionary attitudes seems predictable and programmed. So, an avuncular priest praises the meal and barely breaks his stride when he starts to talk about AIDS as divine punishment for homosexuality. A series of gross caricatures parade from the head of the table straight into the compost heap in the back garden: the homophobe priest joins a smooth-talking apologist for rape, a pro-lifer, a polluting slob and a Nation of Islam zealot, amongst others. The political attitudes are as broad as their characterisations, obviously drawn as a function of the liberals' own desire to be outraged and, by extension, as the director and screenwriter's vision of the audience who, they wager, will accept the set-up dummies as representatives of various slices of the American New Right.

The political content of the group's self-righteous anger gradually evaporates as their victims quickly become people whose cultural and moral attitudes the group doesn't agree with. In one case, a young girl gets stabbed in the back for admitting that she doesn't rate 'Catcher in the Rye'. But the group's transition from sanctimonious self-justification to reflexive blood-letting doesn't really come over as shocking enough to raise the sort of laughter that barely conceals horror or despair. Likewise, the side plot of the policewoman's search for a missing girl is handled in desultory fashion. The moment of heavily signalled moral dilemma, when it becomes apparent to the group that Zac is the chief murder suspect and the group is suspected of knowing his whereabouts, implicitly suggests that the white-trash psycho deserved everything he got but in very different terms from all the others. But after the cop gets decapitated in the back garden, the whole matter is dropped and the moral dilemma dissolves.

The dialogue only rarely challenges. The TV shock-jock's self-justification towards the end of the film is the nicest and most unnerving moment. He contextualises his rabid right-wing exhortations as part of a tradition of dissent, placating his would-be executioners by being utterly reasonable while giving the game away when he explains that his over-the-top TV rhetoric is 'a ratings thing'. In other words, know your audience: scalding hate-vapour is to be exhaled for the TV audiences, equanimity exuded for the dinner-party circuit. Only Luke, by now the blood-hungry loose cannon of the group, twigs who they have hooked. 'He is Hitler!' he exclaims to the others. Having become the most fervent of the dinner-table vigilantes his breaking down in tears as the group unravels and loses its resolve doesn't come across as very convincing.

The action unwinds within the confines of the shared house and only occasionally strays outside. While this might seem reminiscent of *Shallow Grave* and its murderous sense of enclosure *The Last Supper*, with its concentration on character differentiation through dialogue, feels closer to screen adaptations of Ira Levin's *Sleuth* and *Death Trap*. Where Levin dramatised the deadly verbal parrying of theatrical rivalry, *The Last Supper* recreates a similarly static and theatrical *mise-en-scène*, which nevertheless makes good use of the minuscule $500,000 budget, and populates it with caricatures of current political positions. *The Last Supper* suffers from being over-ambitious, targeting the entire political culture from self-righteous liberals to Rush Limbaugh soundalikes and cramming them into the same living room around the same table.

WHERE IS MY FRIEND'S HOUSE?
DIR: ABBAS KIAROSTAMI IRAN 1987
ORIGINALLY PUBLISHED IN *SIGHT AND SOUND* OCTOBER 1996

SYNOPSIS
The village school of Koker, Northern Iran. Nematzadeh has neglected to do his homework in the designated exercise book. The teacher tells him that if he does it again he will be expelled. That evening, by mistake, his friend Ahmad takes home Nematzadeh's exercise book. Ahmad begins looking for his friend's house in the neighbouring village of Poshteh in order to return the book. He is not helped by adults who either ignore him or lecture him on morality.

Having been to Poshteh once in vain and returned to Koker, he leaves again, following the donkey of a craftsman who he thinks may be his friend's father. Ahmad loses track of him and, as night falls, is helped by an elderly window-maker who leads him to Nematzadeh's house. Ahmad doesn't knock on the door. He returns home late and does his homework.

At school the next morning, Ahmad is late and Nematzadeh has done his homework on a piece of paper again. Ahmad finally shows up and takes his place next to his friend. He slips the exercise book to Nematzadeh, telling him that he copied his homework up for him. The teacher congratulates Nematzadeh.

REVIEW
Where Is My Friend's House? is the first in a trilogy of films set around the Northern Iranian villages of Koker and Poshteh. Its companion films, *And Life Goes On* and *Through the Olive Trees*, sees Kiarostami's neo-realist approach combine with an exquisite self-reflexivity. *Where Is My Friend's House?* appears as the most straight-forward of the films – a young schoolboy realises he has taken his friend's exercise book home by mistake and searches in the neighbouring village to return it. The exercise book is a kind of neo-realist Maguffin, like the bicycle in *Bicycle Thief* and the balloon in *The White Balloon*, a trigger for a story that focuses insistently on its milieu.

Ahmad, a grave and tenacious friend, is beset by problems at every turn in his quest and Kiarostami introduces a sly, quiet comedy into the child's relationship with the older generation, which is shown as either harshly authoritarian – the school-teacher who reduces his friend to tears – or intransigently preoccupied – Ahmad's immediate family. Played out in registers of complication, interruption and delay – basic principles of narrative – it's the way that this simple, fable-like story is told that makes the film so remarkable. Ahmad picks up certain clues on his quest. He is told that his friend's house has a blue door, he notices a pair of pants identical to his friend's drying on a clothes line, he listens for the bell of a donkey ridden by a man he thinks is his friend's father. These prove to be red herrings in his mini-picaresque. The manner in which we come to identify with Ahmad has only in part to do with the sentimental reflex of sympathising with a child's travails in a world of hostile adults. Rather, we do the same thing in watching the film that Ahmad does in his search; we look for significant details.

This procedure is set up at the very beginning of the film. The opening image is a medium close-up of the worn, ugly modern door – which won't shut properly –

to a classroom. The following scene takes place in a courtyard, with Ahmad and his friend at a water pump. In the background is a white horse and beside it a hutch with a door flapping open. Cut to Ahmad's family courtyard, a large white shirt prominently drying on the line marking the transition on a graphic match that humorously replaces and condenses the shape of the horse in the previous shot. Ahmad enters the courtyard through the door. The jokey ostentation of that match cut momentarily lures our eyes away from the details of doors and windows, of apertures, that will become motifs in the film, symbols of entrapment and exclusion, family and tradition. These never appear as details grafted onto locale, but as integral parts of it, expressive of realities beyond the immediate physical space of the villages.

There is a remarkable sequence set at night in Koker, as Ahmad is guided by an elderly window-maker. On the way, he shows Ahmad the windows he has made. The two of them are, quite literally, being guided by the lights that shine out into the streets through these windows, as well as being shown to be in a projected reality. The shapes and colours of the windows are cast on to stone walls, the inhabitants occasionally throwing silhouettes within their illuminated frames. It is a moment of a breathtaking shadowplay and a vertiginous self-reflexivity, but worked up to and delivered with such economy of means that the film's realism always contains its effects.

One can legitimately call Kiarostami a present-day neo-realist. On *Where Is My Friend's House?* he worked exclusively with non-professional actors living in the villages where the film was shot and elicits a committed performance from Ahmad Ahmadpoor as the single-minded schoolboy. The commitment to location filming and to a long-take deep-focus shooting strategy is also crucial. Kiarostami creates a metaphorical landscape of struggle and obstructions for Ahmad to overcome out of the physical terrain that he covers. He twice covers the hillsides and forest to reach his friend's village. On his second journey though, having reached the door of his friend's house he makes a decision that at first appears self defeating – he doesn't knock on the door and return the book but hides it under his jumper and takes it back home with him. The next day he surreptitiously hands back the book with the homework completed for his friend. Up to the point where he is guided by the kindly window-maker Ahmad has met nothing but obstruction and disinterest from his elders. His journey with this elderly craftsman, whose crippled gait sets a pace to the house that Ahmad finds agonisingly slow, is also the journey to a kind of insight. Ahmad understands, through the solicitous assistance of the old man, that his quest would be incomplete if he were simply to return the book so late. His exhausting and frustrating search has shown him the extent to which his elders will justify themselves at the expense of understanding the predicament. So Ahmad learns a necessary guile, develops a pragmatist's skill at deceit in the service of a greater good. *Where is My Friend's House?* is a jewel of a film, compared to which *The White Balloon* might be viewed, somewhat unkindly, as 'Kiarostami lite'. Kiarostami is the genuine article, a gifted director whose neo-realist approach conceals a coded moral humanism and a hall-of-mirrors approach to inscribing the workings of cinematic identification within his films.

THE EIGHTH DAY
DIR: JACO VAN DORMAEL FR./BELG./UK 1996
ORIGINALLY PUBLISHED IN *SIGHT AND SOUND* NOVEMBER 1996

SYNOPSIS

Georges, a young man with Down's Syndrome, runs away from a residential home taking the institution's dog with him. The dog is run down by Harry, a harassed businessman who is separated from his wife and children. Harry gives Georges a lift. After trying vainly to entrust Georges to the care of the police, Harry lets him stay at his house for the night.

The next morning, Harry discovers Georges unconscious, having gone on an eating binge. He calls a doctor who diagnoses an allergic reaction to chocolate. Harry drives Georges to an address in Holland which he claims to be his mother's house. The occupant of the house tells Harry that Georges' mother died two years ago but gives him the address of Georges' sister. Harry leaves Georges alone at a crossroads to find his own way to his sister's house, but he soon returns. Harry takes Georges to his sister's house. When she tells him that he can't stay Georges throws a fit. Harry decides to take Georges back to the home. They stop at a restaurant on the way where Georges, smitten by a waitress, tries to charm her. When she realises that he has Downs' Syndrome, she backs off, frightened. Harry phones his wife Julie to tell her that he wants to deliver an early birthday present to his daughter. She refuses to see him. Harry drives Georges to see the seaside. Georges wanders off into the heavy fog and almost falls into the sea but is saved by the sound of Harry's car horn. The two men sleep in the car. The next morning Harry leaves Georges in the car and goes to see his wife. Outside the house, his two daughters talk to Georges who accompanies them into the house where he has to restrain the aggressive Harry. Harry takes Georges back to the home.

Back at the home, Nathalie, Georges' girlfriend, leaves to return to her family. On an outing to an art gallery, Georges and his friends steal a car from a car showroom and break into the conference in which Harry is participating. They steal fireworks, pick up Nathalie and break into a fairground. Harry lets off the fireworks on the beach facing Julie's house for his daughter's birthday. Georges and Nathalie make love in a caravan. The police arrive and Nathalie's parents take their daughter away. Georges, in anguish, runs away, pursued by Harry. They go to a disco where Georges tries to dance with several woman but they reject him. Harry and Georges fall asleep on a bench. When Harry awakes Georges has gone, having taken Harry's wallet with him, but leaving the photographs of his daughters. Harry is reconciled with his family as Georges watches from a distance. Georges goes onto the roof of the building in which Harry works, eats a box of chocolates and throws himself to his death.

REVIEW

Jaco Van Dormael's *Toto the Hero* was an extraordinary first film, with a visual flair and a command of its switchback narrative structure that was hugely promising. *The Eighth Day* comes as something of a shock in comparison. Where Toto was a hard-eyed stare at the ambiguous memories of childhood, *The Eighth Day* feels more like a hymn to getting in touch with 'the child within'. The film's premise is familiar from

Rain Man, Forrest Gump, and even from *Being There*: an uptight regular guy undergoes an enlightening, life-changing encounter with a disadvantaged man suffering some kind of disability. But whereas in these other examples, disability is performed – Hoffman's method autism, Hanks and Sellars as remedial holy fools – in *The Eighth Day* it's the performer himself who is disabled. Pascal Duquenne as Georges, the young man with Downs' Syndrome, has the same condition as his character, which gives his performance an unmediated intensity that is the film's strongest point. The successful pairing of Duquenne with Daniel Auteuil, whose screen persona is rapidly becoming that of a man permanently wall-eyed with shock and rigid with repression, saw the duo share the Best Actor award at Cannes this year.

While the authenticity of its casting might help *The Eighth Day* overcome some of the similarities it shares with its American counterparts, the film also ups the ante in its treatment of the emotional tone of the story. It doesn't so much want to tug at your heartstrings as to hammer out sentimental arpeggios on them. In fact, the film searches for a cinematic language to express excessive emotion and in this search runs through a gamut of options. There's a basic melodramatic structure of sundered relationships – Harry with his wife and kids, Georges with Nathalie – embroidered with sequences of hyperbolic stylistic excess. The imagination at work in these moments is often remarkably cinematic. The opening sequence, for example, is a *tour de force*, in which the two characters – Georges on earth and associated with nature, as he will be throughout the film; Harry in the sterile enclosure of an airliner's business class – are linked by the flight of a ladybird. But such pyrotechnics soon become wearing, particularly when the figure of the ersatz Latin crooner Luis Mariano keeps reappearing as the key figure associated with Georges's interior life. These moments are simultaneously naïve in their unrestrained emotionalism, and tremendously artful in their execution. Imagine Douglas Sirk getting Pierre and Gilles to design a fantasy sequence and you'll have a picture of the sort of stylistic terrain the film inhabits.

Dormael's commitment to the idea of emotional honesty and immediacy with which Georges is associated dictates the film's style. But the pay-off, which has Georges dying so that Harry may live an emotionally richer life, seems dishonest and cruel. Particularly when Georges' suicidal leap is followed by an appallingly misjudged 'Singing Detective'-style burst of ensemble singing. Like so many of its moments of stylistic excess, it's a telling one, an indication that, in the absence of the narrative origami that distinguished *Toto*, Dormael seems to be chaffing at the bit of linear narrative, that what he really wants to do is 'sawdust and tinsel' spectacle or old-fashioned musical show-stopping routines. These moments, impressive as they may be, only serve to add glitter to a predictable story underwritten by the highly conventional 'othering' reflex familiar from the film's Hollywood precursors, where the disabled character is always a kind of idiot savant, a repository of humanising influences to be absorbed by the repressed sidekick. Ultimately, it is difficult to tell whether *The Eighth Day* is a film of childish emotions for adults or a film of adult emotions for children.

LOADED
DIR: ANNA CAMPION UK/NZ 1994
ORIGINALLY PUBLISHED IN *SIGHT AND SOUND* NOVEMBER 1996

SYNOPSIS

Southern England, the early 1990s. A group of school-leavers plan to travel to the country for the weekend to make a horror video. The group includes Neil and his girlfriend Rose, the abrasive Lance and his girlfriend Charlotte, Giles, Zita and Lionel, who plans to join them later. Before leaving, Neil, a troubled young man, visits his therapist who he surreptitiously videotapes during the session. They arrive at a large abandoned country house and immediately start arguing about their ideas for the video. They explore the grounds and, coming across a pool, Neil recalls the boyhood drowning of his younger brother.

The filming of the video continues apace but is beset by Rose's paranoia that her character is too strongly based on herself. Neil wants to sleep with Rose, who is a virgin, but is suspicious of her feelings for Lionel. After Lionel arrives, Lance sees him and Rose in the woods and mistakes their friendly embrace for a lovers' tryst. He later tells Neil, who becomes more suspicious. After a day's filming, the group dine together and Lance suggests that they each drop acid and record an intimate to-camera self-portrait. The acid slowly takes over and delirium sets in. Later in the night, still tripping, Neil and Lance drive into a nearby village for provisions accompanied by Lionel on his motorbike. Returning home, the car collides with the bike and Lionel is killed. Fearful of the consequences, and still high, the group bury Lionel in the woods – just as they buried him in the film. Rose accuses Neil of having deliberately killed Lionel. He denies this and the antagonism between them transforms into sex.

The following morning the group have second thoughts about the secret that Lionel's burial has created for them. They decide to return the body to the site of the accident and nominate Neil to explain to the police. Neil, left alone in the house, rehearses his version of events, while the others search for the body. The search proves futile. Rose starts to panic and returns to the house where she finds Neil. Her distress and hopes for Lionel's resurrection makes Neil feel that the truth needs to be told and the group released from its distress. He phones the police.

REVIEW

Originally titled *Bloody Weekend* and having since been re-cut by Miramax, Anna Campion's first feature has languished for two years between its 1994 Venice Film Festival screening and its British release. In the meantime, several of its cast have gone on to important starring roles, Thandie Newton playing opposite Nick Nolte in *Jefferson in Paris* and Catherine McCormack pairing off with Mel Gibson in *Braveheart*. Standing to profit – or suffer – from association with the slew of 'wasted youth' movies headlined by *Kids* and *Trainspotting*, *Loaded* explores an early 1990s youth-culture moment both before and outside the current poles of up-high, down-hard dancefloor euphoria and Britpop optimism. That's not to say that *Loaded* appears dated, just that its characters seem like they'd probably prefer to associate the title with the Velvet Underground rather than with the lad-rag of the same name. The young of *Loaded* are not exclusively defined by their choice of drugs and clothes but are explored as characters mined for their thoughts and feelings.

The group's dynamics, fuelled by a combination of competitiveness and affection, result in games of domination and submission acted out between Lance's Steve Woolley-wannabe, Giles' rationalist art-film enthusiasm and Neil's Romantic anguish. It's less a matter of these being positions taken for the sake of bloody-minded stand-offs and more a case of the film wanting, a little clumsily at times, to signal its themes: materialism versus rationalism versus spirituality. For example, if Lionel's death is to be read, as the director's statement puts it, as 'the death of innocence', it is only so in terms of a character overly representative of a theme and is only partly convincing. Because Lionel only appears late in the film we care less about him than we do about the others, and also because his death serves to trigger Neil's taking of responsibility. That said, these are minor quibbles compensated for by the vigour of the actors' renditions of the male roles. This is particularly so in the case of Ollie Milburn's nicely modulated Neil, whose vulnerability and angst give him Byronic grunge gravitas and whose final act of admitting to Lionel's death becomes a cathartic taking of responsibility on a wider scale in his life.

There's a nice feeling for the 'time' of this group; its rhythm, less intense than the brilliant combination of simultaneously fazed and rampant sensation in *Kids* is true to the late-adolescent combination of longeur and epiphany that hanging out together entails. Acid is the ideal drug in these circumstances and a wiser, more accurate choice than the more fashionable, but much less interesting E. The sense of rhythm is accentuated by the confined setting of the rambling country house played off against the mysterious space of the woodlands, as well as through the dialogue's emerging from and playing out of the group dynamics and the camera's long-take fluidity. Video features here in various guises to play different modulations on what, in the 1970s, art theorist Rosalind Krauss called 'the aesthetic of narcissism'. So, with Neil's craftily-taped video images of his therapist we are in territory familiar from Atom Egoyan films but which is explored less obsessively here, whereas the group's horror video – while its distressed footage and bleached images approximate the look of bootlegged Mexican cannibal pics – is largely an over-emphatic plot device whose events are destined to be played out in reality, fictional roles merging disturbingly with real lives. The group's use of video for to-camera testimonial is deployed to give the narrative a standard postmodern formalist patina.

If the boys come across as alternately energetic and anguished it's partly because the girls are so hardy and sensible. Even the tremulous Rose's desire to shed her virginity comes across as an earnest preoccupation. Neil, Giles and Lance are the strange characters here, their passions seen as exotic in comparison with the girls' steadfast resourcefulness; the boys appear almost as if seen from the girls' perspective as chaotic, excessive others. Which is another way of saying that the girls are less interesting characters: they know themselves, whereas the boys have the advantage of pustular psyches ripe for exploding – witness Zita's horrified discovery of Giles's ghoulish obsession with serial killers. *Loaded* would make the perfect double-bill partner to its 1986 Australian precursor, the equally sympathetic *Dogs in Space*.

SURVIVING PICASSO
DIR: JAMES MERCHANT USA/UK 1996
ORIGINALLY PUBLISHED IN *SIGHT AND SOUND* JANUARY 1997

SYNOPSIS
1943, Occupied Paris. Pablo Picasso meets Françoise and Genevieve, two young art students, in a bistro. He invites them to visit his studio where he pays particular attention to Françoise. She returns several weeks later whereupon Picasso encourages her artistic ambitions, kisses her but doesn't seduce her.

After the Liberation, Françoise informs her father that she intends to devote herself to painting. Her father reacts angrily and, when she flees to her grandmother's house, he pursues and attacks her. Her grandmother warns Françoise of Picasso's reputation with women and Françoise soon discovers that he visits his previous lover Marie-Thérèse, who lives with his child. When she next visits Picasso, he asks her to move in with him and she initiates sex. Before the couple live together, Picasso takes Françoise to visit a previous mistress, the disturbed, enigmatic Dora Maar, to inform her of their plans. Françoise and Picasso travel together to the South of France where she feels isolated and attempts to take off to Algeria. Picasso forces her to return. When visiting a church he insists that she vows that she will love him alone forever. Back in Paris, Picasso plays his dealers off against one another. Françoise has a son, Claude. The couple spend more time at their country house in Valeuris and Françoise invites Marie-Thérèse to the house to make peace. Marie-Thérèse informs Françoise that she takes precedence over all of Picasso's other women.

While collecting scrap for his sculptures from a demolition yard, Françoise meets another of Picasso's previous mistresses, Olga Koklova, now a disturbed and vengeful woman. Picasso joins the Communist Party and travels to a Congress in Poland. While he is away, Françoise becomes anxious about their relationship and, on his return, slaps him, forcefully berating him for neglecting her while she is expecting their second child, Paloma. The couple visit Matisse, with whom Picasso feels a friendly rivalry. Matisse gives Picasso an African mask as a gift. Picasso's chauffeur accidentally crashes the car and, despite twenty-five years of faithful service, Picasso dismisses him on the spot. Now working with ceramics, Picasso becomes involved with another woman, Jacqueline, who works in his pottery. Picasso travels to Paris but, unknown to Françoise, takes Jacqueline with him. Françoise hears that her grandmother has had a stroke and travels back to Paris only to arrive too late. Françoise's friend Genevieve comes to visit her and the two women spot Picasso in a bistro with Jacqueline. Françoise goes to the studio and tells him that she intends to leave him. He responds by slighting her talents as a painter. Françoise packs her things and takes her children with her. Picasso feigns a collapse and refuses to say goodbye to the children. Soon after, he asks Françoise to ride the ceremonial horse in a bullfight organised in his honour. She agrees, calling it 'my personal homage to Picasso'.

REVIEW
Françoise Gilot was a young art student when she met Pablo Picasso. She became his mistress, the mother of two of his children and his muse. According to *Surviving*

Picasso's account of their relationship, to be Picasso's muse was to be used and abused by a monster of arrogant genius. James Ivory's film depicts Picasso as the misogynist modernist *par excellence* and the callous master of his confidants, most notably the put-upon Jaime Sabarthés, his faithful secretary, and his dealer, Daniel-Henry Kahnweiler. Yet the emphasis on the dark side of the artist makes *Surviving Picasso* sound more promising and exciting than it is.

The film frequently resorts to Françoise's voice-over which narrates Picasso's life via his past relationships. The film's Paris bistro opening has an interestingly intimate tone, with Dora Maar throwing a sardonically jaundiced commentary on Picasso's tried and tested chat-up lines while the master works on Françoise at a neighbouring table. Julianne Moore plays Dora Maar brilliantly, like a cartoon of trampled-upon vampdom, but with a touch of pathos. She also has the unnerving habit of playing the Mexican knife-between-the-fingers routine on the table while conversing. None of the other performances come anywhere near Moore's, and this is a serious drawback in a film where her part is relatively minor. Even Anthony Hopkin's bold and brassy Picasso somehow seems familiar, and therefore less impressive. Natascha McElhone has a presence of such serenity that, at times, almost suggests an innate independence to her Françoise. But her character's artistic aspirations are barely developed beyond their narrative function of allowing her an entry into the minotaur's lair. When Picasso coldly dismisses her paintings as displaying only 'a schoolgirl's facility', the comment lacks the personal bitterness of a spurned lover's rebuke largely because Françoise's character has not been developed as that of an artistic disciple.

The film credits Arianna Stassinopoulos Huffington's biography *Picasso: Creator and Destroyer* as its literary source – rather than Gilot's own account, *Life with Picasso* – and it all feels more than a little predictable, like a colour supplement profile of artistic torment, stormy genius, etc. And Bohemian interiors. The Merchant Ivory 'Furniture Restoration' aesthetic is only minimally employed here, just a bit of Parisian attic-clutter well offset by the odd bistro interior and plentiful excursions to the glorious *midi* town of Valleuris. Picasso's work is largely integrated into the story's emotional dynamic. Thus 'Guernica' becomes the canvas that Picasso works away on happily while Dora Maar and Marie-Thérèse fight over him. The too-easy identification of his work's abstraction of the female form as a kind of creative misogyny is all that *Surviving Picasso* has to offer by way of insights into the work. But it's not an insight that's arrived at, more one that's taken for granted, and in that sense the film is a very conventional artist's biopic with a soft revisionist spin on its subject. As an antidote to James Ivory's politely PC conformism, it's almost tempting to imagine Norman Mailer's current biography *Portrait of Picasso as a Young Man* being adapted for the screen by Oliver Stone.

NORMAL LIFE
DIR: HENRY McNAUGHTON USA 1995
ORIGINALLY PUBLISHED IN *SIGHT AND SOUND* MAY 1997

SYNOPSIS

The Chicago suburbs, the present. An armed, bearded man and a blonde woman attempt to hot-wire a car and are unexpectedly jumped by an FBI team. The man listens on the police car radio as his accomplice is pursued.

Two years earlier. Chris Anderson, a young off-duty cop meets Pam Seaver, a young blonde, in a bar. After an altercation with another couple Pam cuts her hand. Chris bandages it and they dance. They start to meet regularly and Pam introduces Chris to her hobby of star-gazing. Watching the night sky one evening, Chris jokily calls her 'crazy', Pam reacts angrily and storms off. They are reconciled and she tells him that her mother died in a car accident. Chris says he wants to marry her. Pam's erratic and compulsive behaviour, her drug abuse and overspending, provokes huge rows between the newly-married couple. After one violent disagreement Chris takes off on his motorbike while Pam drinks heavily and scars herself with a knife. Having taken to her bed for three days, Chris placates her by buying her a pet dog. Chris's father dies and Pam turns up to the funeral in roller-blading gear. Chris loses his job with the police force and takes work as a security operative. Pam goes into drug therapy.

Deeply in debt, Chris uses his police and security expertise to set up a series of violence-free bank robberies. After several bank raids, he buys a brand new house. The TV coverage of the bank raids refer to 'The Bearded Bandit' and, on leaving work one day, having been dismissed, Pam spots Chris in disguise preparing another job. Pam is excited by Chris's exploits and insists on joining his next job. He resists but then acquiesces. On the raid she fires a round of bullets into the roof, the first time any shooting has taken place on one of Chris's raids. Chris wants to stop the robberies and buys a property which he intends to turn into a used book store. Pam, however, wants to continue and walks out on Chris when he refuses. Chris relents and they do another job. They are tracked and Chris is captured by the FBI. Pam is pursued by the police and shoots herself. While being tried for the robberies Chris grabs a warder's gun, shoots two cops and tries to escape but is shot in the back. Lying injured he screams out Pam's name and shoots himself.

REVIEW

John McNaughton's career to date looks like a series of unsatisfactory attempts to recapture the fluency and conviction of his breakthrough film, *Henry: Portrait of a Serial Killer*. But then, how does a director follow up one of the American cinema's most terrifyingly bleak visions of a psychopath? The film's successor, *Mad Dog and Glory* was a star-decked bid for the mainstream that backfired after the low-budget autonomy of *Henry*. With *Normal Life* McNaughton now seems to be consolidating in his attempt to find a format for his dissections of urban anomie.

Normal Life opens promisingly with a botched bank-job that has cop turned bank robber Chris Anderson listening in helplessly to the police radio wavelength as Pam, his wife and partner in crime, is chased by the Chicago cops. It's the film's pivotal moment; the hinge for a flashback to two years earlier when the couple first meet, as well as being the point returned to as the culmination of a relationship that resorts to crime in order to avoid dissolution. It also contains one of those auteur touches with which McNaughton sprinkles his film. The most telling moments are mediated, where the consequences of characters' actions are fed back to them at one remove – through video in *Henry*, via photography in *Mad Dog* and in *Normal Life*, across the radio. It's a motif in the fullest sense then, a recurrent image that is thematically coherent and it wouldn't be labouring things to suggest that the theme that supports all McNaughton's films is alienation. *Henry* is the thematic ground-zero, the serial-killers Henry and Otis embodying the outer limits of white-trash alienation. *Mad Dog* took white-collar alienation as the core theme in an uncertain examination of hard-man/sensitive-guy roles built around the cop/criminal opposition. *Normal Life* brings it all back home, as it were. Suburban domesticity, the 'normal life' of the title, is the grail that Pam and Chris try ambiguously to secure for themselves, only to discover it to be a consumerist mirage in an edge-city wilderness.

Based on the true story of a young middle-class couple's descent into criminality, *Normal Life* has a classic noir narrative; Pam's an unreconstructed femme fatale dragging her man along with her in a deadly tailspin. But film noir's classic cocktail of fatalism and sexual compulsion is deliberately watered down here. Perry plays Chris as a doggedly dutiful husband whose devotion to his unstable wife provokes his turning to robbery; he's more a regular guy gone wrong for want of a good woman than the moth-to-a-flame male beloved of classic film noir. So, the film turns gradually into the anatomisation of a relationship. Pam is a kind of biker-chick Emma Bovary, a hot-wired bundle of hysterical symptoms, and a dope-smoking, Stephen Hawking aficionado – 'Black holes are *so* intense', she coos spacily – and Ashley Judd plays this blonde with a death wish with great intensity. Those who recall Judd's cameo in *Smoke* as Auggie Wren's errant daughter can expect her incendiary turn to be fleshed out in *Normal Life*. But her character is given little in the way of background for her behaviour, we hear that her mother died in car accident, that she can't achieve orgasm (not until Chris starts turning over banks), and while this may be rooted in the facts of the original case, Pam unbalances the film's central relationship. Chris' motivation for staying with her is never explored, his rock-like stoicism becoming less and less plausible as Pam becomes more unhinged.

Avoiding both classic noir dynamics and melodramatic motivations, McNaughton gives the film a clinical, almost documentary feel, situating his characters in a desert of car parks and suburban lawns. He structures the process of the couple's demise in a deterministic loop that closes like a pair of handcuffs. The strange thing is that, with Chris's suicide, the tone attained is that of a quasi-tragic love story. It's a low-key film though, not dissimilar in style to other examinations of domestic discord turning to suburban crime such as *Handgun* and *My New Gun*. Here McNaughton seems to have found a way to weld his detached examinations of alienated losers to a pared-down, modern-day B-movie style that, while not as brutally dour as that of a director like James B. Harris, indicates that *Henry* was not the hopeless cul-de-sac it was beginning to look like and that McNaughton may yet deliver something just as singular in the future.

PUSHER
DIR: NICHOLAS WINDING REFN DENMARK 1996
ORIGINALLY PUBLISHED IN *SIGHT AND SOUND* OCTOBER 1997

SYNOPSIS
Frank operates as a heroin dealer in Copenhagen with his companion Tonny. He hides his drugs at the flat of his prostitute girlfriend, Vicky. One Monday, Frank meets with Rita, a drug courier, and instructs her to pick up heroin from Amsterdam. The next day, Frank is approached by a Swedish man he doesn't recognise but who claims they served time together. The Swede wants to buy brown heroin quickly and offers Frank a high price. To effect the deal, Frank goes to see Milo, an émigré Serb and local gang boss to who Frank already owes money. Milo lends Frank money, at a high rate and on the condition that it's paid back fast. Frank and Tonny turn up early to meet the Swede on the next day but the exchange is interrupted by the arrival of the police. Frank is chased on foot and dives into the harbour with the drugs. Both he and Tonny and arrested. Refusing to divulge anything, Frank is released the next day, but the police show him a signed confession from Tonny. Frank goes to Milo, whom he now owes more money, and explains the situation but Milo refuses to believe him. Going to find money to pay off Milo, Frank finds Tonny in a bar and beats him up savagely. Frank is joined by Radovan, Milo's henchman, in an effort to round up some debts. They threaten a regular junkie client of Frank's so intensely that the man kills himself. Frank promises Milo that he'll have the money ready the next day.

Frank buys cocaine and a gun off another dealer. On the following Friday, Frank expects Rita to return from Amsterdam but she doesn't show. Frank is informed by his connection that she'll be returning on Saturday. When Frank calls Milo he is told that if he doesn't show up the next day he won't walk again. On Saturday Rita turns up and delivers the drugs, but Radovan and another thug interrupt the exchange. They test the heroin, which turns out to be counterfeit. Frank continues rounding up money to pay off Milo, going as far as to visit his mother who gives him what little cash she has. He finds Rita, attacks her, then holds up the dealer who sold him the gun and steals drugs and money from him. Radovan catches up with Frank and takes him to Milo who strips him of his car, watch and gold chain. Frank is then tortured but shoots one of Milo's thugs before escaping. Frank goes to Vicky's flat and asks her if she wants to leave for Spain with him. She accepts. The next day, they go to a rave where Frank does a deal, during which he gets a call on his mobile phone from Milo, who offers conciliatory terms. Frank tells Vicky that he no longer wants to leave. Vicky steals the proceeds of Frank's deal and escapes. Standing outside the club, Frank has a vision of his doomed and desperate life.

REVIEW
Pusher depicts seven days in the life of Frank, a Danish heroin dealer whose girlfriend Vicky is a prostitute and whose closest friend is his accomplice Tonny, a racist thug. The film wants the spectator to feel a certain empathy for Frank, which is elicited through his relationship with Tonny, and there are likeable but sketchy touches here, detailing the two different characters through their tastes. After a Chinese meal,

for example, Frank insists on ordering Armagnac, while Tonny wonders aloud if this might be 'some kind of cleaning fluid'. But the bond between the two dealers is uneasy. This temporary, untrustworthy alliance of scumbags is expressed most effectively through the hardcore in-car banter they exchange about the sexual preferences of their favourite female TV personalities. On one hand this scene reveals the mixture of complicity and prissy disapproval with which Frank reacts to Tonny's bigotry. But it's also a Tarantino touch that coexists with the by now standard set of American pulp movie references through which any self-respecting gangster movie communicates its contemporary credibility. Additionally, Pusher calls on Ferrara's *Bad Lieutenant* for its tight, episodic countdown of a time scheme and on Scorsese and Cassavetes for the edgy, improvisational quality of its take on male partnership.

It is remarkable how the reflex of homage prospers in the modern-day crime movie, with one film constantly slipping back-handers to others of its ilk. But *Pusher* is more than just the sum of its genuflecting parts. The film rapidly becomes a kind of behaviourist study whose strength resides in an unerring sense of rhythm and place. At large in the tough Copenhagen district of Vesterbro, Frank inhabits an increasingly claustrophobic warren of dingy rooms, darkened stairways and dangerous streets. The speed at which Refn pushes him through these locales accelerates until Frank's movement looks like that of a lab rat bouncing back and forth between stimuli. There's a kind of tension and release elasticity to the editing that plays on the film's balance of its interior and exterior action. When shooting the interior scenes the jittery hand-held camerawork is all about conveying the very temporary sense of refuge that these spaces promise. When the action moves outside it is keyed to another, more explosive pacing and scored to a hard rock soundtrack which doesn't so much generate a feeling of criminal euphoria but rather aggravates the sense of threat that develops the film's theme of pursuit. It is this theme that underlies Frank's profession, the pursuit of drugs, addicts and other dealers, as well as his increasingly being pursued by Milo and his thugs. *Pusher* is an absolutely cinematic treatment of the theme as it takes hold in a street criminal's life, because it is understood and expressed as movement. Frank is like a city shark: as soon as he stops moving he is as good as dead; which is the strong implication of the film's ending. Having promised to skip the city with Vicky and make for Spain, he changes his mind at the last minute and Vicky, feeling justifiably betrayed, steals the cash from his last deal and leaves him. Left standing outside a night-club, Frank is immobilised by the demanding rhythm of his life and has a hellish vision of how he is powerless to change it and how it will destroy him.

If the film's screenplay seems predictable this only serves, in a way, to tighten the noose around Frank's neck. Any overly novel events would simply have distracted from the task the film sets itself – to physically convey the tightening corners that trap Frank. A powerful, impressively bleak debut that dispenses rapidly with genre hat-tipping, *Pusher* is a portrait of paranoid criminal fear intensified to the point of existential despair, with Frank's gangster front slowly wearing down until his aggression turns in on itself.

CLOSE UP
DIR: ABBAS KIAROSTAMI IRAN 1997
ORIGINALLY PUBLISHED IN *THE INDEPENDENT* 12 DECEMBER 1997

There are films whose sound and fury signify nothing, the brutality of whose assault on the senses wanes moments after leaving the cinema. Then there are films as limpid and simple as an afternoon spent watching clouds, that haunt the imagination and reveal themselves to be far more complex and suggestive than one ever imagined. *Close Up*, by the Iranian director Abbas Kiarostami, is one such film. Kiarostami is not yet a name familiar to British audiences, although he is lionised on the international film festival circuit and praised by critics and filmmakers. In 1995, Godard harangued the New York Film Critics Circle over the choice of Kieslowski rather than Kiarostami for a foreign film Oscar nomination and at this year's Cannes Festival his most recent film, *Taste of Cherry*, shared the Palme d'Or. *Close Up* is an essential film and an ideal introduction to the cinema of Kiarostami, whose economy of means and apparent simplicity conceals a lucid, ludic meditation on appearance and reality.

'We are the slaves to a mask that hides our true face,' says the protagonist of *Close Up* and it's a statement that reverberates throughout the film. The speaker is Hossein Sabzian, an unemployed movie fan who finds himself on trial for impersonating the major Iranian director Mohsen Makhmalbaf and having won the confidence of a well-heeled Tehrani family, telling them that he intends to cast them in a film. Sabzian's imposture begins casually, almost reflexively, on a bus journey. An older woman, the mother of the Ahankhan family, sits beside him and notices that he's reading the screenplay of *The Cyclist*, a film by Makhmalbaf that she admires. 'Where did you get that?' she asks the man who, without skipping a beat, replies 'I wrote it.' In that instant Sabzian 'becomes' Makhmalbaf and begins the masquerade that will eventually bring him up against the law. But, as Kiarostami's film reveals, in a way Sabzian did write *The Cyclist*, or at least wrote himself into it through his passion for the film – 'Tell Makhmalbaf that *The Cyclist* is a part of me', Sabzian instructs Kiarostami at one point. None of this is fiction but, then, neither is it documentary. Kiarostami not only based *Close Up* on an actual court case but incorporated its leading protagonists into his film, creating a work that deliberately and continually explores the porous boundary connecting fact and fiction, life and art.

Close Up is two films in one, a hugely skilful work of cinematic origami about doubles and doubling. Kiarostami sought permission to shoot Sabzian's trial – even having the gall to request that the trial judge bring the hearing forward to fit the shooting schedule – then reconstructed the events that bought Sabzian to court. 'I read the story [of Sabzian as the bogus Makhmalbaf] in a weekly magazine,' Kiarostami has stated. 'To quote Marquez, one is more chosen by a subject than choosing it. The first point that struck me was that the guy was not a fraud. He was, rather, infatuated by an image. What a filmmaker could do for him was to rehabilitate him, to portray him as a young man who is in love with cinema.' Sabzian is a grizzled autodidact. His courtroom testimony, shot by Kiarostami in unwavering video close-up footage, reveals him as a sympathetic working-class solipsist whose devotion to cinema overtakes his life. Divorced and unemployed, film is as much a reality to him as the brute conditions of his life. In this respect, *Close Up* is a parable of those moments when the life of the imagination become more certain, more tangible, than the uncertainty of the material life that one inhabits.

An American film critic has described Kiarostami's films rather neatly as 'Rosselini meets Pirandello' in which gritty neo-realist humanism combines with hall-of-mirrors self-reflexivity, and *Close Up* is a perfect example of such traits. Kiarostami loops his account of Sabzian's imposture, opening with a reconstruction of his arrest – Sabzian 'playing' Sabzian 'playing' Makhmalbaf. It's a structure that works to give the film richness and density, as well as a thoughtfulness that is barely alluded to at a single viewing. For, as much as *Close Up* is a film about 'the power of cinema', it is many other things as well. It's a telling anatomisation of the cross-class encounter between the wealthy Ahankhan family and the working-class Sabzian, both united by a shared love of cinema and art, at least until the fraud is revealed. It also contains moments of a certain kind of low-key formal daring that one doesn't come across much in cinema, in which Kiarostami takes inconsequential moments and details and lovingly foregrounds them. An aerosol can is kicked down a street and the camera holds on its clattering descent, an aeroplane passes overhead and a character follows it with his eyes. Kiarostami installs himself, with a curiously effective combination of insistence and unobtrusiveness, between the story and its telling. When, on Sabzian's release from prison, the real Makhmalbaf is there to meet him and take him to visit the Ahankhans again, Kiarostami's crew films the encounter from a car across the road. Their ancient sound equipment keeps cutting in and out and, as Sabzian collapses tearfully into his alter-ego's arms, this moment of concluding catharsis is interrupted by the crackle and hiss of malfunctioning electronics. It's an accidental *tour-de-force* that's no accident. The car follows the couple on a motorbike and their conversation is conveyed in partial gobbets of sound. Just seeing Sabzian restored to the world by cinema is, in itself, enough.

THE RIVER
DIR: TSAI MING-LIANG TAIWAN 1997
ORIGINALLY PUBLISHED IN *THE INDEPENDENT* 13 MARCH 1998

A young man meets a woman he hasn't seen since schooldays; they have sex joylessly in a darkened room and don't encounter each other again. A middle-aged man cruises saunas for gay pick-ups and constructs a makeshift drainage system for the water that pours into his bedroom from the seemingly abandoned flat above. A woman, working as a lift operator in a department store, has an affectionless relationship with a man who pirates porn videos. Such are the joys of modern family life in present-day Taipei as depicted in Tsai Ming-Liang's *The River.*

The third film in a nominal trilogy about contemporary life in the Taiwanese capital, its predecessors being *Rebels of the Neon God* and *Vive L'amour,* Tsai's film won the Silver Bear at the 1997 Berlin Film Festival. Sharing characters and performers, themes and settings with his earlier two films, in *The River* Tsai continues to chart the personal odyssey of a young man, Xiao-kang (Lee Kang-Sheng). Drifting and without work, Xiao-kang finds a day job as a corpse. Or, at least, a one-off cameo role on a film shoot, where he's asked to float stiffly downstream in the heavily polluted Tanshui River. Thereafter, he develops an ache in his neck that simply won't go away. The narrative, such as it is, in *The River* concerns his mother and father's attempts to heal their son's complaint.

The River moves steadily and insistently through those moments that wouldn't normally constitute drama in narrative film. It's a film constructed from the moments in between action, of afternoons of listless domesticity in sparse apartments, of urban drift and significance that emerges from banal details. Tsai's camera style is relentlessly observational, locked-down and static, level-eyed and several steps back from the action. The film accrues its density and allegorical texture from a steady elaboration of specific symbols. Xiao-kang's increasingly agonising aching neck has a specific cause, but becomes more than a merely a product of a dip in polluted waters. Tsai has explained it as 'a projection of his rebellion' but it's also of a part with the film's other images of stultified desire. The water that pours into the father's bedroom becomes the chief image of desire denied and re-routed. The father constructs an elaborate system to divert the leak out of his room, without informing his wife or son. But sometime, inevitably, his little dam must break. Related in this way, the symbolism may appear trite and contrived – but Tsai knits it into the locations and everyday activities of his characters so that it becomes telling, forceful and satisfying. Likewise, the attempts to cure Xiao-kang of his aching neck prove useless, the ancestral remedy of acupuncture and the consultation of religious worthies come to nothing. It's tempting for Western critics to see in this some comment on the incompatibility of the present with the past, of the modern condition being more than a match for ancient treatments. It's a conclusion borne out by Tsai's insistence on the environmental background to his story. 'We don't always live happily ever after,' he explains. 'Look around us, the city is growing fast. Materialism boosts human greed to an inglorious height. We have everything we ever wanted, yet there is something lurking in the dark to keep us from being really happy.'

While Tsai's work is largely unknown to Western audiences its tenor is familiar.

And if *The River* shares some of the themes of Hong Kong-based director Wong Kar-Wei, urban anomie and the being-alone-together of a seething metropolitan existence, Tsai's style is not the redemption through camera pyrotechnics that his Hong Kong colleague achieves in his collaboration with cameraman Chris Doyle. Rather, the comparisons might come from closer to home. *The River* might be seen as being the Taiwanese elaboration of art-cinema themes and characters recognisable from Kieslowski, Egoyan and even stretching as far back as Antonioni. But more than being a neon-lit *La Notte*, *The River* ups the sexual ante of art cinema by engaging fully and brutally with the consequences of sexual repression. When Xiao-kang is taken out of the city by his father to consult a faith healer, the pair independently wind up in the same sauna. The gay encounter that ensues is cross-cut with a scene of the mother alone in the apartment. The father's dam has finally burst and water surges into the room and under the mother's chair. It's the climactic image of the film, as a quiet and understated as it might appear, it gathers into itself all the force of the carefully elaborated symbolism that the film has developed. This river, one feels, will run on regardless, all the way to an emotional apocalypse.

ROBERT MITCHUM & OUT OF THE PAST
ORIGINALLY PUBLISHED IN *THE INDEPENDENT* 3 APRIL 1998

In Jacques Tourneur's 1947 classic film noir *Out of the Past*, Robert Mitchum stepped into Humphrey Bogart's shoes. Bogart was initially slated to play the doomed and fatalistic private eye Jeff Bailey but Warner Brothers refused to loan out the star to RKO Pictures. Mitchum stepped in after his first major screen success in William Wellman's *The Story of G. I. Joe* (1945). Later in his career, Mitchum would offer his version of Philip Marlowe in the 1975 remake of *Farewell, My Lovely* and in Michael Winner's disastrous attempt at *The Big Sleep* (1978). *Out of the Past* pitches Mitchum, as private investigator Jeff Bailey, into a criminal sexual triangle that's played out between femme fatale Kathie Moffet (Jane Greer) and shark-like white-collar crook Whit Stirling (Kirk Douglas).

If *Out of the Past* has become a classic of the noir cannon it's because all the elements are glowingly present and correct. Iconically lit and costumed, the trench-coated figures float in and out of cinematographer Nicholas Musuraca's high-contrast shadows like duplicitious ghosts. The narrative is a snare of flashback, double-cross and frame-up that's built in as wide and sufficiently convoluted an arc to trap the fall-guy Bailey. But he's caught to begin with. When Mitchum first appears in the film, he's languishing by a lake with a youthful sweetheart, Ann (Virginia Huston), who is taken with his air of mystery and worldliness. Living under a false name – his real name is Jeff Markham – he is building an equally false life as a mechanic. But Bailey's desire for happiness can't be seen as entirely fake. One of Mitchum's first pieces of dialogue is a short, and for Mitchum, almost florid declaration of his desire to settle down, build a house, have kids with Ann and 'never go anywhere again'. This thwarted desire for security is a thematic spine in the noir genre. If American melodramas homed in on the neurotic inferno boiling under the post-war dream of domesticity, noir might be said to have encapsulated the jaundiced gaze of those forever living beyond the picket fence. *Out of the Past* contains its fair share of little stabs at happiness, domestic stop-overs, log cabins by the roadside, all of them shown to be one-night domestic bubbles en route to destruction. And Mitchum plays Jeff Bailey as an eternal outsider for whom happiness is just bad luck on hold.

As a genial odd-jobs man, Mitchum doesn't convince. Soon the iconic trench-coat and snap-brim will envelop him, cementing this peformance as an Ur-noir moment. Mitchum talks the talk and walks the walk, the one clenched-teeth laconic, the other a former boxer's shoulder-led roll. But the element of his performance that reveals one of the most compelling parts of his persona is the character's passivity. It is world-weariness turned acquiescent: he is the ideal patsy because he has given up fighting fate. When he encounters Jane Greer's definitive femme fatale Kathy Moffet again after she has first betrayed him, Bailey puts her down hard with the words 'Get out. I have to sleep in this room.' But he can hardly look her in the eye. Throughout the scene, Mitchum keeps shifting his eyeline. He is disgusted, but one senses that this disgust has as much to do with the self-realization that he is so much putty in her hands. 'You're going to find it very easy to take me anywhere' are among his first words to Kathy on their initial meeting and when she tries to spin him a story about the 'small matter' of the $40,000 she has stolen from Whit (Kirk Douglas), he gently silences her with the line 'Baby, I don't care."

Headstone words, these. They could be carved over both the character of Jeff Bailey as well as serving as the summing-up of Mitchum's entire career. After all, Mitchum's public persona was fed by a lovingly-nurtured off-handedness about his craft. This was an actor who once defined his screen technique as being 'Read the lines, kiss the girl, take the money and run.' It was a studied indifference as crafted as the on-screen stoicism. But life had prepared Mitchum to take the punches and roll with them, to such an extent that he seemed almost to invite them. Mitchum had serious drifter credentials: a teenage delinquent and runaway, he had done the hobo routine of freight-hopping, winding up on a chain gang following a vagrancy conviction at the age of fourteen. A well-publicised marijuana bust in 1948 for which he did sixty days in the pen – 'Like Palm Springs without the riff-raff' was his verdict – did nothing to impair this boho image of a marginal individualist at the heart of the studio system. One wonders what would have happened had he found *the* director, the one with whom a body of work might have been possible. But, as David Thomson put it, Mitchum worked 'as if he had a fruit machine for an agent'. There were moments, however, in the fifty-three year career where the encounters were happy accidents that both cystallised and really explored the Mitchum image. If *Out of the Past* keyed Mitchum's air of wounds-well-hidden to the warped psycho-sexual world of noir, this element of stoicism was further explored five years later in Nick Ray's *The Lusty Men* (1952) where he played a rodeo-rider again yearning for a domesticity that's beyond him.

It seems fitting that the two other acknowledged classic Mitchum performances should have hinged on his letting himself go rather than reining himself in. In Charles Laughton's *Night of the Hunter* (1955) he plays the psychopathic hellfire preacher Harry Powell with malicious glee. Likewise, his Max Cady in J. Lee Thompson's original *Cape Fear* (1962) played up the element of calculating observation that seemed to lie behind Mitchum's hooded-eye gaze and made it manifest. His Cady is a brutal, sociopathic schemer whose pleaure comes from toying with his prey. The charisma here is deadly and is performed as such. *Out of the Past* secures Mitchum's place in the noir universe of bruised male losers; as Greer explains to Mitchum, 'You're no good and neither am I. That's why we deserve each other.'

2

CINEMA SANS PAPIER:
WRITING ON FRENCH CINEMA

As I write I have the July 2000 issue of *Sight and Sound* in front of me. 'Growing up with Godard' are the words emblazoned on the cover, and within its pages David Thomson muses movingly on the moment of the late 1950s and early 1960s when the *nouvelle vague* added cinéphilia to the long list of significant French cultural exports. Thomson was of that time, in love with the yet-to-be acknowledged glories of late American film classicism – from John Ford to Edgar G. Ulmer – but galvanised, like so many others around the world, by the young turks of *Cahiers du cinéma* and their campaign to claim cinema as an art and the director as an artist. 'We had become a little French, I don't doubt it,' he admits bravely in his account of how he and his friends ploughed through the French magazine in the days when it was known as *Les Cahiers jaunes*. Cinéphilia was a condition, a way of life, a virus that was contracted proudly and with passion. Godard was one of its chief incubators, the living embodiment of the condition as both a blessing and a curse. In the absence of any canon, this breed of enthusiasts and amateurs were instrumental in both writing and making cinema history. They came before such enthusiasm was professionalised in the academy but somehow they announced it. What eventually would go missing en route would be the passion and sense of discovery.

I, too, 'grew up' with Godard but after the fact, two generations removed from the moment that Thomson had lived. For me, the *nouvelle vague* had the force of a kind of living myth of cinema's possibilities. The films of Godard, Truffaut and Resnais were still being shown on British television in the 1970s and I remember seeing *Les Quatre cents coups*, *Hiroshima, mon amour* and *A bout de souffle*, thanks largely to my mother's good offices. These films had liveliness and gravity, lyricism and depth; black and white had never seemed so much like life. They made me understand that what I saw in westerns and crime movies, in the painterly grandeur of the dustbowl and the explosive monochrome claustrophobia of the city, were already mythical images, relatives of the paintings in the art books we were lucky enough to have in the house. So I was the product of a generation for whom it was still possible to see the great European films on television alongside the classics of Hollywood. I had some sense that this was 'important', even then. Not through any parental coercion or dutiful attendance to the idea of the 'masterpiece' but through the silence that fell on the family in viewing and the feeling that these films were different from the rest of the stuff on television – and that difference was a special, privileged and crucial pleasure. As I grew up sex came into it, of course. I knew that, coming home from a friend's house or the pub, there would be late-night European films on television in which the nudity was unabashed. The world of eroticism, of men and women and the sweaty anticipation of adulthood was part of what made me watch. If that wasn't incentive enough, my friends and I became ardent hunters of the strangest and most recondite pleasures buried late in the viewing schedules. 'Difficult' movies became things against which to test the arrogant intellectual hungers of adolescence. There is a particular kind of masculine rite in all this; we were hooligans for meaning, steeling ourselves for Fassbinder, Herzog and Godard, the 'harder' the better. There is also a kind of narcissistic self-identification here, rigour being equated with pleasure, a hair-shirt intellectualism. Which probably explains why the ironic appreciation of kitsch that became the dominant cultural reflex of the 1980s, and that has since hardened into an authoritarian populism, could never be an option.

It would be through French cinema that I found a way to explore this desire for pleasures other than those available on a prescribed diet of Hollywood. My time in Film Studies, as both a student and a lecturer, led me to realise that the French had a particular attitude towards the cinema that was, in the time that I came to start publishing film criticism, almost completely alien to the British. It was an industry, an art and a culture – never one without the other. For a Francophile film writer this was a dream that sustained one's writing even as one realised that it was a dream against the grain of the dominant attitudes towards cinema. However, there was a further influence that compelled me to write about French cinema in the 1990s – the feeling I retained for France as my 'other country'. My mother had lived in Paris through the late 1950s and early 1960s and I had been born there. The family returned often, eventually to settle there, if only for a short period. Back in Britain, the films from France that made it onto screens were crucial communications, and when I came to write about them I realised that what fired my engagement was something closer to the bone that the splendid myth of the *nouvelle vague* that had first got me interested. I was aware that there was more than a little sentimentality and romanticism in my attachment to things French that provided the perfect reflex against which to sharpen any critical faculties I thought I possessed. To avoid Franco-philic gushing meant research and careful viewing. The Frenchness of a given film was no guarantee that it was any good, after all. I am aware that this attempt at self-imposed rigour did not always win out – I was probably too kind to confections like *Chacun cherche son chat* or *Un hussard sur le toit*, for example, and too hard on Tavernier's *L'Appat*. But it was enough of a compulsion to keep me on the case of those films that crossed the Channel and, for the space of about seven years, *Sight and Sound* would routinely send me off to cover the French releases. Over this period I got tired of hearing writers congratulating themselves on their blithe diagnosis that French cinema was dead, art cinema was over, et cetera. This was, and remains, evidence of a self-deceiving collusion with the narrowing of possibilities for cinema in the UK, as well as a betrayal of the audience that exists for such films. It is also, on a broader level, a symptom of our own deep schizophrenia regarding Europe as a cultural idea and as a possible political future. It is no exaggeration to say that the British have become deeply Americanised in their viewing habits and cultural reflexes and this is not simply a matter of not being able or bothered to read subtitles. It goes far deeper and is much more insidious in that it has resulted in almost stripping away what is left of the appetite for discovery of 'other' cinemas. What follows is an attempt to provide a sense of the French context of the films that made it onto UK screens in the 1990s – both the intellectual debates that inform them and the cultural/industrial circumstances from which they emerged.

A SAINTLY HISTORY OF CINEPHILIA

In May 1991 *Cahiers du cinéma* celebrated its fortieth anniversary. On 12 June 1992 the great French film critic Serge Daney died. These are moments in a broader time-span that extends back to the 1980s and beyond in a nominal sketch of, an elegy for, cinéphilia. Who is the cinéphile? And why the elegy? One of the most concise definitions is Jean-Louis Leutrat's: 'The cinéphile joins together the spirit of the col-lector and the competence of the connoisseur, but a collector who would only col-lect in his memory.'[1] To which one should add that the cinéphile is a curiously French creature that has known two incarnations and is headed for a third. The first of these, as critic, partisan viewer and advocate of 'cinema-as-art', was during the period of silent cinema and mutated along with the medium it worshipped. As Raymond Borde has pointed out, 'There was a 'silent majority' among the French public of the 1930s. The rather active cine-clubs of the end of the silent period disappeared little by little, as did the intellectual journals. The cinephile had become an anachronism.'[2] It is the second incarnation that interests me here, and a sketch of its background, around the figures of Andre Bazin and Serge Daney, is worthwhile.

The cultural climate of post-war France was highly politicised. Bazin, involved in the organisation 'Travail et Culture', aligned himself with the Communist Party against the 'Peuple et Culture' group, which had its origins in the Grenoble *maquis*.[3] His gravitation towards cinema was influenced by André Malraux and Roger Leenhardt, who he would replace as film critic on the journal *Esprit*, founded in 1932. In the early 1950s the Cold War had begun to shatter the left-alliance from which Bazin had emerged but, by then, much of what was to constitute the 'second-generation' cinéphile's support-system was in place. Having traversed a variety of journals, Bazin founded – in April 1951, with Jacques Doniol-Valcroze – *Les Cahiers du cinéma et de la télévision*. Although not properly a ciné-club (where film screenings were often accompanied by lectures and debates), the archetypal home for the cinéphile in post-war Paris was the Cinémathèque Française. Here, under the custodianship of Henri Langlois and Mary Meerson, several generations of film-makers and critics received an autodidactic education in the history of cinema. Already, these two names – Langlois and Bazin – alert us to the fact that we are dealing with a specific sort of history in relation to the cinéphile, what Pierre Sorlin has called 'saintly his-tory'. Sorlin writes that 'Cinema history has constituted itself as a saintly/holy history, the edifying tale of struggles needed to get the seventh art recognised and endow it with a language. Unlike sacred history, which clearly delimits the field of authorised explanations and comparisons, saintly history is infinitely extensible; individuals vener-ate their own saints and lend them whatever virtues they prefer.'[4]

That just such a 'saintly history' is recognisable in the most partisan moments of auteur theory is paradigmatic of cinéphilic history. But this does not take into account that this 'second generation' cinéphile was not limited to its incarnation as critic. It is precisely the fact that the cinéphile could be a film-maker (Godard, Truf-faut, Rohmer, Rivette), a curator (Langlois), or could represent a system of thought (Bazin, Daney) that means one can seriously explore this creature as a vital compo-nent of French film culture. Additionally, the cinéphile in the 1980s became very self-consciously the inheritor of this past, one that includes the 'mystical moment', *pace* Sorlin, of the *nouvelle vague*, but that also included, more fundamentally – for it threatened the cinéphile's very being – the status of that object against which the cinéphile defines him or herself – cinema. It is here that Serge Daney is an exemplary figure, because his critical work throughout the 1980s up to his death represents the most sustained auto-critique of the cinéphile's mixed fortunes in the age of what Daney has described as 'post-cinema'. Exemplary, also, because it is tempting to read Daney's critical trajectory as existing in parallel to the passage of the image itself.

Having been an editor on *Cahiers* during the period of its engagement with Althusser and Lacan and one of those critics to attack the Bazinian critical heritage as 'naïve idealism', Daney's work is deeply mined with a sense of its own history. That Daney should have left *Cahiers* in 1981 to write on television for the daily newspaper *Libération* is significant for two reasons. Firstly, as an acknowledgement that cinema's centre of gravity had irrevocably shifted, something attested to in a text central to understanding Daney's importance as a critic in the 1980s, 'Du grand au petit ecran' (From the big to the small screen): 'Nothing is more unanimous (and more satisfied) than the following cry: films are not 'shown' on TV. Yes, of course, television shows them but they 'show' so badly … It is preferable that falling upon '*L'Inhumaine*' by accident, while zapping between two commercials and a videoclip, we thereby discover a beautiful film rather than we should feel obliged to call it beautiful (or worse, 'interesting') because we saw it during a highly mediatised cultural sermon.'[5] This statement has great appeal to someone of my own generation who came across the films of the *nouvelle vague* precisely through television. The awareness that the televisual screening of films is now the norm is the second crucial features of Daney's criticism at *Libération*. Not simply in order to observe the transformation of cinema by television, but also to be in closer cultural and critical proximity to a generation whose own introduction to cinema history would not exist solely through the Cinémathèque Française. 'It's been a greater pleasure for me to write on an old film,' Daney admitted, 'even a poor one, shown on television and seen by many, than on a worthwhile novelty opening to an empty hall. Because for us as well, time has passed and it's tempting to write for that part of the *Libération* readership that is twenty years old, that one doesn't know, and to whom one would like to transmit the feeling that all this has already existed for others before them.'[6] Perhaps this is to over-emphasise the cultural philanthropy of Daney's criticism at the expense of an equally pronounced and vital element, his Bazinian inheritance. When Gilles Deleuze wrote to Daney, 'You have not renounced finding a profound link between cinema and thought … you have thus maintained the grand conception of cinema's first age … cinema as a new art and new thought'[7] – it is in direct acknowledgement of this inheritance.

It was, as Philippe Roger has put it, 'a high idea of cinema's function'[8] that Daney bought to his writing at *Libération*, the Bazinian idea of cinema as a witness of history. Two post-war cinematic events were of central significance to Bazin and *Cahiers du cinéma*. The release of *Citizen Kane* in 1947 (three years after the return of American films to Parisian screens in October 1944) would presage the well-documented championing of American over French cinema. Of the most enduring effect for Bazin would be the premiere, in November 1946, of Rossellini's *Paisà*. As Daney has explained, the influence of Italian neo-realism was decisive both for *Cahiers* and the *nouvelle vague*, 'Between Italian neo-realism and the young turks of the *nouvelle vague* there was fifteen years and a man like Bazin to make the link. Neo-realism had been, for him, a fundamental experience and it was through him that *Cahiers* had inherited this experience, of Rossellini above all.'[9] Bazin devoted seven major essays to neo-realism and across them one finds, better than in the exhausted dichotomy of montage/*mise-en-scène*, the ethical core that resurfaces so urgently in Daney. 'Rossellini directs facts', Bazin wrote. To which one could add 'Cinema, through Rossellini and others, witnessed history'. Daney, offering Bazin and Langlois in a dialectic that synthesises the idealistic, euphoric vision of cinema that the second-generation cinéphile inherited, wrote: 'Langlois had an *idée fixe*: to demonstrate that all cinema was worth preserving. Bazin had the same idea, but in reverse: to demonstrate that cinema conserved reality; and before signifying it and resembling it, it embalmed it.'[10]

Neo-Realism as another 'mystical moment' in a 'saintly history', then? Perhaps. But a moment with a specific function – that of bearing witness to the Italian resistance and liberation. In specifically French terms the issue of cinema's function as witness was given biting topicality by the desecration of Jewish graves at the Carpentras cemetery in May 1990. Part of the French state's response was network television screenings of Alain Resnais' *Nuit et Brouillard* (1955). In an address given at the Galerie du jeu de Paume two months before his death, Daney explicitly considered this issue of the cinema as witness: 'The time of my life and intellectual activity has been very strongly marked by the fact that there have been certain events in the century that only cinema has seen. The camps are the symbol of this. And departing from this, we see very well what happens today. With the Touvier Affair Jack Lang says 'Screen *Nuit et Brouillard*'. The same for Carpentras, 'Screen *Nuit et Brouillard*'. I have been thinking about something for a long time now; the American TV film *Holocaust* is exactly contemporary with Faurisson's first texts … All at once, it's America which has sent back to us an image of the camps. I remember that, at the time, I told myself that we might as well put away *Nuit et Brouillard* because [it] was this little film that had hit people like me right between the eyes at the age of twelve or thirteen, that said to them that cinema existed, that the camps existed, that man existed, that evil existed, and they never forgot it.'[11]

This passage deserves its lengthy citation because it encapsulates, both in its gravity and complexity, the way in which Daney sees cinema relate to history. There are two 'histories' here, that of cinema itself and that of post-war Europe. The second-generation cinéphile was a part of that generation coming to critical and political maturity in tandem with 'modern' cinema, and while it would be easy to attribute Daney's 'mourning' of the end of this cinema to nostalgia, this does not acknowledge that he demonstrates an acute self-consciousness about the entropic effects of such nostalgia. Just as he explored 'the zapper' as representative of a desire to deprogramme television in order to find 'the image that escapes', so Daney figures one of cinema's 'forgotten' functions, something close to the ethnological, as an alternative to the symbolic presence of digital imagery, of the televisual flux of images, as a means to 'embalm' a social reality that these other media would pass over or then reduce to a consensual news-media composite. It is an idea that descends directly from Bazin, but in a revitalised form, one that is useful to the 1980s cinéphile for a variety of possible reasons. The ontological concern with the image was one developed by Bazin that, during a period of mediatisation marked by the symbolic presence of new media technologies, proved to be a critical inheritance too significant to be overlooked. Daney refigures this inheritance with a particular emphasis on ethical and ontological questions – a discourse of origins; basic, global questions of cinema. Such questions are returned to in a completely different environment to that in which they were originally posed. The steady usurping of what Jacques Aumont has named 'cinéma-roi' leads the cinéphile to become even more of a marginal figure than previously and it is fitting that the work of mourning be carried out in the words of the original euphoria.

In the first edition of *Trafic*, the journal he co-founded in 1991, Daney acknowledged that it was the purpose of the publication to address such questions: 'Returning to those sweet but sickening questions that it seemed we would never ask ourselves again. For example: is cinema an art? Will it be conserved, wholly or in part? And what will become of that which we have loved in it?'[12] In his study of cinema and painting '*L'Oeil Interminable*', Jacques Aumont chose to answer the question rather than ask it and to assert that the space of Romanticism remains a tenable one in which to consider cinema.[13] For Daney, justification of the question exists in the imperative to restate it and not necessarily to give a positive answer. It might be tempting to consider such questions in the light of the fortieth, soon to be the fiftieth, anniversary of *Cahiers du cinéma* as indicative of the second-generation cinéphile's doubt-ridden middle-age. Such doubts are reinforced by the fear that the next generation of cinéphilia will be qualitatively different, what Alain Bergala has called 'cinéphilia minus memory'.[14] Bergala's oxymoron successfully condenses the differences between the two generations: the former for whom '*cinéma-roi*' is already a memory, the forthcoming for whom cinema is one, admittedly privileged, station in 'the passage of the image'. Alongside Raymond Bellour, Daney is the single critic of this period to have understood that the crisis of the cinematic image is, at the same time, a crisis for its clerics and to have attempted to arbitrate this transition from one generation of cinéphiles to the next, from those with a memory of cinema to those without.

NOTES

1   Leutrat, Jean-Louis (1986) 'Traces That Resemble Us: Godard's *Passion*', in *Sub-Stance*, 51, 36.

2   Borde, Raymond (1983) 'The Golden Age: French Cinema of the 30s', in Mary Lee Bandy (ed.) *Rediscovering French Film*, Museum of Modern Art: New York.

3   *maquis* – Resistance movement

4   Sorlin, Pierre (1992) 'Cinema: an undiscoverable history?', in *Paragraph*, 15, 1, 36.

5   Daney, Serge (1988) 'Le Salaire du Zappeur', in *Editions Ramsay*, 163 and 168–9.

6   From Roger, Phillipe (1991) 'Le Passeur: Entretien avec Serge Daney' in *Serge Daney, Devant la recrudesence des vols de sacs a main: Cinema, Television, Information*. Aleas Editeur: Lyons, 8 (Roger/Daney hereafter).

7   From Deleuze, Gilles 'Optimisme, Pessimisme et Voyage. Lettre à Serge Daney', in Serge Daney, *Cine-Journal: 1981–1986. Cahiers du cinéma*, 8.

8   Roger/Daney, 201.
9   From 'Andre Bazin' in Serge Daney, *Ciné-Journal: 1981–1986. Cahiers du Cinéma*.
10   Ibid. 172.
11   Daney, Serge (1992) 'Journal de l'an passé' in *Trafic No. 1*, Editions POL: Paris, 5.
12   Ibid.
13   Aumont, Jacques (1989) *L'oeil Interminable*. Paris: 1989. See also Chris Darke 'Rupture, continuity and diversification: *Cahiers du cinéma* in the 1980s', *Screen*, 34, 4, Winter 1993, 362–79.
14   Bergala, Alain 'De la Singularité au Cinéma', in *Cahiers du cinéma*, 353, Nov 1983, 16.

L.627

DIR: BERTRAND TAVERNIER FRANCE 1992
ORIGINALLY PUBLISHED IN *SIGHT AND SOUND* JANUARY 1993

SYNOPSIS

Lucien 'Lulu' Marguet has worked for fifteen years as an investigator in the Seventh Division of the Paris Police. During a surveillance operation, Lulu makes contact with *un cousin* (police slang for an informer), Willy, to gather information about a forthcoming crack consignment. The stakeout is interrupted by Lulu's superior, who calls in the one observation vehicle at Lulu's disposal before the operation can be completed. Furious, Lulu returns to HQ where he accuses his chief of drunken incompetence. As a result he is transferred to a desk job at another station

While in clerical limbo, Lulu receives a call from another *cousin*, a young drug-addicted prostitute who is HIV positive, and for whom Lulu feels a protective affection. They arrange to meet at the Père-Lachaise cemetery where, facing a memorial to the victims of a terrorist attack on an airliner, Lulu makes it clear to Cécile that he considers dealers to be terrorists and that they should be dealt with accordingly. Through the intervention of Commissioner Adore, Lulu is transferred to a neighbouring division where he is integrated into a newly-established team dealing exclusively with drug-related crime.

The chief of *les stupes* (from the French for narcotics, *stupéfiants*), Dominique 'Dodo' Cantoni, is concerned more with filling a quota of convictions than with the penetration of trafficking rings. In the course of a series of raids, Lulu discovers that his commitment is at odds with the lackadaisical approaches of Dodo and his colleague Manuel, but he is supported by Marie, the deputy-chief, and Antoine, who becomes Lulu's partner. The differences within the group come to a head when Dodo, Manuel and Vincent, the youngest *stupe* and a police-college graduate, carry out a raid on a squat without their colleague's knowledge. Although intended to net a dealer, the raid succeeds only in unearthing a user, a young immigrant mother, whom Dodo arrests. Lulu and Antoine hurry to the scene where they attempt to placate the inhabitants, while berating Dodo.

Soon afterwards, Lulu learns that Willy, his key informant, is hiding in fear for his life. Lulu seeks him out to assure him of his protection, but later learns that Willy has suffered a savage knife attack after his whereabouts is divulged by Dodo to a gang of dealers. Still in pursuit of the same dealers, the team is stalking out a café when Lulu, inside an observation van, spots Cécile on the street. Having been unable to locate her for over a year, Lulu abandons his post to speak to her. She is with her new-born child and tells Lulu that she intends to leave Paris. The team is about to set out after the dealers, and Lulu, hurriedly bidding Cécile goodbye, rejoins them. Back in the van, he realises that he has forgotten to ask Cécile for her new address.

REVIEW

Taking its title from the French Code of Public Health that forbids 'all offences linked to the possession, traffic and consumption of narcotics', *L.627* was co-written by an ex-*stupe*, Michel Alexandre, whose collaboration presumably ensures an authenticity of detail and tone in the film's study of Parisian plain-clothes drug investigators.

Released in the same week as the Maastricht Referendum, Tavernier's film is an ambitious examination of 'the state of the nation' in the guise of a *policier*. As such, *L.627* occupies the same territory as Bob Swaim's *La Balance* (1982), Maurice Pialat's *Police* (1982) and Catherine Breillat's *Sale comme un Ange* (1991), although it is, by comparison, occupied by resolutely 'second-string' performers.

Dider Bezace is outstanding as Lulu, the tenacious and committed investigator whose calm resourcefulness and often sentimental attachment to his *cousins* succeeds where the blustering tactics of the team's chief, 'Dodo' Cantoni – played by Jean-Paul Comart as an overgrown adolescent, complete with hyena cackle and water pistol – fail to do anything other than fulfil the statistical requirements imposed by the Ministry of the Interior. This casting strategy is of a piece with the film's overall style, which opts for an anti-climactic, quasi-behavourist realism which concentrates on context and milieu rather than on a lone vigilante cop.

Doggedly unglamorous, both in terms of character and locations, *L.627* studies police procedure at the desk, on the street, in interrogations, and has several strong set-pieces, all of them emphatically focused on the work of surveillance and raids. Tavernier adopts the point of view of the police, a tactic carried over from his previous film *La Guerre sans Nom* (1991), a documentary on the Algerian War seen from the perspective of French soldiers. But he does so unindulgently, concentrating on *les stupes* as a unit existing between official indifference and street-level trauma.

What defines *L.627*'s realist method – as well as its shortcomings – is Lulu's video camera. Used off-duty to film weddings, it becomes an instrument of surveillance on stakeouts. The video-images mark a kind of zero-degree realism that the film can only aspire to and approximate in a scrupulous and unflinching pursuit of the authentic details of street-level police procedure. The video image acts as a reflexive comment on the difficulties of simplicity, a directorial acknowledgement of the drawbacks of realism.

Tavernier's method is, on the whole, judicious, putting the hot subject of drugs, and the racial networks associated with them, in the 'cool' frame of a procedural policier. When Lulu comments, 'I have the impression that filming helps me understand things better', it is tempting to take this as the director's own statement of intent – that audiences will confront their prejudices through his film. *L.627* is a consciously micro-political exploration of urban France at a point when the grand idea of 'Europe' no longer conceals the absence of political will to deal with domestic social devastation.

LES ROSEAUX SAUVAGES
DIR: ANDRE TECHINE FRANCE 1993
ORIGINALLY PUBLISHED IN *SIGHT AND SOUND* MARCH 1993

SYNOPSIS

1962, Vileneuve-sur-Lot in south-west France. Pierre Bartolo, about to leave for service in Algeria, is getting married. He confides to a local school-teacher, Madame Alvarez, that he wishes to desert and asks her, in her capacity as a Communist Party activist, to assist him. She declines.

At the boarding school where Alvarez teaches, the class includes local boys François and Serge (Pierre's brother) and new arrival Henri Mariani, who is Algerian-born and unpopular with both classmates and teacher. François and Serge have an arrangement to help one another with their class work which develops into a brief homosexual liaison. This leaves Serge unaffected but François is unhappily persuaded of his own homosexuality. He confides his feelings to his closest friend, Madame Alvarez's daughter, Maïté. News arrives that Pierre has been killed in Algeria. Serge walks away from the funeral, disgusted by military rhetoric about his brother's heroism – he knew that Pierre wanted to desert. François sends Maïté after him. On hearing the news, Madame Alvarez suffers a nervous breakdown. Her replacement, Monsieur Morelli, offers Henri extra tuition to help him pass his *baccalauréat*. Henri's hostility subsides until he hears about OAS defeats in Algeria.

Raging, Henri leaves the boarding school at night, burning PCF posters as he goes. On the point of torching the local Communist HQ, he spots Maïté within. Hesitantly, she offers him coffee. Henri makes a nervous advance. She refuses him but reads him the letter from his mother that he has never dared open. After Henri reveals his original intention to incinerate the HQ, Maïté orders him to leave. On the eve of the *baccalauréat* results, François, Serge, Henri and Maïté go swimming together. Serge and François come to a reconciliation while Maïté and Henri make love before he leaves. Madame Alvarez, released from hospital, meets Monsieur Morelli for a meal where they discuss Henri. Morelli introduces his Algerian wife. Madame Alvarez watches as they drive away.

REVIEW

André Téchiné's tenth feature, *Les Roseaux Sauvages* was originally commissioned by the Franco-German television channel ARTE as part of the series 'Tous les garçons et les filles de leur age' in which French directors, including Patricia Mazuy, Cédric Kahn and Olivier Assayas, were asked to contribute films based on their recollections of adolescence. *Les Roseaux Sauvages* depicts that time when angst and euphoria go hand-in-hand, but Téchiné contains sentimental and familiar elements by addressing the wider political dimensions of his teenage years: 1962, the Evian Accords and the final actions of the Algerian War of Independence.

As context for the sentimental education of four adolescent characters, Téchiné's handling of this historical moment is delicate and telling. Henri, an Algerian-born French boy whose father died in the Algerian war, is the intercessor. As a self-proclaimed supporter of the neo-Fascist, anti-independence OAS, he brings the war firmly into the consciousness of the other teenagers. But as an unrepentantly anti-social, metropolitan dandy, dismissive of the provincialism of his peers, he takes an obdurate, adolescent pride in his pain, converting it into the badge of his difference from the others. François, in coming to terms with his homosexuality, is briefly smitten by Henri's darkness, whereas Serge, having lost his older brother in the War, regards Henri as the enemy, as does Maïté, the daughter of Communist militant Madame Alvarez.

Just as Téchiné recruits the political to deepen his portrait of adolescent relationships, so period detail is accommodated with an unobtrusiveness that makes the film something other than the familiar parade of period pop nostalgia and fashion curiosity. As Cahiers du cinéma has noted, Téchiné privileges 'the tension of the moment above the recreation of the time, the dramatic detail over faithful historical reconstitution'. Hit records of l'époque yé-yé (The Beach Boys, Chubby Checker, The Platters) and style details (Serge compliments Maïté on her hairstyle being "très Françoise Hardy") add density to characterisation and narrative development. With adolescence defined by the competing forces of sexual yearning and political intransigence, the setting in the south-west of France thus becomes an environment from which the young crave to escape – all except Serge who flatly states his intentions to marry and settle down in the region to lead the ancestral peasant life.

If Henri is the film's most enigmatic and disturbed character, François is the one with whom the filmmaker seems to feel the greatest affinity, presenting his sexual confusion, self-loathing and intellectual excitement with great sympathy. François brings people together, encouraging Maïté to comfort Serge after his brother's funeral and, less intentionally, enabling the consummation of Henri and Maïté's furtive and impossible love. It is not that Téchiné gives François anything as straightforward as a preponderance of point-of-view shots, it is simply this trajectory that interests him most. In this sense, Les Roseaux Sauvages gathers its force from the careful assembly of social moments and everyday locales – weddings, schoolrooms, cafés, funerals. The result is that by the close, when the four go swimming together while waiting for their baccalauréat results, a crucial threshold in their lives has been reached. It is this sequence that best sums up the stylistic virtues of the film – an unforced French naturalism that reaches near-Renoirian lyricism on the banks of the river. Blessed with some finely judged, completely authentic performances, Les Roseaux Sauvages is a film that avoids the potential wistfulness of its subject matter and remains in the mind.

HISTOIRE(S) DU CINEMA PARTS 1a AND 1b

DIR: JEAN-LUC GODARD FR./SWITZ. 1989
ORIGINALLY PUBLISHED IN SIGHT AND SOUND JULY 1993

SYNOPSIS

Godard narrates a montage of images from different media and genres – painting, photography, cinema and video, fiction and documentary – to present some of the possible stories in the history of cinema.

Part 1a: *Toutes les histoires*. Godard ranges back and forth between post-Revolutionary Soviet cinema and the growth and consolidation of Hollywood to the birth of television. The power of Hollywood as represented by studio bosses Irving Thalberg and Howard Hughes is contrasted with the equal social importance of cinemas in Soviet Russia and Nazi Germany. The outbreak of World War Two, the Occupation of France, the Holocaust and the aftermath of the war are traced through images from painting and film and the effects of war on Europe's national cinemas.

Part 1b: *Une histoire seule*. Godard turns back to cinematic pioneers, the Lumière brothers and Muybridge, while in parallel analysing 'the two great ideas: sex and death', with particular emphasis on the allure of the starlet. Considered as the inheritor of photographic realism, cinema is also seen in the light of industrial development and imperialism.

REVIEW

Originally commissioned by the French cable channel Canal Plus, *Histoire(s) du cinéma* is a project which seems always to have been latent in Godard's work. From the profligate citation of the *nouvelle vague* films onwards, the director's relationship to cinema, its history and to the other arts have been enduring motifs. *Histoire(s)* – of which these are the first two parts in a proposed ten – originates from a series of lectures that Godard gave in 1977 in Montreal and later collected in a book *Introduction à une véritable histoire du cinéma*, in which he wrote that such a history, in order to be 'true', must be made of 'pictures and sounds, not of illustrated texts'.

The method of these lectures – associating, juxtaposing, synthesising his own films with others – is carried over into the present work and elaborated by references to painting, newsreels and television. In short, this is Dr Godard's True History of the Image, but a history refracted decisively through cinema. In terms of technique, tone and technology, *Histoire(s)* is another chapter in the adventure that Serge Daney called 'Godardian pedagogy', one that has been marked by its thorough engagement with video. But these programmes, while they continue the hybridisation begun with *Ici et ailleurs* (1974), have less in common with the sense of impotence and despair that clouded *Numéro deux* (1975) than with the creative and conceptual liberation demonstrated to dazzling effect in *Scénario du film Passion* (1982).

The images in *Histoire(s)* can be read either vertically as palimpsests concealing many other possible images within them, in the hope that 'the miracle of watching what we cannot see' might transpire; or horizontally, as 'cells' in the memory of cinema to be recombined into 'one of the histories that might have been, that will be, that have been.' Exemplary of the former approach is Godard's confronting an image of Liz Taylor and Montgomery Clift – 'an image of happiness', he calls it – and another (subterranean) image of horror: 'If George Stevens hadn't been the first to use the 16mm colour film in Ravensbruck and Auschwitz, Liz Taylor's happiness might never have found 'A Place in the Sun'.' Wartime newsreels pervade part 1a, and particularly impressive is the video-mixing of war footage with landscape by Monet. The montage works as a forcefully literal image of 'invasion' (of France by Germany, of Monet's 'light' by the newsreel's bleak monochrome) and as an image of cinema as being suddenly more necessary, more responsive to the call of history than painting, of one art form 'occupying' the function of another.

These newsreel images, the voice-over intones, were 'not shown on a screen, but on a shroud' – a potent reminder that, for Godard (whose influence on End-of-Cinema discourse is immense), this project is indispensable 'mourning-work'. No surprise, then, that, in part 1b, he returns to Le Mépris, his first film to be marked by a developing register of nostalgia and regret for lost mythologies, be they derived from Classical Hollywood or Classical Greece. And while this lamentation has intimate, anecdotal asides – 'Farewell, my lovely,' he whispers to an image of Anna Karina, 'bonjour, tristesse...' – it is the Godardian belief that cinema's grand spectacle and Romantic artistic undertaking is ever endangered that yields up his subscription to the Great Man theory of history. Included here are Thalberg, Eisenstein, Lang, Renoir and Howard Hughes, 'owner of TWA, producer of Citizen Kane – as if Méliès had owned Gallimard and the SNCF'. But then this is history as Godardian mythology, and myth requires gods just as it does devils – the latter here being Hitler, imperial-ism and television.

Just as its images are treated as palimpsests, so Histoire(s) du cinéma deploys the possibilities of video editing (wipes, keying, superimposition, writing directly on the image) as well as a correspondingly dense and polyvocal soundtrack, to become a text with as many layers as there are possible interpretations of history. Godard once again here uses his technology like a video-quill, annotating, scratching out, thinking live on, in and with the images. Here however, Godard stages himself not in front of 'the white page' of the screen, but apart from it, behind an electronic typewriter, beside a bookshelf, from which position he recites the titles of books and films as if bidding the off-screen space to answer back, to open up a dialogue. Histoire(s) is video 'thinking what cinema creates' – to quote French critic Phillipe Dubois – and doing so in the manner of a wake lit by fireworks.

MADAME BOVARY
DIR: CLAUDE CHABROL FRANCE 1991
ORIGINALLY PUBLISHED IN *SIGHT AND SOUND* JULY 1993

SYNOPSIS
Village doctor Charles Bovary meets Emma Roualt while treating her father's broken leg and they marry shortly after. Emma is happy at first, but an invitation to a society ball kindles her social aspirations and she becomes discontented. Her deteriorating health leads Charles to abandon his practise in Tostes and take another in Yonville, a larger town. Emma's condition improves and she gives birth to a daughter, Berthe.

Charles falls under the influence of Homais, the local pharmacist, and Emma is attracted to Léon Dupuis, a law clerk. The attraction is frustrated when he leaves for Paris to study and, feeling stifled at home, Emma increasingly loses interest in caring for her husband and daughter. She begins an affair with the dashing Rodolphe Boulanger, a local landowner, which offers her the passion and excitement lacking in her domestic life. Enlivened by the affair, Emma becomes more attentive to Berthe and Charles, encouraging her husband in his efforts at pioneering surgery. But when an operation goes disastrously wrong, she regards him with contempt. Becoming more desperate, Emma persuades Rodolphe to run away with her, but he reneges on his promise whereupon she succumbs to listless depression.

At the opera in Rouen with Charles, Emma encounters Léon. The two start a passionate affair. Emma buys more and more expensive clothes, incurring debts with the unscrupulous haberdasher, Lheureux. As the debts spiral she persuades her husband to grant her power of attorney over their financial affairs, using their situation to find excuses for visiting Léon in Rouen. The debts are called in and, when they cannot be paid, the town bailiff arrives to repossess the Bovary property. The distraught Emma turns to Léon and Rodolphe, but neither is willing to help her. In despair, Emma poisons herself with arsenic from Homais's pharmacy and suffers an excruciatingly slow death, her uncomprehending husband at her side.

REVIEW
Chabrol's declared intention in filming *Madame Bovary* was 'to make the film Flaubert would have made had he had a camera instead of a pen'. The film received a favourable response from French critics for its fidelity to the original. But what gets lost in adapting a literary classic for the screen is often as revealing as what remains. It's here that the 'Chabrol touch' surfaces in what is otherwise strictly 'filmed Flaubert'.

The beginning and end of the novel have gone – Charles's childhood, the repercussions of Emma's suicide and her husband's discovery of Léon's and Rodolphe's letters to her are elided, which reduces identification with Charles. The director has also transposed the collective narratorial voice of the novel – the Flaubertian 'we' – into the Olympian objectivity of the Chabrol camera. The process of condensation involves reorganising details from the novel; for example, Charles's garbled giving of his name as 'Charbovari' is relocated from his schooldays to his first meeting with Emma. This marks the catastrophic mutual misunderstanding that characterises their marriage.

It is surprising that Chabrol should come to Flaubert so late in his career, since the novel is the Ur-text of themes in his work from *Le Beau Serge* to *Les Bîches* and *Masques*: stultifying French provincial life, the self-destructive pursuit of illusory desires and bourgeois duplicity. Isabelle Huppert seems to have replaced Stéphane Audran as the director's *actrice-fétiche* – this is her third role for Chabrol following award-winning performances in *Violette Nozière* and *Une Affaire des Femmes*. Chabrol has whittled away the viewpoints of the other characters to install Huppert centre-stage. Her Emma alternates between terrifying self-absorption and Charcot-style *attitudes passionnelles*. At the same time she displays a combination of petulance and defiance, crystallised in a moment when – having swallowed a handful of arsenic – she turns to the camera, her mouth smeared with the white powder, an image of her final gesture of impetuosity and indulgence. The film is extremely well-decorated, a sumptuous addition to the French heritage cycle, superior to the picture-book aesthetic of Claude Berri's Pagnol adaptations and offering a diseased Romantic vision which runs counter to the heartiness of Rappeneau's *Cyrano de Bergerac*. Chabrol's film was only made possible by the last-minute intervention of the television channel FR3, and there are aspects of its formal organisation – its pace and cutting, emphatic punctuation-by-fades and redundant narrative voice-over – that make it suitable for television serialisation. The irony is that Chabrol has here made exactly the sort of faithful literary adaptation that the *nouvelle vague* once condemned as *le cinéma de papa* – respectful, luxurious and eminently forgettable.

LES ENFANTS DU PARADIS

DIR: MARCEL CARNE FRANCE 1945
ORIGINALLY PUBLISHED IN *SIGHT AND SOUND* SEPTEMBER 1993

SYNOPSIS

Part One: *Le Boulevard du Crime* (The Boulevard of Crime). Paris, 1840. The beautiful adventuress Garance is discontent in her relationship with Lacenaire, a suave
murderer who masquerades as a public scribe. She attracts the attention of Baptiste Debureau, a mime at the Funambules theatre, who prevents her being wrong-
fully arrested during one of his street performances. Baptiste, however, is adored
by Nathalie, another actress at the Funambules, and has a rival for Garance's affections in the ambitious Romantic actor Frédérick Lemaître. Baptiste traces Garance
to a bar where he publicly humiliates Lacenaire by dancing with her. When they are
alone together that night, Baptiste panics and leaves her; Garance finds solace with
Frédérick. The wealthy Count Edouard de Montray sees Garance's performance at
the Funambules and declares his love for her; she is uninterested but her admirer
insists that he will always remain her servant. Later, when police accuse her of being
implicated in a murder that Lacenaire has committed, Garance turns to the Count
for protection.

Part Two: *L'Homme Blanc* (The Man in White). 1847. Baptiste, now a famous
performer, has married Nathalie and has a son. Frédérick, the most popular actor of
his time, becomes friendly with Lacenaire. Garance, who has been travelling with the
Count, has returned to Paris; she secretly visits the Funambules and realises that she
has only ever loved Baptiste. Frédérick, although jealous, abandons hope. Despite his
wife's pleas, Baptiste arranges to meet Garance for one last time. Lacenaire, after a
public altercation between Frédérick and the Count, murders the Count. Nathalie,
accompanied by her child, discovers Baptiste and Garance together; Garance, decid-
ing that she cannot split up the family, leaves Baptiste and flees into the carnival
crowd on the Boulevard. Baptiste, pursuing her, is swallowed up in the throng.

REVIEW

While criticism has successfully recuperated the fortunes of 'overlooked' masterpieces of the inter-war years – notably Renoir's *La Règle du Jeu* and Vigo's *L'Atalante*
– the reputation of the 1945 *Les Enfants du Paradis* in France seems to have comes
about less through the good offices of critics than through its consistent popularity
and steady accumulation of prestige. This process culminated in its special 1971
César award as 'the best film in the history of talking pictures in France', thus cementing its status as myth, monument and *monstre sacré* of French cinema. It is as a
monument, a French *Gone with the Wind* (as it was advertised by post-war American
distributors), that it tends to be received abroad.

Dubbed 'a megalomaniac of decor' by André Bazin, Marcel Carné had gained
a reputation for excess during his previous film, the medieval fairy-tale romance
Les visiteurs du soir (1942). Despite the material constraints on production under
Nazi occupation, the director further embellished this reputation with *Les Enfants*
by expansively recreating Restoration Paris on a budget five times that of the standard wartime production. Carné not only recreates the city's infamous Boulevard

du Temple, where the majority of Paris's theatres and – legend has it – unsolved felonies were concentrated; but also populates it with crowds of extras, and draws his principal characters from personalities of the time: the famed mime Debureau, the period's leading romantic actor Lemaître and the notorious gentleman-assassin Lacenaire. This applied recreation of historical characters and milieux was, in part, a strategic manoeuvre in the face of German edicts on style and subject matter. Realism – of the 'poetic' or sociological variety – was out.

The success of Carné's change of style was no doubt assisted by the enduring core of his production team, initially assembled for *Drôle de drame* (1937), including Jacques Prévert as screenwriter, Joseph Kosma as composer and Alexandre Trauner as set designer (the latter two, both being of Hungarian Jewish background, collaborated on *Les Enfants* clandestinely). The film features an ensemble of leading actors – Arletty, Barrault, Brasseur, Herrand – all of whom Carné had worked with previously in different configurations. *Les Enfants*, then, is a film of multiple authors but also the apex of collaborative efforts and working relationships forged in the traditions of French studio production; Carné's follow-up *Les Portes de la Nuit* (1946) was a commercial failure and indicative of how rapidly tastes had changed.

Multiple authors and multiple pleasures: the film's abiding richness resides in the orchestration of each individual's technical mastery. Carné's camera is classically self-effacing, serving the ensemble and its environment rather than itself. When Lacemaire murders the Count and the camera refuses to go with the action, focusing instead on the appalled reaction of Lacenaire's henchman Avril, the scene is unusually forceful precisely because of the unexpected archness of its execution and the sudden assertion of personal style.

'It seems more modern now than it did in 1949', wrote Raymond Durgnat in 1965, and the impression persists. Perhaps this is due to French cinema's return, over the last decade, to the values of extravagant decor, historical spectacle and literary adaptation, with films from *Cyrano de Bergerac* to *Les Amants du Pont Neuf* among the (il)legitimate offspring of the tradition crystallised in *Les Enfants*.

The feature that has intensified with time is the film's vertiginous self-reflexivity, and while one would expect nothing less of a work that consciously explores the art/life duality, *Les Enfants* delivers this and more in a structural origami of doubled allusions. This is visible in its two-part structure but equally in the shot that opens each part, that of the Funambules proscenium arch, the frame within the frame coldly, formally composed as the classical signal of the *mise-en-abîme* and mined here for all it is worth. If this image is set up with its counterpart in the image of the teeming boulevard, they are not so much opposed as developed as functions of one another, as interchangeable 'stages'. Just as the film folds the boulevard onto the stage and back again, so too the roles and identities 'performed' in one space are picked up, inverted or intensified by the other. The current that links these principal circuits of the film is desire, here given its purest incarnation in the character of Garance, who represents a desire that resists being fixed or captured, and that can mobilise (Lemaître's robust actor's ego immediately transforms his jealousy into the key to his Othello performance) just as much as immobilise (Baptiste literally freezes onstage when he glimpses Garance in the audience, his muteness extending to become immobility).

While these reflexive elements are present in the film's first part, it is the second – with its change of tone from lightheartedness to sobriety, from youthful ambition to the mixed blessings of mature success, from love to death – that really puts them to work. The film ends with Garance pursued by Baptiste and borne away from the crowd. By this time the resonances of each 'stage' have become so inter-linked for this moment to suggest overwhelmingly contrasting emotions of loss and renewal, of the end of the affair and Garance's joyful returning home. It is a moment that might also stand metaphorically for the film's present power, less as a monu-ment marking the 'end' of a filmmaking tradition than as a 'return' for a film whose structural complexity re-emerges as astonishingly rich.

LE PETIT PRINCE A DIT
DIR: CHRISTINE PASCAL FR./SWITZ. 1992
ORIGINALLY PUBLISHED IN *SIGHT AND SOUND* MAY 1994

SYNOPSIS
Violette Leibovich, the ten-year old daughter of a happily divorced couple – Adam, a doctor and Mélanie, an actress – is taken to stay with her mother while her father is in New York. On the way she feels dizzy and collapses. On Adam's return, Mélanie berates him for not having noticed their daughter's medical condition earlier, and a medical examination is organised. During the examination, Adam secretly observes the images of the brain scan from the next room and eavesdrops on the doctor's conversation. It transpires that Violette has a brain tumour. Adam abducts her from hospital and the pair take to the road. Staying in hotels, buying food from service stations, they travel to Milan to see Mélanie in rehearsal, and continue from Milan to Genoa. On the way, Violette's condition worsens. It is agreed that the family, including Adam's mistress, Lucie and stray dog adopted by Violette, congregate at the family home in Provence. There, the happy atmosphere is disrupted by the dog's disappearance, Adam's insistence that Lucie leave and by Violette's petulance. Finally, however, mother and father unite at their daughter's bedside as, exhausted by the evening's events, Violette falls asleep.

REVIEW
Legend has it that when asked why the Cinémathèque de Paris possessed a wall-to-wall screen, its founder Henri Langlois replied that it had been specially conceived 'for the films of Renoir and Rossellini, because their shots have the tendency suddenly to burst out of the frame, upwards, downwards and to the sides'. Films, in other words, that acknowledge their limitations in representing the chaotic flux of life. The formal attributes of deep-focus cinematography, and of replacing the scene with the shot in such movies became reified in Bazin's post-war theories of cinematic realism, contributing to the formation of a recognisably 'European' cinematic style, one concerned less with the three-act dictat of the narrative arc than with the contingent encounter and the appearance of improvisation.

This cinema has been described as less concerned with telling a story than illustrating a situation, and so it is with *Le Petit Prince a dit*, whose emphasis is more on character exploration than plot extrapolation. It is none the worse for it, when one considers the saccharine possibilities of the story-line: dad abducts terminally ill daughter from hospital for one last (broken) family reunion. When considered structurally, the film is a case of the episodic held together by the tragic, of events in thrall to the premise. But it is the delicacy and sly circumnavigation of the sentimental that allow it to deal with the intense self-consciousness that comes with a subject such as this, when every fifteen minutes or so brings the possibility of Violette suffering a relapse or of fatality further postponed as the narrative pay-off.

The film's centrepiece is the 'voyage to Italy' that father and daughter undertake after her abduction. Wonderful moments here include the luminous rendition of the daughter's experience of transubstantiation, and a choking breakfast-table routine that manages to be both moving ('When am I going to die?' Violette asks

87

her father over coffee as if she were asking to get down from the table) and knowing (the father wears dark glasses throughout, and you want to see his eyes). It also features some of the best shots of out-of-season hotels in recent European cinema, with the exception of Wenders' *The State of Things*.

The journey originates in and arrives at versions of the same moment, that of the respective parents' reactions to the news of their daughter's condition. Each is 'staged' in a particularly telling way: the father's, appropriately enough, in a medical mise-en-scène with him surreptitiously watching and listening in on the brain scan via a tiny monitor in an adjoining room; the mother's moment played out on stage during her rehearsals in Milan, with both father and daughter present unobserved in the stalls. As academic as these scenes might sound, both moments work. What is it that is constrained by the monitor and the proscenium arch alike? It is life, the free expression of the emotions and, in the case of the medical imagery, it is the body itself that is transformed and reduced. All those elements, in fact, that the cinema takes on in the task of representing life over death, whether it be the medical image of death that provokes the father's abduction, or the deathly masking of emotions paradoxically required of the mother on stage.

The emotional threads are tied together in the closing sequence in the family's country house, but this is not a straightforwardly feelgood finale. When Adam eases his mistress out of the domestic picture, for example, one senses that he knows he is doing the right thing but is not 100 per cent happy about it. Likewise with Mélanie's hysterical, overcompensating gestures. All the good intentions of mother and father alike, volubly broadcast and exaggeratedly displayed, end up in tearful spats and broken glass. But things come right slowly on the verge of Violette's (final) sleep. The film's resolute lack of sentimentality is crystallised in the penultimate shot of Adam's knuckles whitening as he kneads a pillow taken from his daughter's bed — as much an image of mercy-killing passion as of grief.

GODARDVILLE: ALPHAVILLE, THE NOUVELLE VAGUE AND 1960s PARIS

ORIGINALLY PUBLISHED IN *SIGHT AND SOUND* JULY 1994

Alphaville opens with a screenful of flashing light; a strident, ominous music underpins its pulse. A voice, at the same time gratingly electronic and glottally human, declares: 'There are times when reality becomes too complex for oral communication. But legend gives it a form by which it pervades the whole world.' Apart from *A bout de souffle*, *Alphaville* is probably the most complete of Godard's genre pieces. Its science fiction tone is held in satisfyingly parodic balance by the pulp fiction narrative so beloved of the *nouvelle vague*. But the 'too complex reality' to which the film gives 'legendary' (i.e. generic) form is a precise one. It concerns post-war French modernisation and urban expansion – a reality populated by technocrats and consumers and, for the *nouvelle vague* at least, all taking place in Paris.

Alphaville (1965) is the story of special agent Lemmy Caution, played by American actor and naturalised noir icon Eddie Constantine, who has voyaged (in his white Ford Galaxy) across time and space to Alphaville, the capital city of a distant planet. His mission: to bring back the scientist Professor Von Braun. The Professor, however, has since become king of the city by creating Alpha 60, the computer that controls Alphaville along harsh technocratic lines: weeping is outlawed and poetry goes unrecognised, words such as conscience and love have been erased from the lexicon. Add to this Anna Karina as Natacha von Braun, daughter of the Professor and Programmer (Second Class) of Alpha 60, a number tattooed on her neck, who is loved by Lemmy; Constantine's whisky-drinking, poetry-spouting, outrageously over-determined hard man of a special agent whose fight sequences, as Wim Wenders noted in his essay on the actor, 'are like dance sequences in a bad musical'; and Raoul Coutard's cinematography, the luminous opposition of its Expressionist black and white matching the film's abstract absolutes of good and evil, love and death, conscience and technology, poetry and science. Plus, of course, Paris.

Alphaville is Paris, 1965. Or rather, Paris 1965 is Alphaville, a modernist nightmare of post-Bauhaus functionalism where the curtain-walled skyscraper becomes the simultaneous symbol of progress and apocalypse. With *Alphaville*, the *nouvelle vague* aesthetic of shooting in the streets reaches an apotheosis. There is no question here of ethnographic realism in the style of Jean Rouch's *Chronique d'un été* (1961) or Chris Marker's *Le joli mai* (1963), nor of Italian-style realism. *Alphaville*'s is a short-circuited realism applied to the least likely of genres – science fiction – that serves to make strange a real already so strange that it positively demands the strategy.

Alphaville is something of a curio in the catalogue of Godard's city films. Of the fifteen features he made between 1959 and 1967, only four – *Le Petit Soldat* (1960), *Les Carabiniers* (1963), *Le Mépris* (1963) and *Pierrot le fou* (1965) – are shot outside Paris. Yet despite the familiar location, *Alphaville* looks different. With its flashing neon arrows and the tyrannical right angles and aggressive curves of its modern architecture it comes closer to Jacques Tati than to the films of the other *nouvelle vague* directors, not to mention the more representative film set in what we might call Godardville.

Along with *Metropolis*, *Blade Runner* and *Akira*, *Alphaville* is one of the definitive works in the cinema of dystopian cities. Each film proposes its vision of a dehumanised society as the corollary to technological progress within the style of its period: Lang's epic-scale 1920s Expressionism supplies a female robot with a supermodel figure and a vision of Berlin as a machine-age tyranny of power and control; Scott's film gives cyberpunk its founding retromediaevalist look; Otomo's manga-influenced hyperbole of the viscerally brutal and the peachily sentimental creates a contemporary animated vision of the apocalyptic city – neo-Tokyo. As science fiction each of the others dramatises the question 'What would it be like if...?', each proposes a future latent in the present, *Alphaville*, by contrast, says 'Forget "what if...?" Look around you! "If" has already taken place!'

It may seem curious to associate the *nouvelle vague* with a dystopian vision of Paris. After all, the early films render the city as a (shot from the) hip 1950s *carte postale*. From the twin manifestos of *Les Quatre cents coups* (1959) and *A bout de souffle* (1959) to the last-gasp revivalism of *Paris vu par...* (1964), the *nouvelle vague* redefined the look of Paris. But it is Godard's films that focus most consistently on the city in the late 1950s and 1960s, to the extent that Tony Rayns can suggest they are 'so much of their particular time that they'll need explanatory footnotes before long'. Here are some footnotes.

Suggesting that a film is 'of its time' can be a politely indirect way of saying that it looks dated, and *Alphaville* does not escape the implication. In the same way as Ray Harryhausen's monsters and Japanese Godzilla movies now epitomise 1960s SFX-kitsch rather than high-tech screen terror, so Godard's vision of futuristic technology might appear more steam-driven than streamlined. But such an observation is wide of the mark. These films were precisely, insistently, almost fetishistically of their time, and this holds as true for the films of other new wavers as it does for Godard.

Part of the modernity of the *nouvelle vague* can be attributed to the use of new lightweight Eclair cameras and Nagra sound-recording technology to bypass the convention of studio-based shooting associated with the despised *cinéma de qualité*. This allowed the new filmmakers to take to the streets and the boulevards, *quartiers* and apartments of the real city, all the better to mythologise its historic centre. Georges Sadoul, writing on Louis Malle's *Ascenseur pour l'echafaud* (1957), asked, 'How many cinematic poets has Paris had? One would be forgiven for thinking that it was impossible to renew this theme'. For Sadoul, Malle already possessed the eye for detail, for the life of modern objects, that was to characterise the 'Young French Cinema': 'Wall-to-wall carpeting, rubber-coated castors, a cast-iron diamond-shaped trapdoor, a lighter, a parachutist's knife, an empty blue packet of Gitanes ... No need for dialogue here. All these objects speak.' Enhanced by the swooning melancholy of a Miles Davis score, by Jeanne Moreau's city-sphinx persona and by the black and white cinematography of Henri Decaë (who also photographed *Les Quatre cents coups*), the objects in Malle's film anticipated the *nouvelle vague* by a year and spoke perhaps the first words in a dialogue with the grandest modern object of them all: Paris itself.

This dialogue between the cinema and the city was nowhere more insistently developed than in Godard's films of the 1960s. In her key essay 'Godard', Susan Sontag recognised the 'casually encyclopaedic' nature his work; in the January 1967 issue of *Cahiers du cinéma*, the young Bernardo Bertolucci wrote of Godard's 'vulgarity', adding that for him this was a positive quality: 'I call "vulgarity" his capacity and his ability to live day-to-day, close to things, to live in the world as does a journalist, always aware of the right time to arrive on the scene.' But what for some was a 'journalistic' sensitivity to the moment was to others simply superficiality and love of novelty. Writing about *Alphaville* in the leftist cultural journal *Les Temps modernes* in 1965, Pierre Samson found fault with Godard's archetypically *nouvelle vague* shooting style: 'He shoots without long preparation, and improvises against a very thin canvas which permits him to stay in the current of fashionable ideas, to be at one with the snobberies and curiosities of the moment.' When it came to *Alphaville*'s vision of Paris as a futurist metropolis, Samson was equally scathing: 'Godard only chooses the most exterior details, he contents himself with naming things at the expense of knowing how to show them... he inhabits the level of a sort of exoticism of automation and modernism.'

The characterisation was to stick – Godard the modernist exotic, fascinated by the surfaces, sounds and shapes of modern Parisian life, but not by its substance. It was a barely veiled accusation of profligacy of style and theme, of bad taste, of formlessness and lack of aesthetic harmony – forgetting that in Godard's case the old rules simply don't apply and never did. The issue of 'exoticism' is at the ambiguous heart of the modernist cinema's depiction of the modern city.

In a collection of essays that examines images of post-war European cities, French historian Pierre Sorlin proposes that by the late 1950s Italian cinema had arrived at 'a blurred image of cities'. Sorlin arrives at the metaphor of blurring by way of two assumptions; first that 'a change occurred in the socially constituted images when filmmakers ceased to view cities as potential works of art', and second that this change was related to transformations in the post-war urban topologies that resulted in 'a crisis in the representation of towns'. In the case of Paris, it is in the cinematic representation of the relationship between the historic centre and its peripheries, the new suburbs, that this loss of focus becomes explicit.

The 'blurring' of Paris in the cinema of the *nouvelle vague* is a chronicle of the incursions into the city centre of modernist architecture and of the cultural ascendancy of Le Corbusier and the International Style. As a result, the characters lose their bearings – and worse, their love of the city – because, as in Jean Rouch's 'Gare du nord' episode in *Paris vu par...*, the *grands projets* of the 1960s appear to be steadily obscuring and unfocusing Haussmann's rationally planned centre. It is just such a fear that informs *Alphaville*'s image of an architecturally brutalist future world in the heart of the city. In its despair over 1960s urbanisation, *Alphaville* was part of a wider concern about the perceived dehumanising effects of mass-scale housing and the contemporary renovation of the city. Governmental responses to the French post-war housing shortage – particularly acute in Paris, the 1962 census showing that one flat in four was overcrowded and that sixty per cent of all French housing stock dated from before 1914 – had been slow. State intervention in 1959 led to suburban areas being designated for immediate or future development, but in some cases these became the focus of 'national disgust' at the most pernicious of the mass-scale HLM (*habitations à loyer modéré* or low rent housing) schemes, dubbed in Alphaville 'hôpitaux de la longue maladie'.

The most notorious example was the Sarcelles housing estate, which lent its name to a phenomenon named *la sarcellite*. This blanket term for the malign effects of living in an HLM is the subject of Godard's *Deux ou trois choses que je sais d'elle*

(1966), the *elle* of the title being both Paris herself and the young Sarcelles house-wife (Marina Vlady) who takes to casual prostitution in order to make ends meet. The processes of objectification crucial to the consumer society are shown at their most extreme in a scenario wherein a young woman must sell herself as an object in order to afford other objects. The prostitute, a stock figure of Parisian mythology from Baudelaire and Impressionist painting onwards – returns as false conscious-ness made flesh. The film ends with a series of consumer items – boxes of washing powder, transistor radios and so on – arranged in a rectilinear replication of the layout of Sarcelles. The allure of novelty attributed to such objects in Malle's film is stripped away; Godard's objects offer the economic relations behind the new sub-urban towns as metonymic of consumer society itself. Vlady's Juliette Janson is not physically integrated in the city where she lives, but in a circuit of economic demands and desires that Sarcelles represents.

And yet the critique is ambiguous – as it is in Jacques Tati's films on the same subject, *Mon oncle* (1958) and *Playtime* (1967). Within Tati's satires on modernist architecture, consumerism and urbanisation, the ancestral city disappears. In *Playtime* it becomes a shadow image – something glimpsed only as a reflection in the glass curtain walls of the city set nicknamed 'Tativille' that the director had constructed on the outskirts of Paris and which Serge Daney has called 'La Défense before La Défense existed'. Here the historic city is not simply 'blurred', but has vanished alto-gether. In *Mon oncle*, shot in and around the new town of Créteil, there is still some semblance of community to be nostalgic about. But this is separated from the new town by a *terrain vague* that, by the end of the film, is ominously under development. The ambivalence present in both directors' work comes from their manipulation of the harsh geometry of the new architectural styles to formal ends – their 'modernist exoticism'. The ambiguous fascination with the aesthetic surface of post-war urban modernity in *Deux ou trois choses* was eloquently identified by Eric Rohmer: 'In the suburbs Godard filmed the ugliest, most frightful things and succeeded in making them come alive, in making them beautiful... With a panoramic shot of an HLM at Sarcelles one can make a sublime image and Godard did it.'

By the end of the 1960s Godard had quit Paris, moving to the suburbs for *Deux ou trois choses*, taking the *route nationale* out of the city in the agonising traffic jam that opens *Weekend* (a single-take, mobile camera shot of clotted immobility, the highway as haemorrhage), and retreating to an unlit, undecorated TV studio for *Le Gai Savoir* (1968). The city of tourist-friendly landmarks and easy *parisianismes* that the *nouvelle vague* had reinvigorated, if not entirely reinvented, was being systemati-cally replaced from the early years of the decade by the banal spaces of modernity – spaces conducive to lingering, to urban *temps morts* – and by what Gilles Deleuze calls the 'any spaces whatever' that characterise the cinema of Godard and Resnais, Varda and Marker, Rossellini and Antonioni. In his book *Cinema and Modernity*, John Orr acknowledges Deleuze's recognition that the depiction of this kind of urban landscape began with Italian post-war cinema: 'In Neo-Realism the new open spaces of Europe's ruined cities opened up the cinematic spaces of the exterior location which did not have to define itself as a familiar locale.'

Godard created other masterpieces of Parisian cinema alongside *Alphaville*, of course. Of these, *Une femme mariée*, made in 1964 with Macha Méril in the lead role, forms the second panel in a triptych about women in the city, between *Vivre sa vie* (1962) and *Deux ou trois choses*. Separated from *Alphaville* not so much by its concerns – the automation of personal life, dehumanisation, alienation – as by its tone, *Une femme mariée* is a quasi-sociological exploration of a 'typical' young Parisian couple of the 1960s. Pierre, true to the technocratic impetus of the time, is an engineer. Charlotte is a housewife with a young son and a lover. Together they live in a newly-built apartment block packed with the latest consumer durables. Emotionally, Charlotte is divided between her husband and her lover, a fragmentation intensified by that which she undergoes among the multitude of consumer images of women within which the film places her.

The Paris of *Une femme mariée* is 'anonymously modern', its 'any spaces whatever' those of Orly airport and the department store Printemps-Nation, where Charlotte – the post-Baudelairean *flâneuse* (and the only female character in the triptych not to play the Godardian Holy Whore) – finds herself both reflected in and refracted by the images of feminine perfection and inducements to consumerism that multiply around her. As for Godard's 'modernist exoticism', clearly it became too unbearable a contradiction for the director simultaneously to aestheticise and condemn. So the ambiguous fascination with the modern city populated by the objects and alienated characters of consumer society devolved first onto the anguished auto-criticism of *Deux ou trois choses*, then into the savage disavowal of *Weekend*, and, after May 1968, into the militant agit-prop and chic Maoism of 'le groupe Dziga Vertov'.

Towards the end of *Alphaville*, just before being shot dead, Professor Von Braun, the man of the future, says to Lemmy Caution, the man of the past: 'Look at yourself. Men of your type will soon be extinct. You'll become something worse than death. You'll become a legend.' The words apply with unnerving accuracy to Godard himself. And in the continuing absence of any recent Godard on our screens there remains the city films, a highly personal series of Pop Art news bulletins from 1960s Paris. For 'of their time', read 'dated', 'extinct'. Read glorious.

L'OMBRE DU DOUTE/A SHADOW OF DOUBT

DIR: ALINE ISSERMAN FRANCE 1992
ORIGINALLY PUBLISHED IN *SIGHT AND SOUND* SEPTEMBER 1994

SYNOPSIS

Twelve-year-old Alexandrine and her younger brother Pierre are playing in the woods. When Jean, their father, approaches and attempts to touch her she runs away. At school, a story that Alexandrine has written alerts her teacher to the possibility that the girl's home life is not all that it might be. When the teacher talks to Alexandrine's parents, Jean and Marie simply attribute their daughter's behaviour to her age. Following her teacher's advice that she should tell someone if there is anything wrong, Alexandrine goes to the police and informs them that her father molests her. Jean refutes the allegations. Finding it hard to gain the confidence of the children, Sophia, a counsellor, meets Alexandrine, who admits that she feels tiny and helpless. At home, Alexandrine overhears Pierre asking Jean to leave him alone. The two children run away. After spending a night in a disused building, Alexandrine goes to the police. Marie and Jean are questioned. The mother is blamed for negligence but is not charged; the father is released from custody but is instructed not have any contact with his children pending investigation. However, Jean tells Marie that he needs to talk to his daughter; she takes him to see Alexandrine secretly and leaves them together. On Alexandrine's birthday, Jean visits them, much to Marie's annoyance. He justifies himself with a hysterical outburst.

Sophia and the magistrate argue over the court case; he tells her that he can do nothing without concrete proof. Later Alexandrine admits to Sophia that she has seen her father and Jean is imprisoned. When questioning Alexandrine the magistrates hear her talk of a black threatening shadow; when they ask whether it is Jean, she is silent. Marie, undergoing family therapy, is starting to see the truth. Jean receives a letter from his sister that reveals that both of them were abused by their father. After the trial Jean sees two therapists to whom he explains his silence during the trial as one bred of constant fear, his memory of seeing his father abusing his sister, his uncontrollable abuse of his own daughter and his desire to be cured. At the beach, Alexandrine and Pierre play; she is no longer terrified of the water.

REVIEW

If there are subjects that prove to be limit-cases when it comes to their cinematic treatment, child abuse is certainly among them. In *A Shadow of Doubt* Aline Isserman opts to treat the subject by way of a psychological thriller that hangs on whether the allegations of the young daughter against her father are taken seriously by the police and judiciary. In this way Isserman shifts the emphasis away from the potential sensationalism of the act of abuse itself towards its repercussions within the family and in the wider society. Such an approach makes the film's action necessarily reactive, having as its centre a black hole of implied horror, exactly the shadow of doubt that generates the film's dynamic of guilt, recrimination and legal machinations.

In the film's use of the shadow as a symbol of individual evil and of a generalised aberrant 'other', Isserman is to some extent recalling Fritz Lang's *M*. But where Lang used sociopathic desire as a means to focus on an equally ruthless opportunism at work within criminal and judicial worlds alike, Isserman, while cultivating the silences and suspicions of the psychological thriller, inserts her film within the more *intimiste* vein that Ginette Vincendeau has identified as a master-narrative of French cinema, that of the father-daughter relationship. It is in the rendition of this relationship that the film is most interesting. *A Shadow of Doubt* is a film of faces shot in CinemaScope and in set-ups where close-ups and shallow-focus two-shots predominate. This approach is judicious and striking and has an intense cumulative power because its close-up strategy accommodates a host of elements central to the film. The seismic shock that Alexandrine's allegation sends through the family transforms all their interactions into barely concealed negotiations with, and reactions to, the doubt and fear that come to infest the home. Hence all the close-ups become part of one prolonged set of reaction-shots played out with various modulations. Which is as it should be, for as Jacques Aumont demonstrates in his excellent study of the face in cinema *Du visage au cinéma*, the close-up is an invention of the silent cinema that offers the human face as a 'readable landscape' of clues available for scrutiny in the absence of the spoken word. When, as is the case with Alexandrine's repeated allegations, the daughter's words carry less weight than the father's denials, Isserman's camera brings us the faces on which the unspoken, unspeakable drama is being played out.

This strategy gets the highly focused and concentrated performances it requires to be effective from the central couple of Sandrine Blanke, who oscillates as Alexandrine between hypnotised entrapment within her own fear and resolute attempts to flee it, and Alain Bashung, whose sallow, aristocratic features ultimately crumble under the pressure of cultivating composure. Mireille Perrier as the mother is somewhat marginalised by the film's concentration on father and daughter, but her performance is stronger than Bashung's, simply because she nevertheless manages to make her ultimate submission to the truth of her daughter's allegations plausible.

Bashung's transformation from pseudo-schizophrenic abuser to jailed repentant is welcome, if less convincing. This has to do with a shift into melodrama in the latter part of the film that sits uncomfortably with high stylisation and beady behaviourist observation. The latter dominates the film so effectively that the departures from it – which include an uncomfortably unimaginative 'imaginary' sequence with Alexandrine as a bird trapped in the cage of the house and the de rigeur camcorder sequences of the father's objectification of his daughter – fare less effectively.

A Shadow of Doubt, while it holds more than it moves, deserves to be called brave for its content and attack. In the closing sequence on the beach the film revisits that *locus classicus* of cinematic childhood *Les Quatre cents coups*, but withholds its freeze-frame, offering instead a cleansing sense of liberation and possibility that is as palpable for the spectator as it is for Alexandrine.

LANCELOT DU LAC

DIR: ROBERT BRESSON FR./IT. 1974
ORIGINALLY PUBLISHED IN *SIGHT AND SOUND* NOVEMBER 1994

SYNOPSIS

After having failed in their quest for the Holy Grail, the Knights of the Round Table, led by Lancelot, return to Camelot and the Court of King Arthur. Lancelot, the Queen's champion, is fixed on continuing the quest and tells Guinevere that he has sworn an oath to God not to become her lover. She reminds him that there remains a previous oath from which he must first be released.

Arthur entrusts the jealous Mordred with his fear that they have provoked the wrath of God, and Lancelot – although defended against Mordred's intimations by Gawain – again begs Guinevere to release him. Although she unwillingly consents, Lancelot is tempted to arrange another rendezvous with her while Arthur and his knights attend a jousting tournament, thus countering Mordred's plot to either catch him in adultery or to kill him.

At the tournament Lancelot wears neutral colours but is identified by his skill and is wounded by a lance. He rides away into the forest where he is cared for by an old peasant woman. The Knights search for him in order to refute Mordred's slanders but are convinced by a premonition of his death and the Queen's guilt. Lancelot returns to carry her off after killing two Knights, one of them Agaravain, Gawain's brother. Compelled to avenge his brother's death, Gawain is mortally wounded by Lancelot. Lancelot reluctantly returns Guinevere to the king only under assurances that she will not be punished. Soon after, on learning that Mordred has stirred up rebellion, Lancelot returns to Arthur's camp and is among the many Knights slaughtered in the ensuing battles.

REVIEW

Twenty years after its original release, *Lancelot du Lac* is bound to shock, frustrate and overwhelm in equal measure, partly because of its treatment of the Arthurian myth and the trappings of Camelot kitsch that attach themselves to celluloid visions of the Middle Ages. By an uncomfortable coincidence, the recent press preview of *Lancelot* occurred the day after a television screening of John Boorman's *Excalibur* – truly a case of the sublime following the ridiculous – but the contrast is instructive in terms of just those expectations that Bresson has consistently sought to disown in his filmmaking.

In his collection of aphorisms *Notes on the Cinematographer*, Bresson names his entirely individual conception of filmmaking as 'cinématographie... a writing with images in movement and with sounds', and at one level *Lancelot* can be seen as the Bressonian method attaining a particular degree of refinement and consummation. All the elements normally associated with Bresson's film language are present: the use of 'models' in the place of professional actors; un-emphatic and minimally expressive presences denied psychological depth and existing as human surfaces among what the director describes as 'the visible parlance of bodies, objects, horses, roads, trees, fields': a highly-wrought attention brought to bear on the soundtrack and an anti-dramatic attenuation of the narrative.

So much of Bresson's work takes place after the event that narrative convention would consider central. His is always an interstitial reading, on the edges of the action, privileging the ripples on the surface of the water rather than the Lady in the Lake herself. In keeping with this tendency, Lancelot begins at the end of the myth, with the return of the Knights who have failed in their quest for the Grail, and concentrates on Lancelot as the anguished suitor of the Queen and on the bloody decimation of the codes of chivalry. This organising principle covers not only the plot structure but also extends through the arrangement of the sequences down to the manner in which individual shots are attacked. Each of Bresson's films contains moments that stand to both crystallise and characterise such an approach: the oblique effectiveness of the shot/counter-shot exchanges in *Le procès de Jeanne d'Arc*, the eroticised ballet of thieving, caressing hands in the Gare de Lyon sequence of *Pickpocket*, the off-screen robbery conveyed entirely through sound in *L'Argent*. Likewise, in the tournament sequence, *Lancelot* has what might be called its own Ur-Bresson moment. The jousting in this sequence is conveyed through a brilliantly rhythmic montage of shots of the reaction of the spectators, of musicians piping between heats, of the raising of penants, of the horses stamping and charging, the visible impact of lance on shield is withheld until one no longer expects to see it, by which time the impact has gathered in latent power. Sound is crucial to this sequence, as it is to the entire film, armour being sheared by the blow of a sword, the sound of the horses; these participate in an extraordinary orchestration of details, the visual and aural truly interacting.

If *Pickpocket* remains his masterpiece, *Lancelot du Lac* is proof that Bresson cannot age badly, and it is representative of an uncompromisingly singular cinematic vision – discomforting, a little intimidating but thoroughly remarkable and unlike any other in cinema. Godard got it right when he commented that Bresson's films owe their power to 'an idea of the world applied to cinema, or an idea of cinema applied to the world; ultimately it comes to the same thing'. *Lancelot* is the idea given unforgettable form.

LA REINE MARGOT
DIR: PATRICE CHÉREAU FR./GER./IT. 1994
ORIGINALLY PUBLISHED IN *SIGHT AND SOUND* JANUARY 1995

SYNOPSIS

Paris, August 18, 1572. Marguerite de Valois (Margot), sister of Charles IX, the Catholic King of France and daughter of Catherine de Medici, is to marry the Protestant Duke, Henri de Navarre, in a ceremony arranged to appease the two warring religious factions. Marguerite, forced to marry a man she does not love, acquiesces under pressure insisting that she will not share the conjugal bed with her new husband, preferring the attentions of her lover, the ruthless, bloodthirsty Duc de Guise.

Catherine de Medici wishes to neutralise the perceived Protestant threat by killing their leaders. As King, Charles – though indecisive and half-mad – declares that the deaths of the leaders alone is insufficient: he wants all of them dead, so that not a single Protestant survives to blame him. Despite his words being uttered while in the throes of a fit, and under coercive pressure from the Dukes of Anjou, Guise and Tavanne, they are taken as the royal assent to what will become known as the Saint Bartholomew's Day Massacre. On August 23 and 24 a militia of Catholic courtiers and the Parisian people indiscriminately slaughter over six thousand Protestants, including many of the Huguenot guests at Margot's wedding. Navarre is saved from the bloodshed by the attentions of Margot and her courtiers. However, she also attends to a badly wounded young Protestant, La Môle, who she realises is the same man she picked up several days previously when scouring the streets for casual amorous encounters. They fall in love and she helps him escape to Holland.

During a hunting accident Navarre saves the life of Charles and earns the King's trust, friendship and protection. However, Catherine is plotting to have Navarre killed with a slow-acting poison secreted into the pages of a book on hunting. She entrusts the task to her youngest son, the Duc d'Alençon. Unexpectedly, the King, rather than Navarre, handles the book. He dies a slow and agonising death, attended to by Margot. La Môle has returned from Holland to find Margot but is charged with regicide and is executed with his friend Coconnas. Margot visits the decapitated body, taking his head to have it embalmed. Reconciled with her husband, sickened by Catherine de Medici's savagery, Margot flees the court to join the Protestant camp.

REVIEW

Blood, poison and perfume: *La Reine Margot* is a suppurating broth of all three in which the idea of the 'body politic' receives a highly physical twist. Patrice Chéreau has chosen to film the close, murderous and hermetic world of the French court at the time of Catherine de Medici as a scrum of fluid alliances and shifting allegiances. These are negotiated against the backdrop of a coerced marriage of political convenience (Marguerite de Valois to Henri de Navarre), feral, in-bred desire (Catherine de Medici for her son Henri, Duc d'Anjou, the brothers for their sister Margot), merciless religious hatred (the court is Catholic, Navarre is Protestant), focused by the growing horror and despair of the young queen.

Despite having failed as the French entry to set the 1994 Cannes Festival alight

– the Best Supporting Actress award to Virna Lisi being widely (and condescend-ingly) seen as a token bauble – *La Reine Margot* has gone on to reap both critical and commercial acclaim in France. As yet another in the seemingly interminable cycle of heritage films with which Claude Berri – here in the role of producer – has become synonymous, the film arrives here trailing the baggage of expectations associated with others of its genre, but succeeds in satisfyingly short-circuiting them.

Chéreau himself has stressed his desire to avoid reproducing in his own film what *Cahiers du cinéma* has referred to as 'retro-nostalgia', and has spoken in inter-views of using a 'prophylactic measure' to circumvent it – 'Every time an image from a TV film on Catherine de Medici came to mind I would think of the *Godfather* films, of *Mean Streets* and *GoodFellas*.' The Medicis as Mafia clan – it's a nice idea, and one that has clearly shaped the film's depiction of the family as the arena of morbid power-play, while also allowing it to pull clear of the influence of its generic satellites. The heritage film tends to rely on set-ups that maximise its qualities of spectacle – high angles, mid-long shots – to the end of privileging illustrative tableaux, while also plac-ing the spectator in an Olympian and curiously touristic position (it is no coincidence that the 'heritage film' coincides precisely with the trend for restaging national his-tory and culture in theme parks). Conversely, the Mafia film comes in close and claustrophobic, privileges close-ups, two-shots and interior spaces. That this strategy places the spectator in a more intimate relationship with the action is something that has not been lost on Chéreau, who brings his camera in among the bodies, knitting in and out of the bloodlines and circuits of power. The *mise-en-scène* of *La Reine Margot* is one in which the spectator experiences a physical disorientation to match that of the characters themselves and interestingly, the few moments when the film does lapse into a kind of painterly academicism (Vermeer, Zurburan) are those when the action shifts beyond the walls of the Palais du Louvre to Holland.

The uncomfortable intimacy that the film encourages brings out some remark-able performances. Lisi, clad in black throughout, plays Catherine as a woman whose mourning is as constant as her venomous affections. When it becomes clear that the poison she intended for Navarre has mistakenly infected her eldest son, the vacillat-ing, bloodthirsty Charles, a low-angle shot has her lurking in the gallery of the Cathe-dral casting a vampiric shadow – Queen Nosferatu, her hair scraped cruelly back to show a Max Schreck pate. Anglade's Charles is one of the film's real revelations; those with memories of his dream-wimp boyfriends in *Betty Blue* and *Nikita* will barely recognise him here. His is a performance of real range and authority, half slob-bering dungeon freak barely ennobled by filthy lace and half strangely sympathetic victim of his mother's appalling plots. And at the centre of all the mayhem is Adjani's Margot, her face a set of nested ovals that coalesce to express muted horror, her white robes forever absorbing the blood of others including that of La Môle, her Protestant lover, whose severed head she cradles in her lap after his execution, just as she absorbs into her clothes the sweated blood of the slow-poisoned king.

Grand guignol, cloak-and-dagger, cruel Mafia claustrophobia; *La Reine Margot* is nothing if not explicit about power and religious hatred. Its currency is blood, its disguises perfume and lace; parricide, regicide and genocide its manifest destiny. Close to the bone, this is the shocking, slightly cold but undeniably powerful apothe-osis of the French heritage film.

UN HUSSARD SUR LE TOIT/THE HORSEMAN ON THE ROOF
DIR: JEAN-PAUL RAPPENEAU FRANCE 1995
ORIGINALLY PUBLISHED IN *SIGHT AND SOUND* JANUARY 1995

SYNOPSIS
Provence, 1830s. Angelo, a young Italian Hussar and supporter of his country's Nationalist cause, hides in a French town from Hapsburg agents. Having been set up by a friend and almost trapped by his pursuers, Angelo flees into the Provençal countryside. He comes across a village ravaged by disease where a dedicated doctor treats the dead and dying. Angelo assists and sits with him as he succumbs to cholera. Angelo falls in with a governess and her two charges, striking up a friendship with the young woman. Quarantined, he is able to escape because of the cholera-induced panic. Arriving at Manosque, Angelo is immediately suspected to be a poisoner by a rampaging lynch-mob of paranoid locals. He is pursued through the streets and across the roofs both by the locals and the agents who have caught up with him. One of the agents is caught by the mob and Angelo takes refuge in what appears to be an empty house. He is surprised to find the house inhabited by a single occupant, a dignified, unflappable young woman named Pauline de Théus who feeds him.

Waking up alone, Angelo leaves the town discovering that the governess and her children have died. He finally meets Guiseppe, his compatriot, who explains that he was coerced into giving away Angelo's whereabouts to his pursuers. Reunited with Pauline, the pair breach a military cordon sanitaire and escape into the countryside. They encounter a peasant-huckster who travels with them. Angelo and the huckster wait outside a noble house while Pauline is within and Angelo overhears that Pauline is married and is searching for her husband who, it seems, is quarantined in Manosque. She intends to return to locate him. Angelo attempts to dissuade him but relents and accompanies her. They are both quarantined but, unable to find her husband, manage to escape. The pair make their way to the de Théus household where they rest and drink hot wine. Pauline starts to show symptoms of cholera which Angelo treats by massaging her. Her husband arrives and Angelo returns to Italy. The pair exchange letters and Pauline is seen standing alone facing the mountain frontier with Italy.

REVIEW
Fifty different locations, 130 days of shooting, over 100 sets, nearly 1,000 costumes specially made; according to the press kit these were some of the elements that contributed to *The Horseman on the Roof* reputedly being the most expensive French film ever produced, with a budget of FF176 million. Thankfully, that's not its only distinguishing feature. That Jean-Paul Rappeneau's *Cyrano* effectively revived the sumptuously dressed historical drama as a highly exportable staple of French film production – the last time it had been so central was post-war and pre-*nouvelle vague* – means that depending on what one thinks of the genre the director has either a lot to answer for or a lot to live up to.

Horseman succeeds by virtue of working into the French tradition of *films de cape et d'épée* (cloak and dagger films) elements of both the Western and the Disney movie. Figures on horseback set against gorgeous Provençal horizons abound, giving the film's visuals a neo-Western mythic quality that it fully exploits. The concentration on horizons, frontiers and borders also relates to Angelo's exile from his Italian homeland. The adventure element generates a confident sense of narrative drive that is unashamedly old-fashioned in its disregard for plausibility – while all around them are wracked by pestilence, Angelo and Pauline gallop blithely on into the next adventure. The cholera catches up with Pauline only when they reach the de Théus chateau, Angelo's night-long, life-saving *frottage* of Pauline acting as a spot of sexualised healing, a barely sublimated release of erotic tension between them.

Rappeneau took the calculated risk of casting a relatively unknown young actor against Binoche, but Olivier Martinez is given a fair amount of screen time to establish himself before happening upon Binoche's Pauline. His Angelo is dashing and agile, a mother-obsessed young Italian patriot whose single-minded devotion to the cause of his country's independence is the source of his invulnerability as well as an obdurate dedication to duty that oscillates between gallantry and petulance. Binoche plays Pauline as resourceful and mysterious. More mature than her gentlemanly escort, she gently mocks his peevishness when he learns she is married to a much older man. Theirs is a relationship that develops through encounters with adversity that neatly dovetails into a growing companionship such that their final separation can only be read as being temporary. There are some pleasing second-role performances en route; François Cluzet's driven, doomed medic, Isabelle Carré's attractive young governess and, particularly, Depardieu's near-burlesque cameo as a harried magistrate and Jean Yanne as an untrustworthy huckster.

The film's locations alternate between the detail-drenched depiction of enclosed towns and the parched splendour of the Provençal mountains but with a particular emphasis on the reconstructed roofs of Manosque. The town was the much loved home of the novel's author, Jean Giono, whose prolific literary output rested on an abiding investment in *la France profonde*. Pantheist, pacifist and fervent believer in the virtues of peasantry, Giono, like Marcel Pagnol, was one of French literature's devoted regionalists. In choosing to adapt Giono's 1951 novel *Le Hussard sur le toit*, Rappeneau taps into two levels of literary patrimony, not only that endowed by Giono's own particular brand of peasant fabulation but also that of Stendhal, the nineteenth-century novelist whose close relation with Italian affairs of the 1820s strongly informs Giono's depiction of Angelo's exile. The film's headlong narrative thrust derives from the well-balanced combination of Angelo's flight from cholera and his pursuit by Austrian agents, his yearning to return to fight in Italy and his progress as stymied by the plague. Themes of exile and disease, selflessness and monomaniac dedication propel the story forward through its numerous bottlenecks in a tension-and-release dynamic, surging through towns teeming either with plague or a feverish panic of the plague and bursting out into landscapes patrolled by platoons of soldiers. Although treated relatively lightly – Horseman has little of the suppurating and claustrophobic grimness of Chéreau's *La Reine Margot* – plague, death and political terror are set off very effectively against the beauty of Provence, itself a gift to any director with a budget the size of Rappeneau's and assisted by Thierry Arbogast's cinematography. *Horseman* is a more than capable and entertaining romp. Fascinatingly, Giono himself cherished a project for an avant-garde version of Sartre's *La Nausée* filmed in slow-motion. Now that would have been something to see in the ever-expanding catalogue of French cinema's literary adaptations.

L'APPAT/THE BAIT
DIR: BERTRAND TAVERNIER FRANCE 1995
ORIGINALLY PUBLISHED IN *SIGHT AND SOUND* SEPTEMBER 1995

SYNOPSIS
Nathalie is eighteen and works in Paris as a model and shop assistant, sharing a flat with Eric, her unemployed boyfriend, and Bruno, his dim-witted pal. In the evening, she chats up affluent-looking men, collecting their business cards for her address book. The boys dream of moving to the US and setting up in the clothes business. To subsidise this dream they plan a series of robberies using Nathalie to lure men whose cards she has collected back to their apartments where she can let the boys in. The trio bungle the first three robbery attempts. When the next target, Antoine, a lawyer and writer, insists that he keeps no money in the flat, the boys torture and kill him. With another target, Alain, the boys are initially foiled by an internal locking device but they gain access on a second visit. Again the victim insists there is little of value in the flat but Eric suspects him of having slept with Nathalie the first time and so Alain is tortured and killed. The trio ransack a pile of Christmas gifts and Nathalie leaves the apartment wearing a Star of David ripped from around Alain's neck.

Nathalie and Eric argue and she becomes increasingly uneasy with the way their plan is progressing. The police call in at her work and then take her to the station for questioning. They show her images of the victims. When it is explained to her that Alain was repeatedly stabbed with a blunt letter opener, she reveals the identity of the killers. She asks the chief inspector if she will be released in time for Christmas.

REVIEW
The Bait sees Tavernier returning to the street-level realism of *L.627*, whose sure-footedness came from a semi-documentary emphasis on the everyday gestures and operational dilemmas of its drug-squad *flics*. In *The Bait* this former perspective on criminality is switched, the focus here being on the adolescent protagonists of a story closely modelled on a cause célèbre series of killings that took place in France in 1984. The case involved a teenage trio; a girl who procured wealthy Parisians to take her back to their apartments where they would be jumped by her two adolescent male accomplices. Casual pick-ups became hold-ups that culminated in murder. Tavernier retains the characters and facts of the case, re-situating them in present-day Paris to provide a snapshot of current metropolitan criminality. *The Bait* partakes in the contemporary obsession with violent crime in a number of ways.

Tavernier's teenagers are identikit victims of contemporary consumer-society, and when it comes to assigning symptomatic reasons for their casual criminality it's a matter of rounding up the usual suspects: modern American cinema, video culture and game shows are proposed as participating in a culture of celebrity and hyper-acquisitive capitalism. Tavernier's take hardly deserves to be called an analysis, more a knee-jerk reflex of symptomatic moralism with the film condemning a soulless, 'international' (read American) visual culture for having corrupted the youth. It is significant that the dream these young would-be entrepreneurs covet – and for which they are prepared to kill – is of moving to the US and setting up in the rag trade.

In the director's statement Tavernier accurately asserts that America still exercises a strong hold on the imagination of French youth, but – in the fashion of a vaguely left-wing Frenchman of a certain age – he castigates as pernicious the same fascination that he himself has explored in his two volume *History of American Cinema*. It is not so much that the sociologist in Tavernier overwhelms the cineaste, it is more the case of moralism dominating his imagination. This is indicated not only in the easy targets the film elects to home in on, but also in that it chooses – almost as an index of its despair – to pinpoint a young female character as somehow archetypal of current criminality. *The Bait*, then, is of a piece with recent films such as *Fun* and *Heavenly Creatures*, in taking William Golding's founding narrative of childhood as a receptacle of a kind of primal evil, relocating this within specific social arenas and giving it a very nineties gender-spin. Each film, then, is a kind of 'Young Ladies of the Flies', answering to specific fears of the moment. In the case of *The Bait* the answers are unsatisfactory and tediously moralistic with the only panaceas being hinted at on two levels: a barely explored notion of community is suggested when Eric is confronted by Alain's assertion of their – victim and aggressor's – shared Jewishness. The film might appear to offer itself formally as an antidote to the 'irresponsible images' that are presented as symptom and cause of an irresponsible society. How? In its realism to a certain degree, and to the extent that it calls upon a particularly French vein of *intimiste* drama. That this is hardly a domestically popular cinematic form is acknowledged in the boys' addiction to De Palma's *Scarface* and their comments when out foraging in the local video store that a certain film is not worth the effort with the words – 'C'est Français, c'est nase' ('It's French, it's fucked').

Tavernier's exhausted political puritanism is also evident at the level of the film's treatment of Nathalie. Although Marie Gillain's performance is excellent – coltish and waveringly of-the-moment – one has the sense that Tavernier sees Nathalie not just as the bait for the crimes, but also as a kind of blank on which to project all manner of social misgivings, and thus the film serves her up as the butt of his own censorious middle-aged, mainstream guilt and fears. One understands why *L.627* worked, or at least maintained a level of consistency and integrity of tone: the director was alongside the police – physically and, one suspects, in spirit. As *Cahiers du cinéma* noted, in *The Bait* Tavernier films once again 'from the point of view of the law' and the judgement he delivers has all the insight of a *Daily Mail* – or should that be a *Figaro* – editorial.

LA SEPARATION
DIR: CHRISTIAN VINCENT FRANCE 1994
ORIGINALLY PUBLISHED IN *SIGHT AND SOUND* OCTOBER 1995

SYNOPSIS

Paris, the present. Anne and Pierre live together as an unmarried couple with their two-year-old child, Louis. At the cinema one evening, Pierre reaches to take Anne's hand and she rebuffs the gesture. Later the same night he asks her why and she responds dismissively. Pierre dwells on the moment and, some time later, after a party, Anne reveals that she is in love with another man. Pierre attempts to deal reasonably with the revelation, only alluding to the fact that Anne spends evenings out with her new lover. When the two of them and their close friends, Victor and Clare, travel to Normandy to look at a holiday home things come to a head in an argument. Pierre seeks solace in advice from Victor, who is hardly forthcoming, and when he and Clare announce that after years of being a couple who have lived in separate apartments they intend to marry, this precipitates Pierre to become publicly aggressive towards Anne. Later, Pierre further antagonises her by suggesting that they consider separation, an option that shocks her particularly in what it would mean for Louis.

Pierre takes Louis out one evening and arrives back late at the flat. Anne, having been worried, explodes, telling Pierre that she has consulted a lawyer, that she has right to custody of the child and that she is leaving. Devastated, Pierre traces her to her mother's house where he spies on Loulou playing in the garden. When the child senses his presence, Pierre flees. Time passes and when the couple meet again in a bar it seems a rapprochement might be possible. Anne recounts a sentimental anecdote from their past and follows up by reporting that her affair is over. Pierre, friendly but seemingly indifferent to her overtures, does nothing to bring them together again. We last see Pierre on a street corner trying to hail a cab and lost in an unfamiliar corner of the city.

REVIEW

Christian Vincent's *La Discrète*, a comedy of sexual manners akin to a modern-day version of *Les Liaisons Dangereuses*, was a considerable success in France when it was released in 1990, making celebrities of its young director and Fabrice Lucchini, the Rohmer regular who played the film's obsessive seducer. *La Discrète* never made it across the channel, whereas *La Séparation* has, thanks no doubt to the combination of Huppert and Auteuil. Dispensing with the previous feature's cruel comedy, in *La Séparation* Vincent opts for the intimiste mode that characterises so much of current young French auteur cinema.

La Séparation's study of the breakdown of a long term, unmarried relationship between two former *soixante-huitards* is in a resolutely minor key, concentrating on the exchange of telling glances and pregnant silences that degenerates into painful ultimatums. Anne's refusal to take Pierre's hand when out at the cinema – watching Rossellini's *Europe 51* – unleashes Pierre's doubt, Anne's admission of an affair and the slow mutual spoiling of their relationship. Vincent's approach allows for two nearly faultless performances from Auteuil and Huppert and the background against which their strife is depicted is wilfully etiolated. This is a defiantly interior drama largely played out in the couple's awkward room-to-room negotiation of their apartment. When the action does shift beyond these suitably claustrophobic confines one gets the sense of everything arriving as if filtered through Pierre's almost solipsistic preoccupation with his own pain and uncertainty. Played by Auteuil in a combination of prissy withdrawal and inkwell-eyed bleakness, Pierre's is the dominant perspective on the increasingly irresolvable rift. Anna comes across as infuriatingly selfish, and yet utterly convinced of the justice of her actions, no doubt because of the film's dedication to the hapless Pierre's point of view. Huppert has perfected a quality of stillness in her acting that allows her to appear both unknowable and utterly at one with herself. As Anne, she acts with the courage of her compulsions, while at the same time appearing to remain palely indifferent to their consequences.

The presence of Loulou, their young child, serves to focus the growing feelings of anger and despair but thankfully with a minimum of sentimentality, reduced by the use of a camcorder. A commonplace technique perhaps, but one that yields a telling moment towards the end of the film when Pierre, filming Loulou, wonders aloud about how, in the future, he is ever going to look happily on couples with children again. If Loulou occupies the film's foreground, in its background is a meditation on the emotional legacy of May 1968. While Pierre and Anne's latter-day radical chic is inevitably eroded by comfortable bourgeois stability, it is nevertheless clear that Pierre tries hard to overcome his feelings of jealousy and possessiveness in the name of a former ideology. But he is shown to be clutching at straws, particularly when Victor and Clare, long-time friends and fellow veterans of *les évenements*, announce that they intend to marry to please Victor's parents. Pierre's feelings start to get the better of him, he begins to force the situation, widening the rift, preferring that the awkwardness between he and Anne solidifies into outright hostility, that their emotional isolation from one another becomes physical separation. But we recognise that his is a gamble taken in the hope that Anne will back down and return to him on his terms, an emotional brinkmanship that serves only to decisively split them apart.

Although painstakingly crafted, there is a curiously bloodless quality about *La Séparation*. It is as though the film's emotional reticence is motivated not so much by a larger programme, as in Antonioni or Bresson, but through a kind of ascetic cinematic good manners. Vincent desperately avoids confronting the moments that reside at the story's melodramatic heart; passion and, in short, excess are absent. *La Séparation*, then, is a weepy *sotto voce* and strained because of it. While an anti-melodramatic treatment is understandable given the familiarity of the storyline, the film's reserve extends even to withholding the sense of a new beginning from Pierre, imprisoning him at the end of the film indecisively on a street corner. In attempting to demonstrate the emotional application of that May '68 slogan 'Freedom begins with a prohibition – do not interfere with someone else's freedom', Vincent refutes its passé idealism through the treatment of his characters, but however precious it may be, *La Séparation* is still undeniably poignant.

LA HAINE

DIR: MATHIEU KASSOWITZ FRANCE 1995
ORIGINALLY PUBLISHED IN *SIGHT AND SOUND* NOVEMBER 1995

SYNOPSIS

A public housing estate in Paris has been shaken by rioting for twenty-four hours because of injuries suffered by Abdel, a youth from the estate, while in police custody. Vinz, Hubert and Saïd, three local friends, have all been involved. Hubert, a would-be boxer, discovers his training area has been wrecked. Vinz tells the others that he has the pistol lost by a policeman during the rioting and that he intends to avenge Abdel's injuries if he dies. The boys go to Paris to visit a dealer, known as Astérix, who owes them money.

Vinz endangers the deal by provoking Astérix with his gun. Leaving hurriedly, Hubert and Saïd are grabbed by the police, while Vinz gets away. Hubert and Saïd get a brutal going-over at the police station. They are released and miss their train back to the suburbs, but meet Vinz again in the station. The trio walk around the city and unsuccessfully attempt to steal a car. They sleep in a shopping mall and wake to a news broadcast informing them that Abdel is dead. Hubert and Saïd restrain Vinz from threatening a traffic warden. Angry with Vinz, the other two leave him but they are attacked by FN skinheads. Vinz arrives and threatens the skinheads with the pistol and all but one flees. Vinz threatens to shoot the remaining skin but can't manage to pull the trigger. At the entrance to Hubert's block, Vinz hands Hubert the gun and asks him to get rid of it. A car draws up and a plain-clothes policeman gets out. Vinz and the cop tussle and the cop's gun goes off, shooting Vinz in the head. Hubert advances on the cop, and they face each other with guns drawn. Saïd looks on in horror as gunfire is heard.

REVIEW

It's the French phrase for the 'Fuck the Police' (*nique la police*) that reverberates throughout the *La Haine*, provocatively stating where the film stands in its account of the aftermath of a riot in a Parisian *cité* (suburban housing estate). Having represented France at Cannes this year, where Kassovitz took the Best Director prize, *La Haine* went on to do excellent business and garner unanimous praise from French critics. Released in early June, the film became a media event of such proportions that its director eventually went into hiding, with sensationalist press coverage and dubious political manoeuvrings by the extreme-right Front National combining to cast *La Haine* as a celluloid incendiary device. Not bad for a film with a medium-sized budget of FF15 million that, as its director describes it, 'has no stars in it, is about the housing estates and is shot in black and white'. Already being pushed as a Parisian *Boyz N the Hood*, *La Haine* is an angry adrenaline-fuelled film; its poster image of Vinz's thousand-yard stare neatly summing up its combination of in-your-face bravado with the resentful glare of one on the outside looking in.

In an interview with *Positif*, Kassovitz explained that his film was provoked by the death in custody of a young *banlieusard*: 'What I wanted to do was tell the story of a guy who gets up in the morning and by the evening has got himself killed.' So, *La Haine* unfolds over a troubled twenty-four hours, an uneasy morning-after calm having settled on the estate where Vinz, Saïd and Hubert live. As media-vultures and riot police infest the estate awaiting reactions to news of Abdel, it emerges that a police weapon, lost during the rioting, is in Vinz's hands. The gun becomes the film's dramatic motor. Kassovitz observes the growing tension from within the trio, and the film's depiction of the group's cluster-bomb dynamics is its strongest point, aided no doubt by the fact that both Vincent Cassell and Hubert Koundé acted in *Métisse*, Kassovitz's debut. Saïd, a fast-talking, Tachinni-wearing young beur and Hubert, an impassive, introspective African who channels his aggression through his boxing skills, are constantly restraining Vinz, the loose cannon who threatens to go off in all their faces. The film's rhythm is their rhythm, edgy and wired, its camera's restless mobility giving the sense that wherever the group comes to rest they'll be moved on or banged up.

Scorsese's *Mean Streets* and Spike Lee's *Do The Right Thing* clearly serve as Kassovitz's models, but *La Haine* is more than simply a capable reworking of its American models. Just as French rap artists like MC Solaar and Les Sages Poètes de la Rue understand rap to be a musical space where *verlan* (backslang) can collide with Verlaine to comment on the specifics of French street life, so Kassovitz pays a similar attention to the 'prose combat' (the title of one of Solaar's recordings) of his characters' speech. This element of the film, along with its pseudo-documentary sylisation, delivers an authentic sense of detail that more than fleshes out the recognisably generic frame. *La Haine* also avoids the potential pitfall of becoming an overextended promo for French rap stars by minimising the use of music – with the exception of a virtuoso helicopter shot over the estate as a local DJ blasts its towers with a mix of *nique la police* and Piaff's *Je ne regrette rien* – and concentrating instead on a dense stereo-mix of ambient sound.

The lengthy central section in which the trio travel into Paris is a speed-fuelled picaresque that becomes increasingly nightmarish. *Le monde est à vous* ('The world belongs to you', recalling *Scarface*) runs the slogan on a Parisian advertising hoarding which they later alter to read *est à nous* (to us), and when one of the trio tries the old routine of switching off the Tour Eiffel by clicking his fingers (as first seen in Eric Rochant's *Un Monde sans Pitié*) it remains stubbornly illuminated. The point being made – by a sideways swipe at the mythologised city of Rochant's film – is that Paris emphatically does not belong to them. This is Paris as a bleak assault course culminating in the trauma of Hubert and Saïd's harrowing police interrogation; effectively staged with the cop's inquisitorial thuggery played off against the boys' mixed emotions of braggadocio and vulnerability as an ashamed rookie cop looks on.

The French commentary on *La Haine* has tended to overlook one of the best of its pioneering predecessors, Mehdi Charef's *La Thé au harem d'Archimède* (1985), a film that dealt with generational divides within *beur* families in the *cités*. Charef's films also focused on a trio of young males but, unlike Kassovitz's, delineated their environment through their relationships with their families and women. In *La Haine* women are either mothers or sisters, except when the boys attempt to pick up a group of young female sophisticates at a Parisian art gallery but find themselves so out of their depth that they react violently and offensively. The only serious relationship that Vinz, Hubert and Saïd share, apart from with each other, seems to be with the police. This is a minor criticism of a film that brings such a searing portrait of urban despair to the screen, joking nihilistically right up to its final Mexican stand-off.

Kassovitz's take on his trio does attempt to be inclusive, at least within its masculine perspective – Saïd is an Arab, Vinz Jewish and Hubert black African – while avoiding vacuous Benetton-styled, one-world tokenism. Although *La Haine* ends bleakly, it doesn't set out to provide a liberal overview, opting instead to go with what Kassovitz feels he knows about best. It's a mark of his assurance and skill as a director that he manages to avoid over-indulging his sympathies for the trio.

LES RENDEZ-VOUS DE PARIS
DIR: ERIC ROHMER FRANCE 1995
ORIGINALLY PUBLISHED IN *SIGHT AND SOUND* FEBRUARY 1996

SYNOPSIS

Le Rendez-vous de Sept Heures (The Seven O'Clock Rendez-vous) – Paris, the present. Esther, a law student, and her boyfriend Horace arrange to meet later the same day. Esther bumps into Felix, who tells her that he often sees Horace meeting another woman in a café. Disturbed by this news, Esther arranges to meet her friend Hermione to prepare their law papers together. They end up discussing Horace's clandestine rendez-vous. The next day Esther goes to the market where she is chatted up by a charming young man. She eventually agrees to meet him at the Dame Tartine café at Beaubourg at 7 p.m.. After he has left, Esther realises she has lost her wallet. Returning home, a young woman called Aricie returns Esther's wallet. They discuss Esther's losing it; she suspects that the young man at the market stole it. It transpires that both have a rendez-vous at the Dame Tartine. On arriving, Aricie goes straight to a table where Horace is sitting. Esther says nothing to dispel Aricie's illusion that she and Horace have never met before and awaits her own rendez-vous. After waiting for some time at the same table as Horace and Aricie, Esther leaves. Horace follows her and attempts to persuade her that he intended to bring his meetings with Aricie to an end that evening. Esther dismisses him and departs. Moments later Esther's date arrives.

Les Bancs de Paris (The Benches of Paris) – A young philosophy professor meets with a young woman by the Seine. She is in a steady relationship but the professor desires that she leaves her boyfriend for him. Declaring that she is bored with her relationship she continues to meet the professor but always refuses to go back to his apartment with him. Their rendez-vous continues across various locations, but she is uncomfortable in some of the meeting places, as they have become associated in her mind with her long-term boyfriend. Eventually, the couple decide to pretend to be tourists in the city and to stay overnight at a hotel. He meets her as arranged at a railway station, and they go to the hotel. Insisting that she sees her boyfriend arriving at the hotel with another woman she refuses to enter. She instructs the professor that they cannot meet again.

Mère et Enfant, 1907 (Mother and Child, 1907) – A young painter at work in his studio is visited by a young Swedish woman. She is a tourist in Paris and has been sent to the painter by a Swedish former girlfriend of his. She is an interior decorator and it becomes clear from their initial conversation that they have very different ideas about art. He takes her to the nearby Musée Picasso but declines to accompany her, saying that his new canvas requires his full concentration. Walking back to his studio his attention is caught by a young woman whom he follows. She goes into the Musée Picasso where she sits before a canvas entitled *Mère et Enfant, 1907* and takes notes. The Swedish woman notices him and he walks around with her, steering her back to the room in which the other woman is seated. In earshot of the other woman the artist delivers an ostentatious commentary on the canvas. She gets up to leave. The artist hurriedly makes an excuse to the Swede, arranges to meet her that evening and follows the other woman. Approaching her on the street they talk. She tells him that she is newly married and that her husband publishes art books. When she learns that he is a painter she expresses an interest in seeing his work. She accompanies him to his studio where they talk and she resists his advances. After she has left, a friend calls inviting him to a party that evening. He accepts. He waits for the Swedish girl to show up for their rendez-vous but she fails to do so. Calling his friends he declines the party invitation, choosing to return to the studio to work.

REVIEW

There is one piece of survival equipment vital to living in Paris: *Paris par arrondissements*, the *A to Z* of the City of Lights. On the strength of Eric Rohmer's thirty years of filmmaking, there could easily be a companion volume entitled *Paris by Rohmerian Rendez-vous*. More than almost any other of the *nouvelle vague* directors. Rohmer's cinema has been frequently, almost defiantly, Paris-based. *Les Rendez-vous de Paris* recalls his very earliest treatments of the city in *Le Signe du Lion* (1959) and the short conte moral *La Boulangère de Monceau* (1962) and is quintessentially Rohmerian in its theme of amorous *flânerie*. Here, the rendez-vous – as a missed or accidental meeting – is both theme and structuring principle and is treated across three short films. Each independent of the other, the films are shot in 16mm with a deliberate anti-professionalism such that, at times, one can hear the sound of the camera's motor on the soundtrack. This apparently casual shooting strategy includes an emphasis on camera mobility that suits the path-crossings and wanderings of the characters perfectly. Additionally, the predominantly street-based shooting includes moments in which passers-by are caught idly glancing into the lens. So characteristic of the *nouvelle vague*, such unsolicited eye contact marks Rohmer's cinema as seeking a kind of continuum between documentary and fiction, between the contingent and the structured, as well as retaining something of the charm of its sources in early cinematic technique. Hence French film historian Jean-Pierre Jeancolas's naming of such moments as 'the Feuillade effect'.

When the *nouvelle vague* took French cinema out into the streets it did so with a confidence that came partly from its antagonism towards the classical French cinema's studio-based replications of certain *quartiers* but that derived equally from an understanding that they drew on the examples of Balzac and the Surrealists as well as on Impressionist painting. In the face-off with urban fact each found a way of sharpening their creative sensibilities. Rohmer uses this to his advantage in drawing his characters against the locales through which they move. In *Les Bancs de Paris* – an episode of nicely modulated cruelty – the reference to a former Surrealist hangout is not the dusty museological reflex of an antiquarian, it thickens the texture of sexual frustration that drives the philosophy professor to pursue and cajole the woman he desires. The influence of André Breton's *Nadja* – the classic Surrealist novel of the city as a labyrinth of eroticised détournement– is played off here against the frozen passion of the lovers in the Medicis fountain of the Jardin du Luxembourg. Desire and its fulfilment are kept achingly separate with the professor suspended in hopeful agony between them. Rohmer doesn't restrict himself to classical references and ancestral locations; he has often demonstrated a fascination with the way in which modern architectural urbanism is knitted into the city, witness *Les Nuits de la Pleine Lune* (1984). So, the excursion into Le Parc de la Villette in *Les Bancs de*

Paris uses the sterile postmodernist architecture to comment on the wavering and indirectness of the emotions at hand.

Rohmer gets spirited, natural performances from his cast, all of whom are under thirty years old. Clara Bellar in *Le Rendezvous de Sept Heures* is particularly effective as the confused Esther, as is Aurora Rauscher as the manipulative young woman in *Les Bancs de Paris.* There is an overall impression of effortlessness here; the frequent accusation that Rohmer's films are slight confections is understandable but inaccurate. *Les Rendezvous de Paris* is as seemingly casual and elegant an entertainment as any Rohmer has made. But within and behind this the spectator is being as subtly manipulated as the characters. It is through the lies they tell one another and the information that we presume to be true – that, on examination, need not be so – that the unflustered naturalism of the image is complicated, given a density that as much resides in the unforced relationship between dialogue and plot as between what is said and what we see.

NELLY ET M. ARNAUD
DIR: CLAUDE SAUTET FRANCE 1995
ORIGINALLY PUBLISHED IN *SIGHT AND SOUND* APRIL 1996

SYNOPSIS

Paris, the present. Nelly is a 25-year-old married woman whose husband, Jerôme, is unemployed and is making little effort to find work. Nelly does part-time jobs to make ends meet but is plagued by money worries. One afternoon she meets her mother for lunch to discuss her situation. They are joined by an impeccably dressed, charming elderly gentleman who Nelly's mother introduces as Monsieur Arnaud, an old friend. Arnaud, interested by Nelly's predicament, offers to help her with a gift of money. Nelly declines.

Soon after, Nelly loses her part-time job and arranges to meet Arnaud again. Having been a businessman, Arnaud is writing a book on his previous experiences as a judge in the former French colonies. He proposes that she works for him as a secretary. She accepts. Increasingly frustrated by Jerôme's inactivity and bored by their marriage, Nelly calmly tells him that she wants a divorce and that she intends to move out of their apartment. She moves into the spare room in a friend's flat while searching for a new apartment. Arnaud is extremely solicitous towards her, offering her help and more money as well as taking her out to dinner at an expensive restaurant where the others diners look askance at this unlikely couple.

Arnaud asks Nelly to deliver part of the manuscript to his publisher, where she meets Vincent, a young editor, who is immediately attracted to her. Vincent pursues Nelly, inviting her to dinner and making clear his feelings toward her. Nelly, equally attracted, is hesitant and initially refuses his advances. Arnaud learns of Nelly's meetings with Vincent and angrily demands to know if they have slept together. Outraged, Nelly lies that she has in order to provoke him further. They argue. That night Nelly and Vincent sleep together. Arnaud goes away on business and leaves Nelly the keys to his apartment. Continuing work on the manuscript, she receives a visit from the mysterious Monsieur Dollabella who reveals details of Arnaud's previous life as a ruthless businessman. Arnaud returns and Nelly moves into a new apartment. One evening they work late and Arnaud suggests that she stays in the guest room. During the night, Arnaud enters the room and watches her sleeping. Nelly hears that Jerôme is in hospital after a suspected suicide attempt. Visiting, she learns that he has not attempted suicide, that he is back at work and has a new partner. Soon afterwards Vincent ends their relationship. The work on the manuscript is nearly completed when Arnaud's former wife arrives unexpectedly to tell him that her husband has died. They leave together for Switzerland to deal with family matters. When they return, Arnaud reveals that they are going away together on a long excursion and tells Nelly that she can stay in the flat. At the airport, Arnaud reaches into his pocket for his passport, hesitates for a moment, then extracts it.

REVIEW

An elderly, sombre-looking gentleman sits beside a bed in which a beautiful young woman is asleep. Hesitantly extending his hand he strokes her naked back, fingers hovering inches above her flesh. This is the central image of *Nelly et M. Arnaud*, itself the exploration of an image that Claude Sautet claims to have been fascinated by for years, that of an old man and a young woman sitting together on a café terrace. The emotional and erotic life of the French bourgeoisie has been Sautet's stock-in-trade subject matter since Les Choses de la Vie (1970) and with Un Coeur en hiver (1991) he injected new life into his examination of the terrain. The casting of Emmanuelle Béart in that film, as well as in Nelly, recalls Sautet's working relationship with his actrice-fétiche of the 1970s, Romy Schneider, with whom he made five films between 1970 and 1978. The British success of Un Couer en hiver might be put down, not altogether cynically, to the film's knowing combination of high culture and emotional cruelty. But there was the sense of something at stake for its characters – emotionally, creatively and professionally – the feeling that passion must out in ways other than bloodless manipulation.

If Un Coeur had the music of Ravel as its (s)core, Nelly comes across as being both far more desiccated and yet, strangely, down to earth. The closed, specialised world of professional musicians is here swapped for a less specific haut-bourgeois milieu, its trappings of refinement less clearly signalled than in the former film. Béart's professional duties here exchanges mastery of the violin for a touch-type command of the word-processor into which she transcribes Arnaud's memoirs. Serrault's performance of Arnaud, the former colonial judge-turned-businessman, gives us an old fox who has steadily divested himself of most of his ties with the world. Divorced, uneasy with his offspring, installed in an apartment slowly being stripped of its extensive library of rare books, Arnaud appears as a man who wants only the beautifully cut clothes he stands up in to remain. Sautet's commitment to observing the surface of this well-healed world cumulatively delivers the ambiguous pulsations that reside below it. If he is the official cinematic chronicler of the French bourgeoisie it is because he films characters for whom hiding their feelings is both a social prerequisite, a sign of breeding, as well as being the only skill that remains to them towards the end of their seemingly arid lives. Nelly, then, is something of an interloper in this world. Herself separated from an unemployed husband, and casting about for work, she accepts Arnaud's offer of employment well aware of the inequality of the relationship she has become involved in, yet becomes increasingly fascinated by and dependent on Arnaud's companionship.

If the film poses one question above all it is: what do we call such a relationship? Béart is both the conventional feminine muse, as she was in Un Coeur and Rivette's La Belle Noiseuse, and a kind of daughter-confessor for Arnaud. It becomes increasingly clear to both of them that the public performances of their relationship – as employer and employee, as vieux protecteur and young charge – do not begin to describe its complexities. Feelings overwhelm their lucidity and they fall into the protection such roles offer. When Arnaud dines Nelly in a conspicuously refined restaurant the game reaches a particular pitch of simultaneous self-deception and public display; Nelly, as the old man's beautiful trophy, turns censorious heads but keeps her composure. Their relationship is paralleled by the visits to the apartment of the mysterious Dollabella, played by a wonderfully lugubrious Michael Lonsdale, who haunts the flat like an apologetic inquisitor. Dollabella, it is gradually revealed, is trying uselessly to blackmail Arnaud over underhand business dealings in his past. The relationship between the two men is like a strange kind of vassalage and Arnaud's motives for tolerating Dollabella are opaque and ambiguous; guilt over his former unscrupulousness or an old man paying for a memory of days when his pulse raced? Likewise, his relationship with Nelly comes across as a similar kind of contract, a paid-for reminder of vitality. If this is so, then the extent of the feelings that the young woman stirs in him become more than he bargains for. The film bears this thesis out when Arnaud's wife visits him unexpectedly and the two leave for a long holiday together. Nelly, now abandoned, has revitalised the old man who retreats back into the security of a relationship he thought of as dead.

French *intimiste* film alternates between two modes; the withdrawn dissection and observation of predominantly bourgeois characters – Christian Vincent's *La Séparation* (1995) is a recent example – and the uncomfortably penetrating psychodrama – Noémie Lvovsky's extraordinarily intense and harrowing *Oublie-moi* (1995), for one. While the work of a younger generation of French filmmakers appeals to intimiste avatars such as Maurice Pialat and André Téchiné, as well as to the considerable influence of John Cassavetes, all of whom include a dimension of social critique in their portraits, Sautet cannot be ruled out as being a father, if not a grandfather, of this tendency. *Nelly et M. Arnaud* is very much of this school, filmed with a restraint that, at times, reaches a degree of asceticism that, while it focuses rewardingly on the outstanding performances of Serrault and Béart, delivers a far starker, more compelling anatomisation of the emotions than that offered by *Un Coeur en hiver*.

N'OUBLIE PAS QUE TU VAS MOURIR/DON'T FORGET YOU'RE GOING TO DIE

DIR: XAVIER BEAUVOIS FRANCE 1995
OCTOBER 1996

François Truffaut described Jean Vigo's *L'Atalante* as a 'a film whose feet smell'. This tradition of 'smelly', uncompromising French filmmaking is celebrated annually in the Prix Jean Vigo, which was awarded last year to Xavier Beauvois' *N'oublie pas que tu vas mourir*. A film of ill-mannered singularity, very much in the recalcitrant spirit of Vigo, *N'oublie pas...* is a provocative Grand Tour through present-day *mals de siècles* that might have been titled 'To Live and Die in Europe 95'. The film's English title, *Don't Forget You're Going to Die*, stays true to the original French in its jarring combination of conversational informality and fatalistic imperative (the French pointedly uses the familiar, second-person singular *tu* address). At once intimate and apocalyptic, it's a phrase from bar-room banter between friends, with the Grim Reaper serving the drinks.

Beauvois' first film, made when he was twenty-five, was *Nord* (1991), the portrait of a family in crisis under the grey skies of Calais. In interviews, Beauvois made no secret of the fact that the film's alcoholic father suppurating in self-hate, the suffering, too-loving mother, the crippled daughter and the slow-burning would-be parricide of a son, were more than a little autobiographically derived. An impressively austere debut, *Nord* was rapturously received for its cool Pialat-style naturalism, winning prizes at numerous festivals and being nominated for the 1992 Cesar for Best First Film. While *Nord* placed its Oedipal drama against a background of provincial domesticity, its intensity made all the more excruciating for being so rooted, in *N'oublie pas...* the canvas is broader, the scope more ambitious , the subjects – HIV, drugs, Bosnia – more self-consciously controversial. And, as in *Nord*, Beauvois writes, directs and takes the lead role.

N'oublie pas... tells the story of Benoît, a twenty-something Parisian art-history student who, on receiving his call-up for national service, tries to get himself exempted. Taking sedatives to give the impression of mental instability doesn't fool the military. Desperate, Benoît slashes his arm. A blood test reveals he is HIV positive. From hereon in, Benoît embarks on a deliberate itinerary of self-immolation. Meeting Omar, a young *beur*, brilliantly played by Roschdy Zem, he is initiated into the world of drugs and casual sex. They travel together to Amsterdam where they visit a sex club and Benoît smuggles cocaine back to Paris. With the money from drug trafficking Benoît travels to Italy, where he meets and falls in love with Claudia (Chiarra Mastroianni). A brief, peaceful interlude in sun-drenched Tuscany follows but Benoît realises that their relationship is impossible. He takes a train loaded with UN personnel and arrives in Split where he joins up with Croatian partisans. On his first sortie with the troops he throws himself into enemy fire and dies in a hail of bullets.

The idea for *N'oublie pas...* emerged from experiences that Beauvois outlined in a *Cahiers du cinéma* interview: 'After *Nord* I became very interested in the Romantics. Looking at Victor Hugo's drawings, reading Baudelaire and Rimbaud, you realise how dark Romanticism was... This interest in Romanticism became mixed up with watching TV news reports of wars, our own and those of others. And obviously with AIDS, which has affected me closely and claimed the lives of friends, like the film director Michel Bena and the critic Serge Daney, without who I'd never have become a director. So I asked myself how would someone like me, someone even more banal than me, react in these circumstances? Someone who hasn't lived a great deal who sees their future cancelled out by the illness...'

Fed on TV's diet of fresh foreign carnage delivered daily, provoked by the addition of friends' names to the roster of AIDS deaths and filtered through a head full of Rimbaud, Beauvois conceived Benoît in order to submit him to the thesis that 'the age of Byron is topical again'. Beauvois' style of filmmaking remains rooted in realist observation, however, a style that brings his cultural hypothesis down to earth. Sex and drugs are treated here with an insistence that is both unapologetic and absolutely necessary to prevent the film from spiralling off completely into angst-happy Romantic bucaneering. The sex includes seedy pick-ups and hard-core red-light encounters. The drugs are debilitating and glorious. The film's pace and rhythm is the most achieved element of its form; a controlled, somewhat distanced naturalism that shifts the tone subtly from the initially comic, through long-take observational filming such as in the remarkable scene of Benoît's initiation into crack, to a bleak finale.

This is 'hot' material 'coolly' framed. But Beauvois' formal care didn't prevent the film from getting a hostile reception at Cannes in 1995 where it was among the films representing France. Talking to Beauvois it is clear that he's still smarting from the critical antagonism the film provoked in some quarters; *Première*, for example, dismissed it with a shudder as 'an incoherent and mucky photocopy of *Les nuits fauves*'. When I asked Beauvois about how he sees Benoît's Romanticism, which is treated with a distance that makes Benoît's behaviour appear both comically incongruous and pathetically defiant, he was straightforward about what he took to be the problem that some reviewers had with the film. 'I think Benoît behaves in a way that one might call 'Romantic',' Beauvois explains. 'Certain passages of the film really correspond to that idea of Romanticism; the discovery of pleasure, drugs, homosexuality and things about which he knows nothing. The Romantics were people who were ill in relation to society – this is what *spleen* meant for Baudelaire - to burn up one's life without being condemned to death. Byron going to fight with the Greeks against the Turks, for example. It was a game, to play with life without being condemned to death. Byron was unlucky, he died. But for it to be possible to risk your life means that you have a life to possess. When I was in Bosnia I risked my life, like an idiot, but it was a real risk. When you're condemned to death you no longer risk your life, it doesn't belong to you any longer. So Benoît's behaviour no longer works in the old way, it's obsolete. Rimbaud and Baudelaire weren't condemned to death. It's difficult to talk about such things with some of the French press, there's an incredible lack of culture. *Première*, for example, only go to the cinema where they only see American films. But try talking about Byron with them and they don't know who he is. The same with Delacroix. They're not open and art requires being interested in the other arts and being inspired by them. I like football, Formula One, fishing, bullshit like that. I'm not always in the cinema. But these journalists, because of their lack of interest, don't have any cultural references. So they're not critics, they're just journalists. If I make a shot that holds a reference to the history of art or literature, they don't get it. But a guy like Serge Daney could have written twenty-five pages about it. The same goes for Jean Douchet, you could talk with him about anything, these guys have a great breadth of cultural references. If the spectators don't get the references, that's understandable. If you work for a living you don't always have the time for culture. I make a film from time to time so there's the chance to go to exhibitions, to read, to travel. We're privileged. If you're a doctor, you don't necessarily have the time to study the history of art. The role of the critic is therefore to explain the relevance of certain references. But it's the reverse now, it's me who explains to critics.'

Beauvois' reverence towards critics Serge Daney and Jean Douchet, the latter having played in both his films, is part of his sense of belonging to a certain tradition of French filmmaking. Daney described himself as *un cinéfils*, 'a son of cinema', and Beauvois, like many other directors of the new young French auteur cinema, sees himself as one of the sons and daughters of the New Wave. Like his predecessors, he knows who his fathers are, those illustrious intransigents Rossellini and Godard; Jacques Doillon and Philippe Garrel being exemplary older brothers. Equally, there is the characteristic sense that this cinema draws from and exists alongside the other arts, and that French auteur cinema is the immediate cultural heir to the great tradition of French painting. It is this sense of belonging to a tradition, one that is both critically central and commercially marginal to French film culture, that in part informs Beauvois' insertion of Romantic painting and literature into *N'oublie pas*....

Art, in the film, is both a bulwark against and an incitement to nihilism. It represents beauty as the unbearable. This is 'the sublime' in the proper sense, the recognition in beauty of something that appals, that sends you away with your head spinning, gives you back to yourself with an overwhelming sense of simultaneous limits and possibilities. For Benoît, however, the possibilities are nil. This feeling runs throughout the Italian interlude where Benoît falls in love with Claudia. He's a dead man on leave, traipsing through the sunlit landscapes of Italian Classicism with his heart in his mouth at all that useless beauty. Every image that confronts him, from Pierro de la Fransesca's *Madonna del Parto* in Monterchi, to an exhibition of skull drawings, to Claudia's body poignantly beautiful in sleep, is another step towards the inevitability of his death.

Bosnia comes as an afterthought, the necessary terminal station on his journey. Its treatment is one of the most provocative moments in the film, possibly gratuitous and certainly eliciting the most misgivings. We are accustomed to TV images of the war in Bosnia, but Beauvois' cinematic treatment of the Balkan killing grounds is deliberately extreme, almost an admission of incomprehension in the face of this, the defining European disaster (before the next) of the end of the twentieth century. Up to this point, the cinematic style has been naturalistic. During the Paris and Amsterdam sequences the camera is often static, the reframing unobtrusive. In Italy, the camera becomes more fluid and mobile, tracking with the lovers, and Caroline Charpentier's cinematography takes full advantage of the Tuscan light. In Bosnia, as Benoît throws himself suicidally into the gunfire, the image melts into slow-motion and the soundtrack becomes a booming aural assault of treated explosions. For a moment, the film seems to treat Benoît's death in the vernacular of the war film, as a self-aggrandising martyrdom. But martyrdom in the name of what?

AIDS is not mentioned by name. The omission might be taken as a failure of nerve but could equally be seen as crediting the audience with a modicum of intelligence, indicating that this is not an 'AIDS film' à la *Philadelphia* or *Les nuits fauves*. Rather, it is a film about death and, in a way that strikes me as ambitious but might just as easily strike others as pretentious, a film about millennial fears. 'Europe 95', reads the first title in the film: ninety-five and counting. *N'oublie pas...* pushes its death fixation so insistently that it's virtually a memento mori, a celluloid *vanitas* project. As Benoît stresses during a presentation he gives to his fellow art history students on Delacroix's painting *The Death of Sardanapalus*: 'All aesthetic and philosophical systems take death into account. But Romanticism isn't sensible, it isn't prudent. It doesn't wait for death. It anticipates it. It speeds it up or slows it down. Romanticism eroticises death.' During Benoît's presentation the camera tracks slowly back through the auditorium, revealing the breach that Benoît is opening up between himself and the world. He fills it with his last words, a testament that explains his self-destruction as much to himself as to the other students. It makes a kind of sense that the film should be equally obsessed with transcendence. After all, what was the Romantic passion other than the quest for escape from the self, for the creative disordering of the senses through communion with nature, of self-annihilation through drugs, drink and sexual excess? Benoît systematically explores both extremes, the sordid and the sublime, the downward drag and kicks of low-life, the ethereal urge and heavenwards pull of high art. The significance of Beauvois' film is that it explicitly recognises and provocatively explores the residual Romanticism that has remained implicit in the rampant *nostalgie de la boue* of films such as *Trainspotting*, *Kids* and *Leaving Las Vegas*. Whether the cultural reflex underlying these other post-Romantic paeans to nihilism needs to be made explicit is another question. But it's precisely Beauvois' desire simultaneously to show (in Benoît's petit bourgeois slumming) and tell (of what the cultural arbiters are for his behaviour) that makes his film so fascinatingly risky an experiment – to take the thesis and see if it stands up to its cinematic elaboration.

As a film about death it is ideally suited to a moment when every fear is a millennial fear, every catastrophe a premonition of worse to come. But it is also a film that responds to the present-day culture of death in which the nihilist is simply the man who has faced all the facts and to whom remains only a gallows melody with which to dance on the volcano. And the song goes 'Don't forget you're going to die'. Altogether now...

CHACUN CHERCHE SON CHAT

DIR: CÉDRIC KLAPISCH FRANCE 1996
ORIGINALLY PUBLISHED IN *SIGHT AND SOUND* NOVEMBER 1996

SYNOPSIS

Paris, the present. Chloé is a young make-up artist sharing a flat in the eleventh *arrondisement* with her gay friend Michel. Intending to take a holiday, Chloé searches for a local cat-minder for her cat Gris-Gris and is put in touch with Madame Renée. On the street, Chloé exchanges looks with a hip young man.

Returning from holiday Chloé is told by Mme Renée that Gris-Gris is missing. Chloé's concierge introduces her to the local handyman, Djamel, who will help her look for her cat. Mme Renée recruits a network of friends to help. Chloé meets a neighbour, a painter nicknamed Bel Canto. Djamel, Michel and Chloé go out postering in the neighbourhood in the search for Gris-Gris. One night, Chloé is woken by the sound of Michel having sex with his new boyfriend. Unable to sleep, she watches Bel Canto painting as she prepares to go out. Chloé searches for a friend in a bar. Unable to find her she returns home.

At work, her colleagues tell her that she's letting herself go and that evening, planning to go out for the night, she tries out various outfits. She settles on a short summer dress and a leather jacket. She sees Djamel searching the alleyways for Gris-Gris. In a bar, Chloé notices the hip-looking guy again. He offers her a light but they are interrupted by a drunken barfly who chats her up. Chloé angrily flees to the toilets where the barfly's girlfriend, who turns out to be a colleague from work, angrily berates her. The woman bursts into tears and Chloé leaves. On the way out of the bar, Chloé is harassed by a group of men and Blanche, the barwoman, offers to accompany her home. At Chloé's door Blanche tries to kiss her and Chloé refuses her advance.

That night, out of loneliness, Chloé sleeps in the same bed as Michel. She has a nightmare. The next morning she discovers a stranger in the flat, who turns out to be Michel's new boyfriend, Claude. Chloé gets a telephone call from a friend of Mme Renée's friends who tells her that a cat's body has been found on some derelict ground. They meet, but the body is not Gris-Gris. Arriving back at her apartment she sees Djamel climbing onto the roof in pursuit of a cat. The cat is not Gris-Gris and Djamel almost falls off the roof. Chloé meets the hip guy again and they go to his apartment where they have sex. As it becomes clear to Chloé that she is more interested in him than he is in her, she leaves. Djamel finds Chloe and tells her that Mme Renée is ill. They visit her and discover Gris-Gris trapped behind the cooker.

Bel Canto is moving out to the suburbs and Chloé helps him. In the local café Bel Canto says goodbye to his friends. He and Chloé bid each other a lingering, affectionate goodbye and promise to meet soon. Chloé watches Bel Canto's van pull away and runs home ecstatically.

REVIEW

Chacun cherche son chat is the epitome of present-day Parisian cinema. Marketed in France as a youth comedy, it has the slimmest of plots – a lonely young woman searching for her feline companion finds love – on which is hung a bittersweet story of urban isolation and companionship. Sitting somewhere between the sophisticated perambulations of a Rohmer film, the feelgood neighbourliness of *Smoke* and the virtuoso stylistics of *Chungking Express*, Chat succeeds in making its hair-thin storyline come to life through a documentary-like attention to the life of a particular Parisian *quartier*.

The area in question is the eleventh *arrondisement*, known as Popincourt, situated to the east of Paris and bound by Place de la Nation, Place de la Bastille and Place de la République. During the late 1980s, and since the development of the Bastille Opera House, the area has undergone a process of gradual gentrification, *un quartier populaire* becoming *un quartier branché*, a working-class area turned fashionable. It is in the observation of this transformation of the urban fabric that Klapisch roots his film, a central motif of which is the demolition of the beautiful old church, Notre Dame d'Espérance. Gentrification is seen as an ambiguous but unstoppable process. The film returns repeatedly to rubbish-strewn wastelands awaiting development, and compares the merits of the local cafés – the ultra-hip Pause Café is unfavourably compared to the local café de quartier by Mme Renée, who can't understand why people should choose to go to a place where a coffee is four times more expensive than at her local. Mme Renée is herself treated as something of a representative icon of the old area; authentic, aged and soon to be replaced by new money and fashionable young things. Likewise, Bel Canto's decision to move out. It's often the case that gentrification can be foretold by the popularity of an area with artists – a case of studios first, speculators follow – and the eleventh *arrondisement* had a reputation with artists before rents increased and many were forced to move out.

The rootedness of *Chat* in a particular neighbourhood has led to its being identified by *Cahiers du cinéma* as part of a tendency of the young French cinema to combine the street-level shooting style of the *nouvelle vague* with a concern for the lightly-handled, social-observation comedy that characterised the French cinema of the 1930s and early 1940s. In this respect, *Chat* is close to Pierre Salvadori's *Les Apprentis*; these characters are of a certain time and place. Benoit Delhomme's cinematography works well to convey both the frequently cramped apartments within which the older generation lives and the fugitive encounters and glancing exchanges with strangers of Parisian street life. In fact, Chloé's encounter with the hip young guy she keeps noticing on the street – a cooler-than-thou fashion victim whose vocabulary barely extends beyond 'ouaiis, mortel' ('yeeah, wicked') – is one of the hoops of contingent encounters that she has to leap through on the way to the promise of a relationship with Bel Canto. There is much here that is observationally acute about the way people live together in the city. The casual cruelty, for example, extended to Djamel, the good-hearted *beur* , when Chloé sees him searching for Gris-Gris in the alleyways of a trendy street. The comedy pitches itself quietly, juxtaposing unlikely types, and through careful pacing and some neat editing. Chloe's holiday is given as an interlude, a sunny beat between entering and leaving the same Metro stop, she barely has time to breath between strokes in the sea before she's back on the Paris streets, her holiday over in a flash. The only misjudgement is her bad dream, which provides unnecessary access to her interior life, and about which the most nightmarish thing is its resemblance to a particularly tacky perfume ad.

Alternating between wide-eyed self-possession and city-stressed vulnerability,

Chloé is a perfect contemporary *gamine* heroine. Oscillating between the shallow-ness of the fashion world and the authenticity of her local neighbourhood, Chloé's character is slowly revealed as melancholic, capable of much love and a little horri-fied when, an old maid before her time, she is drawn into the network of older, lonely women gathered around Mme Renée. Like the films of the *nouvelle vague*, *Chat* has that ambition characteristic of much 'Young French Cinema' in its desire to create cinematically compelling protagonists derived from contemporary Paris-ian life. Chloé is both anonymous and singular – she's as generically une parisienne as Renault's Nicole, but her experiences are so recognisably urban as to translate to London, New York and Hong Kong. Despite the slightness of the story, there is the cumulative sense of people's loneliness being held at bay by street-level encoun-ters and café congregations. The euphoric final image of Chloé running through the street, propelled by the promise of love in bloom, arrives with an unexpected force that indicates that, for all its appearance of off-the-cuff improvisation, this is a carefully structured, charming film that makes the city feel like home.

IRMA VEP
DIR: OLIVIER ASSAYAS FRANCE 1996
ORIGINALLY PUBLISHED IN *SIGHT AND SOUND* IN FEBRUARY 1997

SYNOPSIS

Paris. Actress Maggie Cheung arrives three days late at the chaotic production offices of a film in which she is to star. She goes to meet the director René Vidal who wants to cast her as Irma Vep in a TV remake of the French silent serial film *Les Vampires*. Maggie tries on her black latex costume and meets Zoé the costumer.

During the first days shooting, Zoé and the production assistant Maïté argue. After the dailies, René walks out in disgust. Zoé takes Maggie for a meal at a friend's apartment. Zoé confides in her older friend Mireille that she finds Maggie very attractive and believes that the attraction is mutual. To Zoé's chagrin, Mireille tells Maggie. Maggie is amused and a little shocked. Back at her hotel Maggie discovers René has been calling her. She goes to René's apartment where the police are in attendance. René has attacked his wife and is under sedation. He tells Maggie that he despairs of the project and then passes out. Maggie returns to her hotel and prowls the corridors in her Irma Vep costume. She creeps into another woman's room and steals a piece of jewellery. Escaping onto the hotel roof Maggie drops the jewel over the edge.

Maggie is late on-set the next morning and Maïté blames Zoé. Maggie is interviewed by a French journalist who dismisses Vidal as an elitist director. Laure, another actress, tells Zoé that Maïté told her that Zoé slept with Maggie the night before. Zoé is furious. Laure adds that she has received calls from another director, José Murano. René does not appear and the day's shooting is cancelled. On the way back to the hotel Maïté tells Maggie that Zoé is pushing drugs on-set, which Maggie refuses to believe. Laure meets José Murano. He tells her that René has had a breakdown and that he has been approached to step in. Murano wants to replace Maggie with a French actress and offers Laure the role of Irma. Later that night Maggie and Zoé drive to an night-club and Maggie recounts her afternoon meeting with René. Maggie declines Zoé's invitation and leaves in the taxi. Maggie leaves for the US the next day. Murano watches the footage that René has shot and edited.

REVIEW

Shot in four weeks on a minuscule budget and written by director Olivier Assayas especially for the Hong Kong action starlet Maggie Cheung, *Irma Vep* explodes like a firework over its thematic terrain of mourning for cinema's past. Cheung plays herself as cast by René Vidal, a burnt-out, middle-aged French auteur, to play Irma Vep, the black-clad Parisian criminal from the French silent serials *Les Vampires* directed by Louis Feuillade between 1915 and 1916. Vidal's *idée fixe* is of Musidora (the original Irma Vep) as the icon of cinematic grace and of Feuillade as cinema's brilliant primitive. But his attempt to revive such cinematic 'purity' is little more than a futile seance, and he knows it. Assayas, at times, seems to concur with Vidal's obsessions and seeds his film with telling glimpses of cinematic moments that indicate that such 'innocence' has been and is still yet possible. A video-screening of the 1968 militant film *Classe de lutte* stands in as 'politicised purity' and Vidal's own terminal film-poem that closes the film is its 'poetic' equivalent.

It would be easy to see *Irma Vep* simply as a satire of French auteur filmmaking. After all, the stock characters are present and correct – an unhinged, autocratic director, bitching crew-members, conniving, narcissistic actors, and a Schwarzenegger-lauding journalist. However, this would be to short-change a film that skilfully interweaves character relations and thematic concerns, wrapping them in an exhilarating improvisational style. Eric Gautier's fluid hand-held camerawork and crepuscular lighting – the film was shot on Super 16 then blown up to 35mm – as well as Luc Barnier's supple editing makes the film fairly dance across the screen in a kinetic flurry. The film's on-set atmosphere is acrid with petty rivalries and myopic arrogance and Maggie Cheung emerges from it as grace incarnate. She plays herself with an innocent guile, deliberately demystifying her star persona. 'It's all done by stunt men,' she says when René describes her Hong Kong action routines as being 'like an acrobat'. Yet she displays a touching faith in her washed-up auteur, played by Jean-Pierre Léaud as a truculent loon and melancholic visionary who eventually gives up on the project. René's (and Assayas's) intuition was right; in her black latex catsuit Cheung makes a splendidly slinky Irma.

If Assayas succeeds where René fails he does so because he invents René as a surrogate to shoulder the weight of film history for him. This is the film's central and winningly paradoxical strategy. René is creatively exhausted by his fidelity to the past whereas Assayas displays utter stylistic vitality. His film doesn't work out its mourning with the romantic nostalgia of Godardian wakes like *Le Mépris* and *Passion*, it is more like a Mexican Day of the Dead, remembrance as an act of celebration. The theme of cinematic history as a dead weight is crystallised by the film's ending. When the replacement director, José Murano, watches René's edited footage he is confronted with a viciously experimental squall of film. Shots of Maggie-as-Irma are bleached and out-of-focus, scratched and defaced; the obsessive attention paid to every frame speaks volumes about René's state of mind. He's like a child who colours in every letter of a favourite book before trashing it in a fit of pique. He cannot possess Maggie – Irma is inviolably distant anyway – so he vengefully imposes himself like a spurned lover on his flimsy celluloid material.

Assayas isn't just using Lettriste tropes of experimental cinema for expressionistic atmosphere here – compared to the opening credits of *Se7en* – there's a thematic coherence to René's black and white film-poem. A torrent of scratches, scored onto the film, pours from Maggie's eyes. Her gaze becomes like a fusillade that echoes from Feuillade's day down across a century of cinema. On one hand, the sequence expresses the impossibility of rejuvenating silent cinema's 'innocence' – a theme alluded to when René damns the idea of the TV-remake of *Irma Vep* as 'blasphemy' and when Zoé demands 'why must we do what's already been done?' On the other hand (the remake is entitled *Les Yeux qui fascinent* (The Eyes that Fascinate)), it is about the mystery of cinema's attraction. Maggie sums this up neatly: 'Desire. It's what we make films with'. But it's also what we watch films with. This circuit of desire unites those who cast lifelike shadows on a wall with the audience that re-animates them in their heads.

It is this circuit of desire that is played out and projected on and off the film set. Zoé, the bisexual costumer – sympathetically played by Nathalie Richard – develops a crush on Maggie around which is developed the intrigues and desires of others. Maïté, the production assistant, attempts to poison Maggie's attitude to Zoé; Mireille vicariously exploits Zoé's attraction to Maggie and René himself harbours barely suppressed desires for his lead. When Maggie prowls the hotel corridors in her Irma Vep outfit and steals an item of jewellery from another room, she is not only losing herself in the character she'll never perform, she is also enacting the play of desire that the whole film so effortlessly works through.

Formerly a critic on *Cahiers du cinéma*, Assayas made five films before *Irma Vep*. His previous film, *L'eau froide* (1994) was a particularly impressive example of that style of *intimiste* portraiture in which the 'Young French Cinema' excels. But *Irma Vep* is both a departure and an experiment that has paid dividends. Assayas seems to have found a freedom in his filmmaking that makes his future work a fascinating prospect. Having made a film that feels like a divertissement but that acquires richness on reflection, that has style, wit and depth in equal measure, he must now be seen as one of the most exciting European filmmakers currently at work.

INTERVIEW WITH OLIVIER ASSAYAS
FEBRUARY 1997

CD: What was the inspiration for *Irma Vep?*

OA: The film is a kind of meeting-place for different ideas but I think the point of departure for me was the meeting with Maggie [Cheung]. We met at the Venice Festival in 1994 where she had come to present *Ashes of Time* by Wong Kar-Wai and I was on the jury – we really met only very briefly. I thought that she had something very different from other actresses that I knew; she had, let's say, a type of grace, beauty, a radiance that I associate with performers from that cinema which I adore, that is to say silent cinema. I thought that she had something that one doesn't find in the French actresses that I've worked with, who have something else – a kind of realistic, everyday quality. At the same time, there was something of this initial inspiration that remained with me. if I had met an actress different from other actresses with whom I'd worked, could this in turn inspire other stories and another way of making films? I found this idea exciting and it was from this that the film was born.

CD: Your film is about the making of a film but at the same time it's about cinema, and the history of cinema.

OA: You know, I've written a lot about cinema – I think that my life has been divided in three, my first inspiration was really painting, from a very early age I was painting and drawing and then, at a certain moment, it was something that I gave up completely in order to concentrate on cinema. At the same time there was this parallel strand, which was writing – screenplays for other directors and writing about cinema, theoretical reflection about cinema. There was a time when this was very important for me. It was like my school; my training as a filmmaker came from having the opportunity to think and write about cinema. But I've always had this idea that the theory was a necessary part to the practice of an art – afterwards one might do things in a completely intuitive and spontaneous way but the moment of reflection is important. From the moment when I started to make my own films I completely abandoned my theoretical reflection on cinema, with the thought that now I'm talking about my perception of the world through my characters and stories. I think there was a moment with *Irma Vep* when something happened which I needed – which was to find a way, in cinematic terms, of reconciling those things that I'd abandoned – the plastic arts and theory, to conduct a reflection on cinema in movement. I had a lot of misgivings about doing a film about cinema. There was a danger of it being too narcissistic, too asphyxiating. I thought that making such a film as a comedy would be a way in but I was venturing into tricky territory – to make a film about cinema but one with a lightness of tone. Comedies were also a completely new genre to me. So this put me in a position of risk, of danger such that I had to forget what I knew, to abandon all the tics that I'd acquired and obliged me to reconsider everything that I'd learnt about making films.

CD: This new way of making films – was that achieved through a particular way of shooting?

OA: No. It was present almost at the moment of writing. I wanted the film to have changes of tone, style, material. I didn't want the film to follow a traditional drama-turgical line, I wanted it rather to be like a chain of thought where one idea leads to another and yet another... I wanted the background of the film to take in a sense of the history of cinema but, at the same time, for the film of be like a Polaroid of a moment of my vision of the world through cinema.

CD: There's a great lightness of touch to the film.

OA: For me it was essential that nothing weighed too heavily. It was a film that I wrote very quickly and with a great deal of pleasure, in two weeks, and the shooting lasted four weeks. The important thing was the speed but also the fact of working with very little money and therefore to be beyond the worries of a major budget. The film was made outside the commercial system and only made because Canal Plus gave us the money, four million francs, which is very little. This freedom became part of the film and is evident in it.

CD: When Maggie says 'It's with desire that we make films', is she talking for you?

OA: I adopted a comic tone and obviously Jean-Pierre Léaud played certain scenes in a very comedic tone but at the same time the questions posed are real questions. When he talks with Maggie about how he makes films these are exactly the same sort of questions that I would ask myself. And Maggie's statement points to the fact that if the desire is there then that's enough – it's the most important thing. But he replies 'I feel nothing'. I think I have to become a little abstract here, it has to do with the element of sexual fantasy that is involved in artistic creation. I use this metaphor in order to talk about the physical rapport that's involved in creation, it has to do with the libido but it's also beyond that. The character of Rene Vidal represents a man in the grip of a sexual fantasy, purely and simply, which is the way that Feuillade conceived and filmed the character of *Irma Vep*. And it's this desire that Vidal recog-nises. At the same time when he films this straightforwardly, when he reconstitutes it, he discovers that the shooting of the film is enough of a response. Does he really need to make the film? From the moment that he sees his fantasy being played out in costumes before him – has he any need of cinema beyond that? In the same way, Vidal has the same egotistical satisfaction during the shooting as Maggie does when she identifies with the character Irma and steals the jewellery in the hotel scene – she's playing out for herself her fantasy of the character. People can lose themselves in this egotistical version of desire. If one is too intimate in the reproduction of desire one remains only in oneself and not in any communication with the other.

CD: Is not the proof of this in Vidal's own footage, his film at the end of the film? Because your film is a completed film about an incomplete film at the end of which is this very experimental piece, the film's been scratched, and so on. Is this not something very personal to Vidal?

OA: Yes, for me the film is the place where I'm asking a question through this charac-ter about the reproduction of sexual fantasies. It's because of this that he gets angry when he sees the rushes – nobody else can understand his anger because techni-cally everything's fine – he realises that his fantasy is only images. And the problem for him is where is the transposition of this desire? The problem that I'm posing through him is how to find the original power of the desire that animates him? At the end of the story there is a solution. I wanted him to find, if not a real response to his question, then... a voice. There's also the element of trying to relocate the first emotions of cinema, so while I'm talking about something quite contemporary which has to do with the element of sexual fantasy, I'm doing so in very archetypical terms that date back to the days of silent cinema, where things were filmed for the first time. How can we rediscover the original power of those virgin images from silent cinema? How to rediscover the moment when one filmed things for the first time? How, today, can one rediscover that sensation in filming the 1915 character of Irma Vep? There's something quite literal in this character – quite unique in cinema, and mythical. She's the original woman in black leather, the spy, the thief, the femme fatale, Catwoman in *Batman*, she's there in Hitchcock's *To Catch a Thief*, Dianna Rigg in *The Avengers* – she's almost like a silhouette who autonomously haunts the cinema. It's in Feuillade that she first appears and the question is how, ninety years later, with all the cinema that's passed since then, can one reconstitute this original sensation of her first appearance? Rene Vidal's response is incomplete and fragmentary. He's trying to do it as though nothing had existed, to simply tear some sense out of the mate-rial itself, to move from the human figure to abstraction. Francis Bacon at a certain moment had to fight with his material, to battle with the matter of paint in such a way that abstraction is utterly present but in the service of the reconstitution of a feeling which is very truthful, deep and human.

CD: Rene's film is like evidence of a struggle for faith. But you also use a little extract from a Groupe Medvedkine film *Classe de lutte*. Why was that in there?

OA: That was a part of the improvisational element of the film.

CD: How is it to make films such as yours in France at the moment?

OA: I think that freedom and space in French cinema is being reduced, the same as everywhere else. The logic of French cinema at the moment is one of suppres-ing and suffocating the spaces in which one can resist the complete industrialisation and professionalisation of cinema. The French cinema wants above all to produce unproblematic films, consensual films.

CD: We see this in the film where the character of the French journalist damns Vidal and praises Van Damme.

OA: It's a bit of a caricature, but only slightly because it's a kind of discourse that one can easily come across in France. It's a profoundly anti-intellectual discourse that is promoted by intellectuals. It's a discourse that is very present in the industry where there is a certain collusion between a certain kind of cinephilia and the most brutal end of the industry. The French cinema is increasingly falling into the hands of large financial groups, who have made a fortune in other areas and are now seeking to diversify by moving into cinema. What follows from this is the cold commercial calculation of rationalising and annihilating all that isn't, to their eyes, profitable.

CD: After having shot *Irma Vep* with a small budget do you think that you'll try to find another way to reproduce that kind of liberty?

OA: The last two films I've made have been with small budgets, *L'eau froide* also had a similar budget and while it was a very different film it was easier to make than *Irma Vep*, which seems like a materially richer film – there's more on the screen. So the answer is yes and no. What has been very heartening is the discovery that I can make films for very little money and do just about what I want, that I'm not a prisoner of the system, I have a margin of freedom. But I don't want to find myself constrained to making films on a small budget. I've two projects that I'm interested in at the moment that are for bigger budget films. So while I value the freedom in which my last two films were made I'm also very attracted to exploring elements of a, let's say, a richer cinema, a more traditional cinema. The question is: is it possible to make such films with the freedom that I need to make films? But that kind of free-dom is like a drug, once you've tasted it, it's very hard to accept anything else. Also, with filmmaking you're always only a couple of steps away from making a film that doesn't work, that's an artistic failure. It's too fragile a medium to make compromises over. Today I'm in exactly that position – can I find that degree of liberty within a form of filmmaking where I'm more dependent on the industry?

INTERVIEW WITH JACQUES AUDIARD
ORIGINALLY PUBLISHED IN *SIGHT AND SOUND* APRIL 1997

'The best lives are invented' says the ageing Albert Dehousse (Jean-Louis Trintignant) as he surveys his long, active life as a liar. And one particular li(f)e stands out – his period as a Resistance hero who never fired a gun, who bluffed and dissimulated his way into the upper echelons of Resistance heroes in post-liberation Paris and eventually secured the position of Colonel in French-occupied Germany. It's this period, with the young Dehousse played by Mathieu Kassovitz (director of *La Haine*), that forms the main part of Jacques Audiard's second feature, *Un héros très discret (A Self-Made Hero)*.

Adapted from a novel by Jean-François Deniau, the film is an elegant disquisition on the pleasures of deceit, into which Audiard knits all manner of fake witnesses – sociologists, resistance veterans, historians – to attest to the relative truth or falsehood of Dehousse's career. But it's also a troubling parable of the still-unresolved French guilt over its immediate post-war record, a guilt that came into sharp focus around the time of former President François Mitterrand's death. French 'revisionist' historians have contributed to the steady undermining of the myth that France was neatly, and comfortably, divided into two camps during and after Occupation – between those who supported the collaborationist Vichy Government of Marshall Pétain and those who resisted the Nazis and their puppets. The result of such revisionism has been an uncomfortable, and ongoing, reckoning, both with the national mythology of Resistance and a history of deeply-ingrained French anti-semitism. Studies such as Pierre Péan's *Une Jeunesse Francaise: François Mitterrand 1934-1947* concentrated on the degree to which the post-liberation period was a snakepit of politically ambitious – and often politically ambiguous – power-broking. It's into just this pit that Audiard casts his quick-to-learn young would-be hero. Under the tutelage of 'le capitain' (Albert Dupontel), a diabolically charismatic gay *resistant*, and the collaborator-cum-fixer Monsieur Jo (François Berléand), Albert sees his main chance and inveigles his way into a group comprised of those known as *les gens de Londres*, the London-based Gaullists – five Resistance heroes. This he achieves with a combination of stealth, quick thinking and a dogged application to detail – memorising all the stations on the map of the London Underground so as not to be caught out. Dehousse has no awkward record of political *parti-pris* – because he was never around to get politicised – and the military establishment soon size him up as an ideal man to be interrogating suspected French collaborators. So Dehousse finds himself a Colonel, subject to the suspicion, envy and admiration of his colleagues, including the attractive and astute Servane (Anouk Grinberg), who quickly sees through his charade. However, the pressure of maintaining a fabricated identity becomes increasingly intense and when it falls to him to dispense summary military justice to a group of Frenchman who volunteered for the German army, Dehousse finally cracks.

Jacques Audiard is a respected French screenwriter – *Un héros* won Best Screenplay at Cannes in 1996 – whose credits include scripts for films by Josiane Balasko, Denys Granier-Deferre and Claude Miller. His father, Michel Audiard, was one of the French school of screenwriters working between the 1940s and 1960s whose contributions were often credited under the title *dialoguiste*. Audiard *père* was one of Jean Gabin's preferred dialogue-writers, writing for the star on many of his films including *Les Grandes Familles* (1958), *Le President* (1961), *Un singe en hiver* (1962) and *Melodie en sous-sol* (1963). Jacques Audiard's first film, *Regarde les hommes tomber* (1994), which featured the first pairing of Kassovitz and Trintignant under his direction, was a sombre film noir with an elliptical time structure and a splendidly sorrowing tone. Winning a 'Best First Film' César in 1994, it was an impressive debut that combined the best of French auteur cinema with a strongly literary take on the structures and modes of the French thriller. But few expected Audiard to follow up with a comedy. And certainly not a comedy – again highly literate and intelligent – about the Resistance. In conversation with Audiard – who often explains his film in the terms of a screenwriter's fascination with mechanics and structure – the director was serious about the motives for his comedy of history-as-deceit.

CD: When you decided to adapt the novel *Un Héros malgré lui* by Jean-François Deniau, were you attracted by the character of Dehousse or by the period it was set in?

JA: Both. The novel is one in which an individual destiny meets up with a collective destiny, that was the element that I really appreciated. I could add to that the fact that I was born after the war and that I was immersed in this period of lies and deceit. Although it was less marked in the novel than in the adaptation, there was also the real possibility of doing a comedy . I really wanted to make a comedy.

CD: You've said that 'I want everything to be false' in the film. Yet, at the same time, the film appears to be quite a faithful reconstruction of the period – in the sense of cars, clothes, food and newspapers all looking authentically of the time.

JA: I wasn't particularly concerned about that aspect of the film, it didn't preoccupy me. For example, when you see Sandrine Kiberlain's character (Yvette, Dehousse's first wife) she's of her time – perhaps. But she could easily walk down a street today and nobody would give her a second glance. And take the character of Captain Dionnet, played by Albert Dupontel. I went to see Dupontel when he was doing costume tests and he had long hair. He asked me, 'What do you want me to do with my hair?' It didn't occur to me to tell him to get it cut. But really, that element of the film didn't interest me. I wanted the film to be a purely fantastic vision of history.

CD: I ask because along with the background authenticity of the objects and clothes, there is also the moment when we see the photograph of Dehousse's father come to life in its frame. He's drunk, and singing. It's a deliberately anti-realist moment.

JA: You remember what the father says at that moment? He throws up and says, 'Vive la France'. You know, when you make a film, there is a moment when certain preliminary questions crop up. And it's always the same questions. How does the time pass in this story? How far can I go visually in the film? And these questions have to be answered very early on because they have to be evident from a very early stage in the film. It's a bit like in mathematics, one has postulates. These questions are the formal postulates from which the film departs. At the very opening you define what the limits of your film are going to be.

CD: At the beginning of the film we also see Trintignant as the aged Dehousse talking to the camera, bearing false witness, as it were.

JA: Right, everything that will recur later is present in the opening. It's like music, you first play the theme, then the variations... at the end of the day I suppose it's a highly classical conception.

CD: Kassovitz and Trintignant played the principal roles in *Regarde les hommes tomber*. What so attracts you to these two actors that you've worked with them again?

JA: I hadn't immediately thought of Matthieu for the role of Dehousse. He kept saying to me during the shooting of *Regarde les hommes* that he wasn't an actor. And I told him, 'Well, that's fine because I'm not a director'. I was seeing a number of actors for the role but I wasn't happy with them and I think it might have been my wife who suggested that I ask Matthieu. Then it hit me that there was a rapport between the role he'd played in *Regarde les hommes* and the character in *Un héros très discret*. He's still a character who's an apprentice. It was that realisation that decided it for me. It was a little different in the case of Jean-Louis Trintignant. Something curious happened on *Regarde les hommes*. The character that Matthieu plays is a killer and for the first contract he must carry out I was looking for someone to open a door so that Matthieu could shoot at them. Matthieu said to me 'Look, it's ages since I've seen my father. I'll ask him to come along to the shoot' – his father is Peter Kassovitz, who also used to be a filmmaker and scriptwriter – 'We can get him to play the guy who opens the door and gets shot.' So Peter came to the shoot and he had three or four day's growth of beard. It was then that I thought to myself that there was a possible resemblance – and if it came to finding someone to interpret Dehousse as an older man or Matthieu as an older man I would naturally think of Jean-Louis.

CD: Something struck me about both your films. They're both about boys learning to be men and following the instructions of other men – who are often pernicious and dangerous examples. Both films seem fascinated by the spectacle of masculine behaviour as it's passed on, as well as with the element of homosociality that accompanies this theme.

JA: It's not something that I'm very conscious of in the films. There's a childish dimension to men that I'm very sensitive to, a sort of 'playground' behaviour. I've enjoyed dissecting this type of male behaviour, yes, that's true. The screenwriter's is a solitary, sedentary job, and when I shoot a film I face a situation that's totally alien. On the set for *Regarde les hommes* I was faced with the on-set power-games that go on and I found the need to constantly prove oneself absolutely infantile.

CD: Tell me about your father, who was one of the key screenwriters in French cinema during the 1950s and 1960s.

JA: I was an editor, then I took a detour via theatre, and after that I became a script-writer. I needed a bit of time to arrive at that stage and perhaps I took a detour because the cinema seemed a natural and easy option. My father's relationship with the cinema was very straightforward. For him it was a job, as simple as that. He wasn't part of the generation of cinéphiles which I think came later. Whereas I was a cinéphile in the etymological sense of the term, the love of cinema. Even though when I was an adolescent this expressed itself as an avid consuming of cinema, what we call *cinéphagie*. But I discover now that I too have this prosaic relationship with the cinema — I'm not possessed by the desire always to create. This allows me to alternate screenwriting and directing at a rhythm that I feel comfortable with. I wouldn't feel happy about only being a director.

CD: How do the twin experiences of having been an editor and a screenwriter affect the task of directing?

JA: Being an editor really taught me about cinema. There is an obvious connection between editing and screenwriting. It's the same analysis of syntax and rhythm. Except that when you're an editor you're not creating, you're arranging. The idea that a film can be saved in the edit-suite is not even interesting. But when you're shooting, the fact of having been an editor is very important.

CD: You show Dehousse's progress more than you judge it. Do you think that this attitude could be problematic, given the period of the film and of the accusations of political relativism that might be levelled at you?

JA: When I think about that period I feel profoundly uneasy. So I wanted my film to be discomforting, to make the audience uneasy. And even better – or worse – I think that if it's a comedy that creates uneasiness... well, that was one of my goals. I didn't want to be politically correct, it's too easy. There's a sort of ready-made thinking and hence ready-made judgement that comes with that attitude. For example, the character that Deniau describes in his novel was a bit more psychologically mature, more manipulative and cynical. Which is to say, that the judgement was implicit in the characterisation, it was given in the definition of the character's cynicism. I thought this approach was too easy. What I wanted to do with *Un héros* was to be empathetic with Dehousse. I wanted follow this character like an entomologist. But what can supersede this approach is the potential for sympathy that a human provides and I have to confess that Matthieu's interpretation of Dehousse lends him more sympathy than I expected. He's even too sympathetic. You know, for people of my generation in France the question is simply 'what did our parents do in this period?' An English kid in the 1970s could have asked its parents the same question and got a simple answer. For a French person of my generation it was not so simple. But my generation has not stopped asking the question. But there is another question, equally interesting: 'What would we have done? What would I have done?' Perhaps I would have been a liar, a bit cowardly and later have lied about my cowardice. I wouldn't have been a complete bastard. But Dehousse is not a bastard of that ilk. I don't judge him in the film because, like a lot of my generation, I can identify with him. I wouldn't, however, like to see myself in the character of a real bastard, a tor-turer, or a collaborator in the deportation of the Jews. This is something unpardon-able. But I would not necessarily have been a hero. No, I could have been a dirty little dissembler. It's true that there exists a certain type of French historical personality – earlier we talked about Mitterrand, for example – and there's a completely literary-romantic side to this personality; its something that the French are quite sensitive to. We'll accept all kind of stuff if there's this romantic counterpart to it. A character like Mitterrand, for example, is truly like a Florentine prince, a Machiavelli, with precisely this romantic literary dimension. The fact is that, in France, one can know that such and such a character is not necessarily a liar, but a crafty bastard or an opportunist, but that he was so brilliant that one ends up thinking, 'shit, he was all right.'

REGARDE LES HOMMES TOMBER/SEE HOW THEY FALL
DIR: JACQUES AUDIARD FRANCE 1993
ORIGINALLY PUBLISHED IN *SIGHT AND SOUND* JUNE 1997

SYNOPSIS

France, the present. Simon Hirsch, a middle-aged salesman, befriends Mickey, a young undercover cop who asks him to help in the stakeout of Donata, a criminal. Mickey is shot and taken to hospital where he is diagnosed as being brain-dead. Simon vows to find the gunman.

Two years earlier Marx, a middle-aged conman, meets a young man named Frédéric. They hitchhike together and when Marx is attacked after a card-sharp operation Frédéric beats up his assailant. Frédéric changes his name to Johnny and offers Marx his dole money. Simon follows the police investigation of Mickey's shooting and meets an informer who tells him that Donata's killer was a professional. Having lost Johnny's money gambling, Marx wants them to split up. Johnny slashes his wrist and Marx returns. Simon talks to the informer who shows him the scars where Mickey tortured him. Later, Simon gets a call from the informer, who tells him of a connection in Lyons that might lead to the identity of Mickey's assassin. Simon leaves home and heads for Lyons where he tortures the connection named by the informant, extracting a description of the gunman as 'an old guy with a bum leg'.

Johnny is working in a pizza restaurant and when Marx gets beaten by Donata's thugs for owing them money, Johnny robs the restaurant safe but gets arrested. He's released and Marx tries to instruct him in tough guy behaviour. Simon goes to the hotel where they stayed, leaving a suitcase behind them. Later, Simon takes a young male prostitute back to the hotel with him. Simon's car is stolen and when its wreckage is discovered all he can salvage is the suitcase. He is fired from his job. Still owing money to Donata, Marx is given the chance to wipe the slate clean by carrying out a killing. At first he refuses but Johnny offers to do it. Simon is now sleeping on the street and picking up rough trade. He bumps into his daughter, Sandrine, who takes him home. Johnny effortlessly carries out the killing and the duo continue to work for Donata as hitmen. When another gangster makes contact with Marx and asks him to kill Donata, Marx accepts. Simon searches through their hotel room and finds photographs of their next targets. He meets Johnny in an amusement arcade and persuades him to go for a meal. Marx spots them and later savagely beats Johnny. Marx is contrite and the pair admit that they love each other as Simon listens outside the door. When they move onto the next hit, Simon is waiting for them. He shoots Marx dead and Simon and Johnny go off together.

REVIEW

Regarde les hommes tomber was Jacques Audiard's 1994 César-winning first feature and gets a British release on the strength of the warm welcome given Audiard's follow-up, *Un héros très discrét*. Mathieu Kassovitz is again in a lead role in *Regarde*, as the slow-witted, blank-faced innocent Johnny, who could be seen as Albert Dehousse's younger, less ambitious brother. Jean-Louis Trintignant, who crops up as the aged Dehousse in *Un héros*, is more central to *Regarde* where he plays Marx, the crippled and fractious card-sharp who takes Johnny under his shabby wing. It's a highly successful pairing. Trintignant's career-long perfection of cold-eyed misanthropy here shading into a portrayal of shambling criminal opportunism as Marx turns the lonely Johnny into a professional hitman who kills simply to maintain their relationship.

Adapted from the novel *Triangle* by Teri White, *Regarde* is an absolutely contemporary French film noir – and the French element is crucial here. There exists a well-loved tradition of French noir that, in films such as Jacques Becker's *Touchez pas au Grisbi* (1954), incorporates a fascination with the group dynamics of its male characters as incarnated by actors like Jean Gabin and Lino Ventura. Additionally, Audiard's father, Michel, was one of the main screenwriters of the tradition. With its focus on the masculine world of petty crooks and killers, *Regarde* is a very much an askance take on these traditions of French noir but, as *Cahiers du cinéma* has pointed out, one underwritten by Audiard *fils'* own meditation on his father's legacy. Or, in other words, how to stake a place within an already hugely self-conscious genre and make it one's own? Audiard succeeds because he has taken risks with the genre in every respect imaginable.

The story is simple: Marx owes a gambling debt which he must pay off by carrying out a contract killing which his accomplice Johnny undertakes. Johnny accidentally kills an undercover cop, Mickey, whose friend Simon Hirsch vows vengeance. In synopsis it's zero-degree noir fare, but Audiard chooses to loop its telling, so that the film opens with the killing that's the catalyst for Simon's pursuit, then switches back to a time, two years earlier, when Marx and Johnny first pair up. From thereon in there's a parallel, switchback time-structure that curves round on itself until it arrives back at the killing and goes beyond it to explore the consequences of Simon's obsessive search for the duo of Marx and Johnny. Formally, the film looks and feels like an investigation, being elliptical in its transitions and favouring disorientating close-ups of objects and action, as well as homing in on faces, particularly that of the grizzled Jean Yanne, whose lugubrious, dead-man-on-leave authority is utterly commanding.

The film's most fascinating feature is its isolation and examination of the latent homo-erotic subtext of the gangster film, often subsumed into violent action, narcissistic preening or geekish logorrhoea. Yet Audiard's characters are the antithesis of gangster glamour. Simon is a somnolent travelling salesman-turned-angel of death, Marx and Johnny are a pair of Beckettian clowns playing out an increasingly ambiguous master-slave relationship. Their world is one of anonymous hotel rooms and provincial streets and they run on exclusively masculine energies. Johnny's unquestioning love for Marx is slowly returned, as Simon's infatuation with Mickey is gradually focused on Johnny. The film is full of cameos of horrifically displaced male affection. Simon meets one of Mickey's informers who describes the young cop as 'handsome... he scared the shit out of me' and then lovingly displays the scars left by Mickey's electric torture routine like an adolescent proud of his love bites.

The film's homo-eroticism is never put over as a revisionist dimension but rather as an unearthing of elements that were always present in a genre so populated by off-the-rail males. And it's this, along with Audiard's evident pleasure in mischievous but purposeful narrative origami, that makes the film such an achievement. *Regarde les hommes tomber* returns the original and vital sense of strangeness to film noir that derived from its German Expressionist roots and the warped externalisation of psychologically disturbed states that carried over into the American cinema of the 1940s and 1950s. For that achievement alone, it ranks above anything that the recent American noir revival has produced.

SELECT HOTEL
DIR: LAURENT BOUHNIK FRANCE 1996
ORIGINALLY PUBLISHED IN SIGHT AND SOUND JULY 1997

SYNOPSIS
Clichy, Northern Paris. The present. In the Hotel Sélect, a flophouse, some of its inhabitants talk to camera about living there. One of the speakers is Nat, a young drug addict and prostitute. Nat's brother, Tof, also lives in the hotel. Denis, Nat's pimp, tells her that she must service a perverted client known as Monsieur St Paul and Nat refuses. When the landlord tells her that she's behind with her rent, Denis pays the arrears and entraps her into doing what he asks.

Tof goes into a nearby shoe shop and is ejected by the shopkeeper, who takes him for a dangerous vagrant. On the street Denis, Nat and Tof sting a guy in a drug deal and Denis beats him up when he questions it. At the launderette Tof meets Clementine, a prostitute who also frequents the Hotel Select; they talk and are mutually attracted. After a night hustling for clients and drugs, Nat bumps into the guy Denis beat up the day before, who attacks her and steals her money. Back at the hotel, Tof breaks into the safe and steals a gun. He goes back to the shoe shop where he humiliates the shopkeeper, his actions caught on a surveillance camera. Pierre, the shopkeeper, returns home shaken, and prints an image of Tof from the surveillance tape. Tof searches for Nat, who has been taken by Denis to Monsieur St Paul. Tof arrives, threatens Denis and the client and saves Nat, who is traumatised. Tof visits Clementine, only to discover a naked man with her.

Pierre sees Nat on the street and follows her to a meeting with a client and asks where he can find her. Denis returns from Spain; he's looking for Tof. Tof replaces the gun in the hotel safe and joins some acquaintances on a drugs binge. Pierre turns up at the hotel; he and Nat go to a rave. Later, Pierre wakes up at the hotel where Nat has discovered the image of Tof in his wallet. He leaves. Tof meets Denis, who bludgeons him to death. Clementine tells Nat of Tof's murder and Nat deliberately puts herself at the mercy of a maniac. One of the hotel transvestites, Lydie, takes Pierre to the hotel, where they find Nat's bleeding corpse. They bury her body in wasteland.

REVIEW
Le misérabilisme français was how a member of the Critics Jury at this year's Rotterdam Film Festival summed up Laurent Bouhnik's debut feature, Sélect Hotel. The film opens in deceptively documentary mode with inhabitants of the Hotel Sélect, a flophouse in the Place Clichy, talking directly to camera. The style then switches to hand-held vérité shot through with moments of hallucinatory excess. The principal characters constitute a gallery of contemporary Parisian street-life: Nat's a young bottle-blonde hooker, played with woozy desperation by Julie Gayet; her brother Tof, given an appealingly faux street-smart edge by Jean-Michel Fest, is the most dynamic of the pair who clearly wants out of the dead-end life they lead. Denis, the mustachioed reptile who completes the trio, is Nat's pimp and the pair's collective nemesis.

Sélect Hotel draws from the well of mythologised Parisian marginals primed by

Prévert and Céline and depicts the Paris of the 'lower depths', where the working class overlaps with what is now offensively dismissed as the 'underclass'. In films such as Mathieu Kassovitz's *La Haine* and Claire Denis' remarkable *Nenette et Boni* – yet to be released in Britain – recent French cinema has portrayed the ever-deepening fractures in French society. For all the mythologised squalor of its depiction, Bouhnik's film certainly includes the issue of class and does so cleverly, through the character of Pierre, the shopkeeper who is humiliated by Tof and beguiled by Nat. Pierre is the well-heeled interloper in this other world of experiences that rubs up against his respectable shopkeeper's domain. Simultaneously attracted and repulsed by its denizens, he is an upright citizen caught in the sexual delirium available from Nat. But he also represents the bourgeois optic of social voyeurism through which French street-life has so often been mythologised. Bouhnik signals this aspect of Pierre's character through two images; there's the surveillance frame of Tof filmed during the robbery that Pierre keeps fetishistically in his wallet, and in Pierre's initial stalking pursuit of Nat into a cul-de-sac where he spies on her smoking crack. Played like a self-hating somnambulist by Serge Blumental, Pierre is a social voyeur and a sexual tourist whose final gesture in the film is to bury Nat in wasteland, hurling a rock down onto her stiffening corpse in a horrifing gesture of disgust and denial. Bouhnik succeeds not in demonising this petit bourgeois outright but by using Blumental's impassive performance to comment on the class that can cross the tracks without consequence for a spot of vicarious slumming.

Bouhnik's desire throughout the film to thoroughly *épater les bourgeois* finds another, gentler, expression in the muted comic subplots. Tof's growing affection for Clémentine, who is unapologetically drawn as a *pute* with a heart of gold, develops with a lightheartedness that is unexpected within the film's general grimness of sentiment. Tof turns up to Clémentine's flat to be greeted by a naked client of hers, and the three take a civil, lightly comic breakfast together. It's a moment that could run perilously close to the sort of misanthropic class-comedy that Bertrand Blier has made a career out of, but Bouhnik gives it an understatement that makes it touching. *Sélect Hotel* is an intriguing portrait of those thoroughly marginalised by French society, a 'Last Exit to Beaubourg'. While it quotes Brecht and is dedicated to Emiliano Zapata (and Arletty), its most symptomatically political element is in its palpable sense of disgust for the bourgeoisie and in its depiction of Tof and Nat as romantic, beautiful losers.

NOUVELLE VAGUE: THE SOUNDTRACK TO
THE FILM BY JEAN-LUC GODARD (ECM RECORDS 1997)

ORIGINALLY PUBLISHED IN SIGHT AND SOUND JULY 1997

'It's a story I wanted to tell.' These are the first words spoken in the soundtrack to Jean-Luc Godard's *Nouvelle Vague*, now released as a two-CD set by the adventurous German jazz label ECM. The *Nouvelle Vague* soundtrack is just that, the film's sound in its entirety and uninterrupted – natural sound, dialogues, sound effects and music. In listening, there is the sensation familiar from other Godard films – think of *Une Femme est Une Femme* and its staccato music editing, of *Prénom Carmen* and the filming of the Beethoven String Quartets – that Godard is uninterested in respecting the conventional hierarchy of attention accorded to the image over the sound. Here, sounds clash, merge and emerge in counterpoint to one another. Voices overlap in polyphony. Music wells, reaches a crescendo and is suddenly silent. A dog barks. Cars screech. Waves crash. This is sound conceived not only independently of the image but as an extra dimension to it, sound composed as another image.

Ever since moving to the shores of Lac Leman in Switzerland in the 1980s, Godard's physical world has steadily contracted. In his recent film *JLG/JLG: Autoportrait de décembre* (1995) and in the ongoing work of the *Histoire(s) du cinéma* series he is the Hermit, the Wizard of Rolle, happily cloistered in his library with his music and surrounded by video machinery, reels of film and the most analytical imagination in cinema. The Alchemist. The Romantic recluse. *Nouvelle Vague* is a key film of this period and was one of Godard's regular forays into relatively commercial filmmaking, shot in 35mm colour and starring Alain Delon. And 'the story' it wants to tell? In the first part, a man, Richard Lennox (Delon), meets Elena, a rich Italian industrialist (Domiziana Giordano). She almost runs him down in her car (an extraordinary sequence, with David Darling's long cello lines merging in dissonant antagonism with a car horn's savage blast) then fails to save him from drowning. In the second part, another man – who is in fact the same man, played again by Delon – appears and a love affair begins. This time Lennox saves Elena from drowning. All of which takes place around Lake Geneva in the luxurious enclaves of the super-rich. The rapacious business of international finance is the backdrop. Love and work, emotion and money, the time-honoured Godardian dialectic is here played out again but with such a degree of sensuous attentiveness – to nature, music and words – that film and soundtrack alike possess a fine, barbed and fragmentary beauty.

Walter Benjamin once dreamt of 'a work composed entirely of fragments'. Of other people's works. Godard finally got there with *Nouvelle Vague* (actually, he got there with *A bout de souffle* but that was only warming-up). This time it's fragments of Gide and Schiller, Faulkner and Chandler for dialogue; a fragment of film history (and a fairly large fragment of the budget one would imagine) in Delon; fragments of music – Dino Saluzzi's mournful accordion, the sweep and drone of David Darling's solo cello, Patti Smith, Meredith Monk and Paul Hindemith amongst others. And fragments of Godard's childhood surely, given that he now lives in the same area in which he was born and grew up.

Does one listen to this as a soundtrack? Not in any conventional sense. As a piece of *musique concrète*, then? Perhaps. Above all this CD is the shadow of an invisible film, a film largely unseen by British audiences, the ghost of a film that never got through. But, in a way, that is as it should be. The CD is accompanied by an immaculately packaged booklet that includes a fascinating text by Claire Bartoli, a blind writer, entitled *Le regard intérieur*, in which she describes her piecing-together of another film in her head, her version of *Nouvelle Vague*. It's the same work that we do when listening to a soundtrack composed with such idiosyncratic care and attention that it does indeed have a life independent of its visual images. I've seen *Nouvelle Vague* and I remember feeling that the sound pointed to another dimension in the experience of watching JLG. The sound seemed not just to alternate between on-screen and off-screen space but to exist in that place where on-screen and off-screen come together in the viewer's head.

PORTRAITS CHINOIS
DIR: MARTINE DUGOWSAN FRANCE 1996
ORIGINALLY PUBLISHED IN *SIGHT AND SOUND* AUGUST 1997

SYNOPSIS

Ada is a fashion designer moving into a new flat with her screenwriter-boyfriend Paul. Paul's co-writer, Guido, refuses to move in with his girlfriend, Stéphanie, provoking a row between them. René, Ada's boss at the fashion house, is recruiting new designers and is particularly impressed by the work of Lise, a newcomer whom he instructs Ada to hire on the spot.

Four months later, Ada and Paul have a house-warming party, where Lise falls in love with Paul. Another friend, Emma, is given a lift home by Alphonse, a film producer. During the journey, Emma discusses the new film by their mutual acquaintance Yves. Guido confides in Paul that he and Stéphanie have split up; he spends a lot of time at their flat. Ada and Paul set Guido up with Lise and on the same evening the couple go out on their first date, Lise calls Paul and tells him that she loves him. Later, Paul meets Lise in a cafe and tells her that her infatuation is fruitless. Alphonse finds Emma in the production office, where she is now working as a script reader. They have dinner together and Guido goes home with Emma. Ada discovers she is pregnant and tells her friend Nina. Paul and Lise make love. When Ada tells Paul that she's pregnant and that she doesn't want the baby he suggests she have an abortion. She soon realises that Paul is having an affair with Lise.

Some time later the group – minus Paul and Lise – go on holiday together. Yves and Nina now have a child. Alphonse and Emma are still conducting their affair and trying to conceal it from the others. The group receives a card from Guido, who is working as a screenwriter in Hollywood. Ada and Yves argue over a news broadcast about war crimes. Ada leaves in tears. March in Paris. Lise's fashion designs are a success. Ada has left the company and Lise has split up with Paul. Ada works as a costume designer on a film which is being shot close to Yves' latest film. Ada watches the shooting of a scene which is based on her break-up with Paul. Later, reunited, Paul and Ada watch the completed film together. It has a happy ending.

REVIEW

Martine Dugowsan's first feature film, *Mina Tannenbaum* (1993), was an engaging, if uneven, combination of adolescent angst and 1970s Parisian period detail. In her follow-up, *Portraits Chinois*, the time frame is present-day Paris and the film concentrates on a group of twenty-something professionals working in film and fashion. An Anglo-French co-production involving Channel Four Films, *Portrait Chinois* stars Helena Bonham-Carter alongside a roster of important contemporary French talent which includes Romane Bohringer, Marie Trintignant and Yvan Attal. Bonham-Carter plays the chief female protagonist, Ada, an English fashion-designer living in Paris. It's a potentially interesting piece of casting that plays to the strengths of Bonham-Carter's persona as the sophisticated yet troubled upper-middle-class Englishwoman. Never the most physical of actresses, she does some nice things with French as her adopted language, mastering Gallic phatic emphases, grimacing and shrugging her way through dialogue that lapses into *franglais* to indicate troubled emotions.

Although Ada is the principal protagonist, the centre around which the other characters revolve, there is the strong sense that Dugowsan's own sympathies are with Romane Bohringer's character Lise, the talented newcomer to the circle of friends (Bohringer also took the lead in *Mina*). She is the only character accorded a past, which we are given access to through an interestingly-shot flashback in a cafe, just as she also has recourse to subjective monologues. This works well with Bohringer's style of interiorised passion but in a film with so many vying subplots and character-relations this divergence of sympathies makes for an uneasy balance. The development of the other characters consequently suffers from being overly-telegraphed; Guido's postcard from Hollywood and Yves and Nina's child appear as a way of signposting the changes over the film's two-year timespan.

There's the overriding sensation here of Sunday supplement lifestyle-psychoanalysis. In Dugowsan's hands, the characters' well-heeled angst seems part of an aspirational package of glamorous jobs and desirable apartments. Nor does Dugowsan do herself any favours by alluding to other directors truly able to put a sting in their depictions of middle-class personal crises. In this respect Portraits Chinois could be said to break down into three parts. There's a Woody Allenesque opening, a Bergman-styled interlude (friendships wearing thin against a stony coastal backdrop, à la *Persona*) and an ending derived from Truffaut in which life is comfortably incorporated into art by way of Yves' film. It's all conventionally bittersweet but utterly conformist, with abortion, infidelity and emotional turmoil treated to this unconvincing life-and-art sleight of hand.

Y AURA-T-IL DE LA NEIGE A NOEL?/WILL IT SNOW FOR CHRISTMAS?

DIR: SANDRINE VEYSSET FRANCE 1996
ORIGINALLY PUBLISHED IN *FILM COMMENT* NOVEMBER/DECEMBER 1997

Y aura-t-il de la neige à Nôël? is a French film which features seven young children, their beleaguered but stubbornly loving mother and a polygamous brute of a father. It takes place on a farm in the rural south of France, its narrative is strongly influenced by fairytales and it concludes over the Christmas period. Given in synopsis, its elements sound unbearably winsome but be reassured, the film is anything but. Sandrine Veysset, its thirty-year-old first-time director, dedicates the film to her mother and, while assiduously avoiding any overt references to the period, the film appears to be set at some indeterminate point in the 1970s, when Veysset herself was growing up. The mother – she is given no name, we'll see what world of archetypes we're in shortly – has had seven children by the father, who is likewise nameless. He employs her and the older children on his farm, where they are squalidly lodged and underpaid. Meanwhile, the father continues to live in the nearby town of Cavaillon with his other family, which he steadfastly refuses to leave.

Veysset's film is stark, simple and beautiful. But as a first film by a young French director what's most unexpected about it is the quality of its realism. *Y aura-t-il de la neige à Nôël?* provides a contemporary experience of a strand of French cinema that is less and less familiar to international audiences. The current crop of the 'young French' are associated with cinematic portraits of callow Parisians parading post-coital tristesse in vying registers of cultured insouciance and hell-for-leather nihilism. The 'young French cinema' of the 1990s is generally Parisian in emphasis and works within a form of *intimiste* portraiture that derives from the hugely influential realism of John Cassavetes, fed through the work of older progenitors such as Maurice Pialat and André Téchiné. Any discussion of French film realism ultimately devolves down onto the French mythical interpretation of their cinema's history, best expressed in that founding binary opposition of Méliès with the *frères* Lumières; primitive cinemas of fantasy and realism being seen as aesthetic paradigms present from the very outset. The Lumières axis extends down the years to include Renoir, Pagnol and, later, Pialat. And now Sandrine Veysset. The force of its application has often been grounded in the filmmakers' attention to the lives of the socially marginalised, with an equal aesthetic attention paid to the pursuit and absorption of authenticity of place, detail and moment. And in these respects, Veysset's film fits the bill.

There is an unforced naturalism to Veysset's filming that recalls the early Pialat of *La Gueule ouverte* (1974) and *Passe ton bac d'abord* (1978) as well as with Agnès Varda's *Sans toit ni loi* (1985) with which it shares interesting parallels. This naturalism derives from Veysset having shot the film on location in the farmlands of the rural south over the consecutive seasons of summer, autumn and winter with a cast largely comprised of local, non-professional actors (with the exception of Dominique Reymond and Daniel Duval who play the mother and father, respectively). This approach, plus weeks of location-based rehearsals, intended the performers to take on as many of the reflexes of the rural labourer as physically possible. Likewise, the camera style was conceived in order to accommodate the children so that they appear as comfortable on screen as possible. It's Veysset's unfussy, focused attention to the authenticity of place, comportment and to the details of rural agricultural life that is initially striking. With little introduction, the viewer is immersed in a universe where there is no immediate central character – the mother only gradually becomes the focus of the film's story. In the meantime, we observe a world every bit as enclosed and autonomous as seventeenth-century French court and we must accustom ourselves to the film's gradual anatomisation of its social etiquettes and peasant codes. Relations of power here are not telegraphed by the angle at which a *peruque* is worn or by the brilliance of the wordplay, but by whose turn it is to harvest the radishes and by the farm owner's arrogance – *le père* as *patron* – which is every bit as pronounced as a feudal baron's. This is not an entirely lazy analogy either; there's the strong sense that the film is reaching for a certain timelessness (more accurately, atemporality), something served both by the phenomenological wager of the seasonal shooting schedule as well as by the deliberately functional costume design. And while tractors, cars, a black and white television and supermarkets are visible, there remains the presiding sense that this story – of poverty questionably redeemed by love – is ancient. This is a mythical, folkloric time after all, that of the cyclical rhythm of the seasons, and it assists the film in two important respects. First, it lends a quality to the film's photographic realism that is crucial to its aesthetic density and qualifies the film in that desperately old-fashioned area of a felt 'authenticity'. Second, it helps avoid any overly specific historical association and the instant kitsch-effect that often accompanies retro-stylisation. It's also of a part with the film's fairytale influence – *Cahiers du cinéma* dubbed it, approvingly, 'Snow White, the Ogre and the Seven Dwarves', through which the slice-of-life vérité becomes cumulatively oneiric.

Veysset comprehensively refuses to damn the tyrannical father. The implication of his sexual abuse of the eldest daughter, Jeanne, is elliptically treated, the specifics of the scene entirely removed to the viewer's imagination, and the scene is more forceful for being so handled. And while it may not quite justify itself in the terms of *amour fou*, of love-as-malady, the film inches towards the horrific suggestion of its ending by constructing a portrait of maternal love as ambiguous as any in contemporary cinema. Veysset depicts the family as part haven, part prison, a collective hallucination of harmony induced under duress. It's a theme most explicitly developed in the mother's telling of a Christmas story to the children –a dream she had at sixteen and one she's recounted many times before but whose reprise the children noisily request again. In the dream she meets God who commands her to run a race with a very fat woman. The Mother loses. 'My punishment,' she tells her rapt audience, 'was to have seven children.' The children love it. They feel special because of the drama of their mother's life, but one wonders at the complexity of her feelings towards them. The eldest children, Bruno and Jeanne, know a little better than their siblings; they have come closer to their father's brutality. Bruno, bawled out by his father over some minor mistake in the fields, has his tremulous adolescent pride permanently offended. Jeanne suffers sexual advances from her father that reduce her to tears and scandalise her mother. From this point on, the mother is repulsed by him and consequently feels even more dependent and imprisoned.

The scene of the Christmas story prepares for the terrible suggestion of the 'open' ending and, in a film that devotes such care to the authentic delineation of gesture and place, to a kind of behavioural authenticity, it's one of the few moments where we are given access to the mother's interior life. In numerous sequences Veysset depicts the mother as an archetype of nurturing fecundity, the shots of her in the fields surrounded by her children give her as the personification of Earth Mother and *mater dolorosa*. But 'mother as the killer of her children' remains a spin on the more acceptable iconography that the film draws back from confronting fully. That's not to say that it doesn't broach this taboo – the closing moments of the film suggest a collective suicide. The mother, having borrowed a gas heater from the sympathetic teacher of her children, gasses herself and the children as they all sleep. It's a strange ending, extremely compelling at the first viewing but somehow lacking in resolve when one sees the film for a second time. It's a deliberately unresolved closure on the potentiality of the character rather than on actuality, on suggestion rather than shocking finality. When the mother awakes – alarmed at finding herself still living or terrified by the dream she's just had? – is this a way of getting the viewer to calculate the probabilities of her actually carrying out the killing? Yes, as an 'open' ending, it must be. At the same time however, the ending preserves a strict ambiguity that corresponds to the fairytale logic of the film's narrative schema, it's an ambiguity of the 'and it was all just a dream' variety. It's here that the film's oneiric and realist elements decisively separate having been, up to this point, so productively meshed.

There is another, and I think more fruitful, reading that might explore the ending as the culmination of the film's gradual journey around and then within the figure of the mother. In the steady, beady-eyed investigation that spirals in on its object (the iris-in on the mother standing alone in the fields clutching her youngest child is the visual declaration of this trajectory), the film has moved from a behavioural observation of the character's place in her immediate environment to interior psychology. What is revealed is a vision of horrific intent that the Mother can only countenance as a nightmare. Perhaps it's this element, that of the approach to its principal female character, that most strongly allies Veysset's film with Varda's *Sans toit ni loi*. And while the extent to which *Y aura-t-il de la neige à Nôël?* may be seen as a feminist film is arguable, it would certainly be interesting to read it in relation to ideas of *femme-filmécriture* that have be advanced in analyses of Varda's film.

LUCIE AUBRAC
DIR: CLAUDE BERRI FRANCE 1997
ORIGINALLY PUBLISHED IN *SIGHT AND SOUND* FEBRUARY 1998

SYNOPSIS

Lyon, March, 1943. Resistance activist Raymond Samuel, known under the pseudonym 'François Vallet', dynamites a train and is arrested. Raymond's wife, who goes under the pseudonym 'Lucie Aubrac', manages to get her husband released by threatening the local prosecutor with Free French reprisals. In facilitating Raymond's release, Lucie is upholding a pact that, come what may, they will be together every May 14, their anniversary. Raymond is renamed 'Claude Ermelin' and is temporarily put in charge of the Resistance's Northern Zone. In June, betrayed by an internal informer, Raymond and others are captured at a meeting by the Gestapo. One of their number escapes. The group is imprisoned and tortured by Police Chief Klaus Barbie, who is intent on discovering the identity of their leader, Max. Barbie knows that Raymond is 'François Vallet', and has him sentenced to death.

Lucie plans a way to liberate her husband and determines to kill the escapee, Hardy, who is assumed to be the informer. Discovering that she is pregnant with Raymond's second child, she asks Barbie to release 'Claude Ermelin' but he refuses. Via a Resistance contact in the Paymaster General's Office, Lucie is finally able to request a marriage in extremis to Raymond in order to spare her family the shame of her giving birth out of wedlock. A meeting between the two is set up by the Nazi superiors and Lucie arranges with her Resistance cell to spring Raymond during his transport back to prison. The plan fails when a getaway car stalls. When the couple are married, though, the plan is successfully executed. Lucie and Raymond escape south where they learn that Raymond's parents have been arrested. The family is flown to Britain, where they are to join up with de Gaulle's Free French.

REVIEW

Most contemporary French films about the Resistance are necessarily revisionist accounts. They attempt to reconcile present-day French attitudes to the past which, when it comes to the still thorny issue of the Occupation, oscillate awkwardly between national shame at collaboration and the celebration of Resistance heroism. Jacques Audiard's *A Self-Made Hero* had the virtue of inscribing the revisionist approach into the fabric of its own deeply sceptical fiction, with its hero airbrushing his personal history to blend in with the Resistance movement.

It's the precarious balance between the first-person, anecdotal account of history and the Grand Narrative approach that always underlies the 'history film'. Claude Berri's *Lucie Aubrac* proves no exception. Based on Aubrac's true-life account of wartime exploits, *Ils partiront dans l'ivresse (Outwitting the Gestapo)*, Berri's film bills itself as 'a true love story'. The instant critical reflex is to dismiss it as yet another lavishly budgeted French costume drama, doing for the Occupation what *Indochine* did for French end-of-Empire traumas. The standard argument against mainstream French film accounts of the Resistance is that they create a too easy, post-hoc identification with the freedom fighters, mythologising the national resistance to Nazi occupation rather than subjecting it to awkward enquiry.

In presenting itself as a true-life love story with a Resistance setting, *Lucie Aubrac* is more concerned with the emotional than the political lives of Lucie and Raymond. In itself, this is a potentially fascinating subject, suggesting a study of the incredible pressures that Resistance fighters had to endure in combining armed sub-terfuge with everyday anonymity. The basic dramatic dynamic is the constant threat of discovery or betrayal but, strangely enough, *Lucie Aubrac* does little to exploit this element. Rather, physical tension arises more from the physical separation of the two characters – Lucie's constant scheming to get Raymond released while he languishes in prison under the threat of execution. Their separation and the promise of their being reunited works to up the emotional ante and delivers one of the film's strong-est scenes. Lucie, claiming she was abandoned by Raymond after he impregnated her, demands to be married to him in extremis in order to avoid shaming her military (by implication, Vichy supporting) family. She confronts him in the office of a Nazi functionary where the couple must act as if they barely know one another and Berri skilfully uses the dynamics of denial and suppressed emotion generated across the film to construct a powerfully emotional scene. Auteuil is well cast as Raymond, and ably reprises his now stock-in-trade depiction of emotional repression previously refined in *Un coeur en hiver* and *La Séparation*.

In fashioning an emotional portrait of Resistance heroism, Lucie Aubrac fits alongside other accounts dramatising the role of women fighting against Nazi occu-pation – notably Réné Clément's *Le Jour et l'heure* (1962) and Jean-Pierre Melville's *L'Armée des ombres* (1969), both with Simone Signoret. Moreover, the film plays explicitly on discourses of the family, featuring both real families and familial social groups, up to the national level. Thus different plot strands concern Lucie, the mother of Raymond's son, expecting their next child, and Raymond's parents, who refuse to conceal their Jewish identity by changing their surname Samuel. These elements are brought together in a scene when, having been saved by the Resistance and in hiding with Lucie, Raymond learns that his parents have been arrested. The implication is clear: they will die for his freedom and as he weeps for them, Lucie cradles his head on her belly, his child kicking inside her.

There's a certain pleasure to be had in the role-reversal that Berri effects in this scene and others, with Auteuil as the terrified Resistance fighter and Carole Bouquet (who replaced Juliette Binoche after a month's shooting) as a ruthlessly resourceful matriarch. But it's a strange kind of war thriller that sacrifices much-needed suspense in order to generate the oceanic feeling of the French as one big anti-Nazi family.

CLUBBED TO DEATH
DIR: YOLANDE ZAUBERMAN FRANCE 1997
ORIGINALLY COMMISSIONED BY *SIGHT AND SOUND* FEBRUARY 1998

SYNOPSIS

Lola, a twenty-year-old French city dweller, falls asleep on the bus home from work and wakes up in the suburbs. A friendly young man takes her to a huge warehouse dance club where Lola takes an Ecstasy tablet and dances until dawn. She meets Emir, a young boxer with a cocaine habit, and the two are attracted to each other. Emir lives with his brother and his long-term girlfriend, Saida, who dances at the club. Emir's brother has arranged for Emir to fight one last bout, in a month's time, for the local drug dealer to whom both brothers owe drug money.

Lola goes back to the city. She thinks about Emir and returns to the suburbs to find him. They embrace passionately but are observed by a distraught Saida. Saida and Lola talk; Lola is frightened by the other woman who extracts her address from Emir. Lola is angry to discover that Emir has a debilitating drug habit; he in turn doesn't want to drag her into his world of drugs and crime. After numerous false starts, Emir announces to Saida and his brother that he intends to kick his drug habit and he proceeds to start sweating it out. Saida visits Lola to tell her that Emir has quit drugs for Lola's benefit, but she refuses to see him.

Emir goes into pre-fight training and is later told that it's to be a gloves-off bout without a time limit and that his opponent is his brother. Saida realises that her relationship with Emir is finished and the couple share a brief, bittersweet moment of parting. Lola appears; she and Emir make love for the first time. In the boxing ring, Emir beats his brother to a pulp but is then floored by him. After the fight, Emir and Lola leave together.

REVIEW

Yolande Zauberman's second feature after her critically well-received debut *Moi Ivan, toi Abraham* is a curiously lightweight affair that looks splendid but soon dissolves in the mind. If Kassovitz's *La Haine* can be said to have established the Parisian *banlieues* as a new cinematic topography to be explored and imaged, a landscape of otherness that serves to focus a whole host of pressing political and social issues – then *Clubbed to Death* is certainly in the current cycle of French *banlieue* films. But where, in *La Haine*, Vinz, Saïd and Hubert visited Paris almost as strangers, in *Clubbed* Elodie Bouchez as Lola reverses the trajectory, happening on the suburbs by accident and finding herself falling in love with Emir, a damaged, impotent boxer with a crippling cocaine habit.

One of the film's disappointments is that it does little to depart from the conventionally Parisian film narrative of twenty-something love angst. This may have something to do with the fact that Zauberman's co-screenwriter is Noémie Lvovsky, who scripted and directed the extraordinarily intense and harrowing *amour fou*-film, *Oublie moi*. Lvovsky's film was a kind of limit-case of amorous psychodrama, pushing post-coital tristesse into a realm of punishing extremity. Sadly, Zauberman doesn't attempt such an experiment. In fact, Lola comes across as something of a cipher – we know as little about her as does Emir, and Elodie Bouchez doesn't have the weight as an actress to invest her character with the degree of enigmatic depth that might compensate for this. Roschdy Zem is the film's most soulfully command-ing presence as Emir – a prowling, saturnine and affectingly bruised male. Zem deliv-ers, even in this underwritten role, on the promise he showed in Xavier Beauvois' *N'oublie pas que tu vas mourir*. It would be a real pleasure to see Zem stretching out, playing a character who is something other than a drug addicted *beur*, he's certainly one of the most interesting actors to emerge from the 'Young French Cinema' of the early 1990s. But he's given little to do here but play the good-hearted masochist, having to fight his brother in a gruelling no-holds-barred, gloves-off bout in order to settle his debts with a local drug baron.

That the film has been picked up for British distribution is probably on account of a combination of factors – the *banlieue* narrative having become a relatively famil-iar component of 'exportable' French film; the presence of Béatrice Dalle, at a pinch, reviving memories of her incendiary role in *Betty Blue* and the contemporary club soundtrack (which includes Massive Attack and The Chemical Brothers) – which will date the film very rapidly. If the music is one of the principal pleasures of *Clubbed to Death* it is also one of its major drawbacks. It's not so much that charges of the dreaded MTV aesthetic can be levelled at the film – more that Zauberman's over-reliance on the music bleeds the film of much needed character development and insight. That said, Denis Lenoir's camerawork is consistently impressive. Lenoir gives the club scenes real verve and renders the any-space-whatever bleakness of the *banlieue* landscapes with a lunar glow. But this doesn't save the film from being a strangely inconsequential experience; it's as if, for ninety minutes, we're watching the grandsons and daughters of Antonioni characters coming down from one too many Ecstasy trips. And who needs ecstasy when you've got angst?

FIN AOUT, DEBUT SEPTEMBRE

DIR: OLIVIER ASSAYAS FRANCE 1997

ORIGINALLY PUBLISHED IN *SIGHT AND SOUND* SEPTEMBER 1999

SYNOPSIS

Gabriel Desheys and his ex-girlfriend Jenny are selling their flat. Gabriel is also arranging for a television documentary to be made on his writer-friend Adrien Willer while also involved in a new relationship with the volatile Anne. Jenny calls Gabriel to hospital when Adrien unexpectedly collapses.

One month later, Adrien, out of hospital, travels with Gabriel to Mulhouse for the filming and admits that his attack signalled the return of a dormant and danger-ous disease. Anne shows up uninvited which leads to a row with Gabriel. Three months pass. Returning to Paris, Gabriel and Jenny dine together and argue. Adrien is admitted to hospital for an operation whose seriousness he admits only to Vera, a sixteen-year-old girlfriend whose existence he conceals from his friends.

Gabriel takes Anne to visit his family where his brother tells him he's a fool for splitting up with Jenny. Gàbriel accepts a job editing the literary section of an encyclopaedia and, with Adrien out of hospital, offers his friend some work. Adrien asks for time to consider. One evening, Gabriel and Anne have an argument when she discovers that he doesn't want them to live together. A phone call from Jeremy, Adrien's agent, informs Gabriel that Adrien has died. Adrien's posthumous book is critically well-received and Gabriel, having completed a ghost-writing assignment, admits to Anne that he has almost finished a novel. Jenny and Jeremy are now a couple.

REVIEW

In many respects, *Fin août, dèbut septembre* can't help but be seen as a follow-up to Olivier Assayas' 1997 cult success *Irma Vep*. And while Assayas could be said to have returned to subject matter characteristic of his previous films, the formal dexterity that Irma had shown to be in his grasp remains intact. *Fin août* follows the effects of the death of the writer Adrien Willer (played by Francois Cluzet with almost Hoffman-esque gravity) on a group of friends. The film's principle perspective is that of a younger friend and would-be writer, Gabriel Deshays, for whom Adrien is something of a mentor. Gabriel persuades Adrien to participate in a television documentary on his work and when the cynical producer asks 'Who reads Adrien Willer?' the film sets itself a task other than being a dramatic catalogue of the effects of bereavement within a tight social circle. *Fin août* is concerned with Adrien's social death more than his physical death, more interested in unravelling the complicated degrees of dependence and emotional vampirism that mark friendships inflected with artistic ambitions.

It would be fair to say that the territory of *Fin août, dèbut septembre* is familiar, not only from Assayas' previous films, but also as a larger strand of French cinema. The refined and psychologically acute depiction of urban middle-class manners is a mainstay of a certain strand of the national cinema. At its most superficial, this deliv-ers films such as Martine Dugowsan's *Portrait Chinois* where the privileged milieux of fashion, art and the media seemed to be the film's flimsy substance rather than its pretext and in which the angst of the characters appeared more as part of an aspirational package than as an acute symptom. But in *Fin août*, Assayas is closer to the world of Annaud Desplechin's *Comment je me suis dispute (ma vie sexuelle)*, an impression partly enforced by the casting of Mathieu Amalric and Jeanne Balibar. Amalric is a sympathetic presence as Gabriel, hinting at being clever but not necessarily smart and shading the character with intimations of the ambiguous power-play that centres on his, probably exaggerated, respect for Adrien's achievements. One feels that Gabriel admires, in a selfishly ambitious way, the fact that Adrien writes, rather than what he writes. His attempts to 'help' Adrien after a major operation are contextualised with rather cruel comedy. It transpires that it's Jenny, Gabriel's ex-girlfriend, in whom Adrien confides most. As Jenny, Jeanne Balibar confirms herself as one of the most fascinating of contemporary French screen actresses. Blessed with an unusual ability to express at least three conflicting emotions at any one time, Balibar has a skittish on-screen presence, all nose, eyebrows and gangling limbs, one that's focused by a repertoire of blazing looks and weird offbeat smiles. The intensity that she bought to the damaged young philosophy student in *Comment je me suis disputé* is here muted. She and Amalric, who are a couple off-screen, are perfecting an on-screen rapport that makes them the modern face of the thirty-something urban French couple and since *Fin août* they have been cast opposite each other in Jean-Claude Biette's *Trois ponts sur la rivière* (1998).

In their review of the film, *Cahiers du cinéma* rightly praised Assayas' *gravité legère*, his lightness of touch in addressing serious, 'adult' subject matter. It's in this feature that the film is most recognisably marked by the experiment of *Irma Vep*. That film's speed and economy, the sense it gave of a narrative assembled as it went along, is here taken further. In *Irma Vep* the over-riding idea might be said to have been the difficult act of relinquishing the weight of cinema history for a filmmaker only too aware of that pressing inheritance (Assayas was, after all, a *Cahiers* writer for many years). In *Fin août*, the act of relinquishing has a more intimate focus, it's not about the 'death of cinema' but the death of a friend and the 'lightness of touch' is worked at. Not that one notices on a first viewing, though. *Fin août* has the sensation and impact of a brilliantly executed meditative flurry. It used to be said of French art cinema that there was too much talking and Assayas seems to have come up with a simple solution to this cliché. His characters expound the best of them but he keeps them moving or surrounds them with an incessant motion that suggests the speed of the life that encircles them and that won't relax to make a reckoning with mortality any easier. Denis Lenoir's camera is almost always on the move, shoulder-borne and shuddering or looking for blurred close-up detail that's put to use in the film's transitional sequences. There's at least one moment of terrific formal control over the hand-held camerawork, close-up detail and editing when Anne, Gabriel's new girlfriend, rides off in a taxi after a row and buys a lottery scratchcard. It's nothing more than a transitional moment, a very brief snapshot of Paris-by-night that's not done by numbers, and it works to gently change the film's gears, to emphasise plasticity and rhythm. It's fascinating to see a director at work who can obviously handle the elegant, Téchiné-style anatomisation of emotions while still being capable of such a moment of stylistic *legerdemain*. Likewise, the film's organisation into four 'chapters' gives *Fin août* what might be called a cubist structure – Gabriel may be the privileged protagonist but the information that we get from his perspective is contextualised, questioned and offset by the perspectives of the other characters and this multi-focal narrative structure leaves much for second and third viewings.

It's probably excessive to suggest that Assayas has reinvigorated, if not rein-vented, the French art film in *Fin août*, but he demonstrates that it's possible still to make a film with character ambiguity, structural ambition and formal audacity that is both rewarding and moving.

ALICE ET MARTIN
DIR: ANDRE TECHINE FRANCE 1997
ORIGINALLY PUBLISHED IN *SIGHT AND SOUND* DECEMBER 1999

SYNOPSIS

Martin Sauvagnac, aged ten, is encouraged by his mother to visit his father, Victor, whom he's never met before. Although illegitimate, the young Martin fits into his real family where he grows up among his half-brothers, François, Frédéric and Benjamin.

Ten years pass and Martin flees the family house after the death of his father. After three weeks living rough he goes to Paris where he turns up at Benjamin's flat. Benjamin shares the apartment with his friend Alice, Martin moves in and falls into modelling, through which he becomes rich and successful. To Benjamin's resentment, Alice and Martin become a couple. They travel to Spain. When Alice tells him she's pregnant, Martin collapses and is hospitalised. Martin recovers and they move into a small cottage by the sea. He declares that, despite having run out of money, he has given up modelling. Terrified by the prospect of imminent fatherhood, Martin reveals to Alice the cause of his father's death. The family business was floundering and François, who was struggling to keep it afloat, committed suicide. Unable to participate in the family's grief, Martin planned to leave. When Victor tried to stop him they struggled and Martin pushed him down the stairs, killing his father. Martin fled.

Having heard Martin's account, Alice attempts to reassure him that he believes the death was accidental. Martin, however, is convinced he is guilty of murder. They return to Paris where Martin commits himself to a psychiatric clinic and Alice undertakes to deliver a letter from him to his step-mother, Lucie. Alice encounters obstruction from Frédéric. Martin declares that he wishes to hand himself over to the police and asks Lucie to testify as a witness. Alice meets Benjamin who tells her that, because of his brother's political ambitions, the family is obliged to testify and that Martin will be tried. Alice returns to Paris and Martin is discharged from the clinic. He turns himself over to the police and is detained. Alice waits for the decision and the birth of their child.

REVIEW

With his thirteenth feature, André Téchiné reveals himself as the French master when it comes to dissecting male hysteria. From the outset Martin, the illegitimate scion of a wealthy provincial bourgeois family is damaged goods. The short opening sequence that sketches his childhood has Martin attempting to persuade his father that he's ill. Victor Sauvegnac, the cold, business-like patriarch who sired Martin on a local hairdresser and then denied his existence for ten years, refuses to believe him. From hereon in, the film charts first the symptoms and then the causes of Martin's frail psychological state. After his father's death – the circumstances of which are only revealed in a lengthy flashback midway through the film – Martin flees into the countryside where he hides out like a hunted animal for three weeks. Picked up by police, then discharged, he hitches to Paris, showing up at Benjamin, his half-brother's, flat. Here he meets Alice, an initially brittle and impatient presence who describes the curious interloper as 'an extra-terrestrial hobo'. She too is psychologically delicate; her sister having died young, leaving Alice to negotiate her warring feelings of residual grief and filial jealousy. But her life with Benjamin, a struggling gay actor played by Mathieu Amalric as the live-wire black sheep of the Sauvegnac family, has allowed them both to find an asexual equilibrium. 'We take turns at being each other's child,' is Benjamin's analysis of their relationship, but this is transformed into barely-repressed anger and bitterness first when Alice and Martin become a couple and then when Alice takes it upon herself to explore the background to Martin's crippling sense of guilt over his father's death.

Téchiné's been here before, most recently in *Les Voleurs* (1997), where he explored the internal dynamics of a crime dynasty. It was the generic element of that film that felt a little forced but it certainly relates to *Alice et Martin*. There's the same concern with an oppressive family inheritance but here the issues of law and 'the family business' (in the case of the Sauvegnac family, local manufacturing and political interests, rather than criminal activity) are more subtly interrelated. In fact, one possible reading of the film is as a complex exploration of issues of blame, personal reponsibility and victimhood.

Téchiné explicitly treats the film as a case study. When Alice asks Martin to tell her about his 'flight' from the family, she uses the French word *fugue*, which has a clear psychoanalytic application here as a state in which the subject loses awareness of their identity and, indeed, flees their usual environment. So, in short, the film is another French examination of a young man's growth, via crisis, to responsibilty and maturity. Martin's 'crisis' is triggered by Alice's pregnancy, unleashing a double-barrelled stock of guilt relating to François' suicide and what Martin has convinced himself is his own parricide. Téchiné makes impending fatherhood the explcit trigger; we go into the flashback off the moment when Martin touches Alice's growing belly.

Alice et Martin is a work of density and powerful emotion, its melodramatic potential contained by superb performances all round. Newcomer Alexis Loret is shifty, pale and sympathetic as Martin. Binoche (who Téchiné has directed once before in *Rendezvous* (1985), early in her career) develops her character with a charged finesse, undertaking her quest with the full realisation that she too has a path to adult love before her, via Martin's self-realisation. If this is 'literary' filmmaking it is so in the best sense; in the richness of its characterisation and the acuity of its structure. Cold melodrama, psyched-up Bressonian case study, *Alice et Martin* is a masterly opening-up of classical French *intimiste* themes.

THE YOUNG FRENCH CINEMA: ON FRENCH FILM IN THE 1990s
ORIGINALLY PUBLISHED IN *SIGHT AND SOUND* DECEMBER 1999

In Alexandre Astruc's 1948 essay 'Towards a new avant-garde: le *caméra-stylo*', he argued for a form of cinema that allowed for as much personal expressiveness as the novel (hence the invocation of the camera as pen). More recently, in *French Cinema since 1950: Personal Histories*, Emma Wilson suggested that 'the phantom of the auteur still haunts French cinema'. Judging from the films of *le jeune cinema francais* (the Young French Cinema), so do the phantom's sons, daughters and grand-children. Throughout the 1990s a generation of French film-makers has been stub-bornly reassessing the myth of the auteur and revitalising its place within an industry and film culture that alternately supports and looks askance at such film-making.

The films of the Young French Cinema (YFC) do not have the 1980s ad-man's gloss of the French *cinéma du look*, and in many ways they can be seen as a reaction against this highly exportable style that exploited the *lingua franca* of television and music video. Nor are they the high-profile, big-budget heritage exercises that French costume dramas so often become. The YFC comprises of up-and-coming auteur talents, but what is meant by 'young' within this sobriquet requires some qualification. One need not have been a twenty-something tyro to be seen as part of this generation. Eric Zonca, whose *La vie rêvée des anges* (1998) is a key film of the YFC, was forty when he made his debut. Yet the term had a currency in 1990s France that has been both positively and negatively inflected, depending on where one stands on the place of auteur cinema within the French film industry. A selective list of representative YFC titles that have been distributed in the UK would include: *Don't Forget You're Going to Die* (*N'oublie pas que tu vas mourir*, Xavier Beauvois, 1995), *Will it Snow for Christmas?* (*Y'aura-t-il de la neige à nöël?*, Sandrine Veysset, 1996), *My Sex Life* ('*Comment je me suis disputé ... (ma vie sexuelle)*', Arnaud Desplechin, 1996), *Irma Vep* (1996) and *Late August, Early September* (*Fin août, début septembre*, Olivier Assayas, 1998). One could extend this selection further back to include other significant films such as *Les roseaux sauvages* (André Téchiné, 1993), *Savage Nights* (*Les nuits fauves*, Cyril Collard, 1992) and *A World without Pity* (*Un monde sans pitié*, Eric Rochant, 1989). There is a decade's worth of work here, and while key films may well have reached a small number of British screens, little sense of their cultural or industrial context has travelled with them. If it is too soon to provide a 'portrait of a generation', it is nevertheless possible to outline the impact and repercussions of *le jeune cinéma français* in France.

At first sight, the 1990s were a remarkably productive decade for French cinema. The 1998 figures for box-office admissions were the highest for thirteen years at 170.1 million and production levels reached the record level of 183 feature films. But explore the figures generated by the Centre Nationale de la Cinématogra-phie (CNC) further and the picture of the French film industry looks decidedly less rosy. Particularly when one learns that the share of these record admissions enjoyed by French films was an all-time low of 27%, significantly down from its regular market share of around 35%. Add to this the unprecedented level of production of first features, 58 in 1998, the highest figure in two decades, and one gets the picture of an ever-increasing number of films competing for an ever-diminishing audience.

From October 1998, two Parisian art cinemas ran a month-long retrospective of sixty films devoted to the output of France's young directors. Covering the event in *Libération*, Gérard Lefort observed 'This movement already has its illustrious elders (Desplechin, Cédric Kahn, Catherine Corsini, Pascale Ferran) and its young newcomers (Gaël Morrel, François Ozon).' Noting how many of the films not only share actors and actresses but also scriptwriters and technicians, Lefort added, 'it's evident that an absent and somewhat traumatic grandfather lurks in the vicinity of these films. In the best cases, it's Maurice Pialat that haunts them all'. Pialat is an important reference; along with André Téchiné, Phillipe Garrell, Catherine Breillat (and, yes, John Cassavetes), he is one of the elder avatars of the YFC. Uncompromisingly confrontational and single-mindedly psychodramatic, Pialat's cinema is characterised by an intimate realism often derived from the gruelling encounter between director and actor. For the sake of a mini-genealogy of Pialat's influence on the YFC, one must invoke Cyril Collard who worked as an assistant director on *A nos amours* (To our Loves, 1983) and whose own feature *Les nuits fauves* extended Pialat's conception of an auteur cinema of first-person emotional directness. Beyond Collard, whose early death from AIDS saw him sanctified as a star-martyr/auteur of French cinema, the cinema of Xavier Beauvois and Noémie Lvovsky continues this strand of self-immolating intensity. It is the overridingly *intimiste* register of the YFC that has frequently provoked hostility in France and which tends to boil down to persistent accusations that this is a cinema that's *intello* and *nombriliste* – 'intellectual' and 'navel-gazing'. To its numerous vocal detractors, the YFC is solely by and about a bunch of privileged, bourgeois thirty-something former students publicly picking over their trivial emotional travails. As gross as this caricature may be, it has given rise to the idea of a kind of YFC genre film – the intimate, polyvocal ensemble piece rendered in the style of choral chamber cinema. In many ways, these are as much actors' films as they are auteur pieces (many of the YFC 'faces' turn to directing as well as assisting with screenplays). The extent to which this cinema's actors and actresses have come to define their 'generation' has passed largely unremarked in the UK but in France it has been this wealth of new screen talent that has lent the YFC a coherent identity.

In May 1997, the French film journal *Positif* published a dossier titled '40 Young French actors' commenting that 'Even more than the directors, screenwriters or producers they [the actors] are shaping the image of our cinema ... none of them is a *vedette*, even less a 'star' in the classic, mythical sense of the term ... when one watches them at work it is not the personality that asserts itself but the character. Not the presence but the role.' Later, and with slightly backhanded emphasis, *Positif* notes, 'It's as if the ever-present second-role personnel of French cinema were stepping into the limelight.' Many of the names *Positif* mentions have featured in French films that have received UK releases during the 1990s. So actors like Mathieu Amalric and Emmanuel Salinger, Philippe Torreton and Charles Berling, actresses such as Jeanne Balibar and Emanuelle Devos, Nathalie Richard and Virginie Ledoyen have, steadily and collectively, become the faces of contemporary French film. If the ensemble style of acting is one of the features of the YFC, this feature extended out to media characterisations of the YFC as a unified 'group' of directors and actors. This was particularly the case with Arnaud Desplechin whose two films *La Sentinelle* (1993) and *Comment je me suis disputé ... (ma vie sexuelle)* explored and extended what became known as *la bande de Desplechin*. Working with Salinger, Seigneur,

Devos, Podalydes, Amalric and Balibar, Desplechin became associated with a hard-core grouping at the heart of the YFC. Each of these actors have gone on to have independent careers beyond this rather claustrophobic 'clan' but the idea of the YFC as a group was well expressed by the veteran French director Romain Goupil who, in an interview in *Le Monde*, observed that 'the films of the young French cinema are often explorations of the idea of 'the group', of generations, of the sense of belonging to self-acknowledging circles, even if it's not always formulated quite like that. The characteristics of a generation can only be perceived retrospectively but a '68 generation definitely exists.'

If the idea of 'the group' persists around the YFC it does so in several ways: as an atomised *groupuscule* (to bowldlerise from the argot of May '68) within the French film industry that has a reflexive cultural-political role; as a manner of dealing with the still-powerful memory of '68 as a moment of short-lived and utopian collectivity; and as a way of reflecting – in an often microcosmic fashion – upon the deep and widening social rifts in France. Whether the 'groups' depicted are those of the medical, diplomatic and academic worlds explored by Desplechin, or the cultural and artistic circles of Assayas, or the underprivileged rural and industrial communities of Zonca, Veysset and Laetitia Masson, each contributes an element of askance social analysis that belies the received idea that the YFC is comprehensively and exclusively hermetic and self-absorbed. In 1998, Claude-Marie Trémois, film editor on the French weekly listings magazine *Télérama*, published a book entitled *Les Enfants de la Liberté: le jeune cinéma français des années 90s* which, while not offering much in the way of critical analysis, isolates the political events of February 1997 as the moment when the YFC as an entity came to widespread public attention. Directors Desplechin and Pascale Ferran responded to the French Court's judgement on one Mme Jacqueline Deltombe, found guilty of having sheltered a Zairean friend whose immigration status, as a person *sans papiers* was deemed 'irregular'. Between them, the two film-makers organised an initial petition of 59 co-signatories against this judgement that was almost exclusively comprised of young French film-makers. Aside from what *Positif* remarked on as the evidently 'powerful feminisation of the profession, 22 of the 59 being women film-makers', this initial petition unleashed an impressive wave of support and mass demonstrations. That a group of 'navel-gazing' cineastes should organise and galvanise such a wide-reaching solidarity campaign calling for civil disobedience was unheard of. This was a demonstration protesting the perceived corruption of the letter of French law but that can also be seen as a generation's focused expression of rage against what was dubbed the 'Le Pen-isation of minds' as well as disgust at a left-wing government's collusion with racist political discourse.

The issue of the YFC as a marginal cinema for a minority audience raises more pressing cultural questions in France than it does in the UK, where the idea and presence of an auteur cinema carries considerably less, if any, historical freight. In the UK, an auteur is cinematically 'other', automatically 'foreign', a provocation to our cinema's tepid populism. What disturbs about the hostility that is levelled at the YFC within France is that a similar discourse has become popularly prevalent, one that is embodied in the accusations of 'navel-gazing' and that bleeds into industry declarations that this a genre that is self-absorbed, over-subsidised and under-frequented. It needs to be demonstrated that this is a party line that operates within the French industry for very specific reasons and has done so for decades, and one in which the role of the scriptwriter is seen to be undervalued, if not entirely neglected, by the YFC. If one approaches the practice of film-making from the historical example of the *nouvelle vague*, and the YFC is in many crucial respects its direct inheritor, then the scriptwriter is either the director or the director's close collaborator. But the conception of the script is as a process, an element in the envisioning of the director's film. It is not seen as a commodity that can be passed from one director to the next (consider, in this respect, Truffaut's polemic against the sovereignty of scriptwriters Aurenche and Bost as characteristic of the academicism of pre-*nouvelle vague* French cinema). The auteur spirit of the original *nouvelle vague*, a movement birthed by maverick critics turned maverick directors, has since become institution-alised in bodies such as the French national film school, FEMIS (Fondation pour l'enseignement des metiers de l'image et du son) and supported by the French state through its extensive system of film subsidies. It does not take much imagina-tion to extrapolate from this that the mainstream of the French film industry, those who Godard dubs 'the professionals of the profession', should mightily resent such recognition and support of French cinema's maverick auteur strand.

The role of script and scriptwriter alike focuses a number of issues concerning the YFC, its investment in auteurist film-making and its 'cultural' position within the French industry. Someone well qualified to respond to the industry characterisation of the YFC as neglecting scriptwork is Pascal Bonitzer. For many years a critic on *Cahiers du cinéma*, Bonitzer has been writing scripts for directors such as Jacques Rivette, Raul Ruiz and André Téchiné for twenty years as well as having taught in the script department of FEMIS (where his students included Noémie Lvovsky and Sophie Fillières] and has recently turned to directing with *Encore* (1996) and *Rien sur Robert* (1999). 'The young French film-makers that I know, on the contrary, do an enormous amount of work on their screenplays,' Bonitzer asserts '[They] devote much greater care to the screenplay than was shown at the time of the new wave. Their screenplays are highly written and very worked at.' As for the mainstream industry opinion of YFC scripts, Bonitzer says 'I think that it's a discourse that comes from the fact that the industry, or the 'commercial cinema', desires screenplays that are formatted on models that come from the 'commercial cinema'. The reproach they level at the young auteur cinema is not to say they don't know how to write screenplays – often they're more intelligent, vibrant and strong than those emerging from 'commercial cinema' – but that they don't write them according to the com-mercial norms.'

An additional perspective on the more general issue of pre-production within the French system is supplied by the independent producer Humbert Balsan. Having produced the first film by the untried Sandrine Veysset *Y' aura-t-il de la neige à noël?*, which was a popular success in France, gaining over a million admissions, Balsam's response to the issue of how a 'small', auteur debut can reach an audience in an over-populated market is highly illuminating: 'One doesn't know for sure if a film's going to work because cinema isn't a rational industry. So, in order to rationalise things a producer requires a little more latitude to develop projects. The system is a little biased: from the moment one starts working on a film one is condemned to make it. For me this isn't so serious as I don't get things wrong too often. But there are enough films that would benefit from being developed further. Why are certain films made? Because a million has been spent in development and it is necessary to make this money pay. If an independent production company does not make the film, it goes under. The single powerful factor that American cinema has in comparison to ours is that it is able to develop its projects infinitely and to stop when necessary.' The YFC, then, is then a cinema rife with productive contradictions. A largely state-subsidised cinema of dissent, whose aesthetic programme is part of a larger one of cultural politics that attempts to resist the American hegemony barely concealed by the term 'globalisation'. A cinema of 'youth' that is consciously continuing an older tradition of film-making inaugurated by the New Wave. An intimist, 'navel-gazing' cinema obsessively focused on groups and the self in relation to 'the other'. A cinema seemingly despised by the maintream industry that has nonetheless served as the forcing-house for a generation of acting and directing talents that this industry then takes up.

3

CINEMA EXPLODED:
FILM, VIDEO AND THE GALLERY

In the 1980s, when a reasonably-sized but rapidly diminishing circuit still existed, I spent my time in London repertory cinemas. In the 1990s I found myself going to galleries, which were themselves being increasingly colonised by the moving image. Was there a relationship between the waning of one and the emergence of the other? Why had cinema migrated into the gallery? The horizon against which this has happened is one shaped by a variety of phenomena; the multiplex monopoly of exhibition ensures that the Hollywood-dominated cinematic monoculture is stronger than ever before; the proliferation of image-toys and vision-machines, from video-games to WAP phones, has further domesticated our relationship to the moving image. The viewer – like the reader – has ceased to be seen as a culturally-engaged citizen and is appealed to as a consumer above all. So the gallery might be seen as having become an alternative site, something of a refuge that resists the speed, flux and technological blur of the spectacular world surrounding it, a still centre in the image-storm.

The overlap of gallery and cinema begs the question of the correct critical language with which to address the interpenetrating worlds of film and art. I may be exaggerating my sense of how 'critical correctness' comes into play here, but I'm aware that it is legitimate for art critics to address cinema; they have had to do so in the last decade, just in order to keep track of the number of artists morphing into film-makers. But why does it seem to be less legitimate for film critics to write about cinematic imagery in the gallery? Perhaps it can be put down to a respectable reticence to engage with work that, once placed in a gallery context, calls upon a range of art-critical precepts that require some familiarity with the vocabulary of conceptual and minimalist art. Perhaps it also has something to do with a generation of critics for whom the tradition of experimental cinema barely registers and which removes a crucial set of references by which to approach the genre of what I will call the gallery-film, many of which are revisiting and reshaping tropes, such as re-filming and multiple-projection, that are familiar from experimental film. However, it seems possible for a film critic to address gallery works that either recontextualise pre-existing film fragments or that employ elements of film grammar precisely because of the critic's presumed familiarity with such grammar.

In the UK during the 1990s, it was probably easier to make a certain kind of questing, low-budget film if you called yourself an artist rather than a film-maker. From this perspective there's a healthy pragmatism at work, one that acknowledges the greatly diminished opportunities available for what used to be called 'independent' film-making, where television has largely given up on commissioning work of an 'experimental' nature and with the possibilities for cinematic outlets being restricted to specialist festivals and underground film clubs. There's also a hybridisation of artistic roles becoming visible that responds to the increasing hybridity of visual media.

Artists, by necessity, cross the borders between corporate and cultural worlds just like film-makers. So, from this practical perspective, the gallery can be seen as having become the *de facto* home for an alternative cinema. It is now, and all at once, the holding-space for the development of what Raymond Bellour calls a future 'other cinema'[1] as well as being a forcing-house for the radical fracturing of the forms of cinematic narrative and exhibition. The gallery is now a repository for the splinters and debris of cinema, which has not so much 'expanded', to employ Gene Youngblood's prescient late-1960s terminology, as exploded. And video is clearly the agent that has enabled the overlap of film and gallery.[2]

Perhaps inevitably, the material in this section has something of a miscellaneous character to it and takes in video-in-film and video-art, essay-films and found-footage work. Such work has either emerged from or been shown in an art context, has existed outside of cinema 'proper', or has, by the skin of its teeth, found some low-level television broadcast-life. What unites such works is less their generic affinities than the way in which video and digital technologies have been used, either to explore cinema as a subject matter or to point to future formal possibilities that call on older traditions of work. This introduction will attempt less to provide a detailed analysis of each of this section's constituent terms – film, video and the gallery – than to describe some of the tendencies that have made it interesting to write about each of them and the passages between them. This miscellaneous collection of works is also somewhat esoteric in nature but, I believe, representatively so. That is to say, such works fall outside of traditional exhibition and distribution systems and have generally to be sought out, otherwise they fall off the map. The function of the critic should, in part, be one of exploration – the uncharted territories of the future will not only be the film festival but the gallery, the website and the low-profile video-distribution agency. In short, for the critic to find the cinema of the future it won't be enough just to go to the movies.

My interest in video began while studying at the University of Warwick, where I was doing researching into the debates around the status of the image that were active in France in the 1980s. And while there was a great deal of writing on video-art available none of it had made much of an inroad within Film Studies, which struck me as an odd oversight. How was it possible to study film in the midst of its absorption into another technological sphere without in some way engaging with the agent of that process? To discover the work of the French theorist Raymond Bellour was therefore something of a liberation. Here was a writer who had long been engaged in highly detailed film analysis and was dealing with the transformations of the image in systematic and imaginative ways. Stranger still, Bellour's work on this subject remains mostly untranslated, ten years after it first emerged in French.[3] He was, however, invited to London to present a lecture at The National Film Theatre in 1991 and it was that event, as well as reading the essays, that made me realise that it was going to be difficult to write about film in the 1990s without broaching Bellour's insights. I was also fortunate enough to have done a number of freelance jobs that deepened my interest in video and the issue of how, as an art and technology, it might relate to film. Between 1995 and 1996 I worked for the London-based Film and Video Umbrella, a body that, then as now, curates and distributes artists' work in film and video. This proved to be a crash-course in absorbing a 'new' genre of video-art which overlapped with the occasional pieces I was writing on video for the art magazine 'Frieze'. It was an interesting time to be engaged with the form partly because, with only a few years hindsight, it became clear that two significant developments had been underway. The first of these involved the increasing visibility of the moving-image in gallery spaces. The high-profile phenomenon of 'young British art' saw video become an absolutely orthodox component of artists' practice. In addition, if slightly later, the arrival of digital video would herald a minor revolution in film production, from Dogme 95's revitalisation of European art-cinema to films such as *The Blair Witch Project* and *The Matrix* being seen as polar-opposite signals of what was possible in American cinema with the arrival of such technology. Later still, I was involved in using digital video to make reportage pieces on film and the arts for a production company providing programmes for pay-TV channels. This exposed me to some of the practical conditions of the media transformations underway. But everything I was trying to work through in writing about video was originally spurred by Bellour's theoretical insights and which require some introduction.

In the winter of 1990, the Centre Georges Pompidou in Paris hosted a major multi-media exhibition, 'Passages de l'Image'. In the catalogue, the curators Raymond Bellour, Catherine David and Christine van Assche, explained that the exhibition arose 'from the desire to understand what has been happening in and between images from the moment when it has become plain that one can no longer speak of the cinema, photography, painting.' They continue, 'because we have entered a time of crisis in the image, touching on the nature of images themselves'.[4] 'Passages de l'image' cystallised those theoretical debates around the image and its 'crisis' that assumed a central significance in French film criticism during the 1980s. Including essays by Raymond Bellour, Serge Daney, Pascal Bonitzer and Jacques Aumont, the catalogue stands as a primer of the positions taken within these debates. The 'crisis' is seen to stem from the modern proliferation of the image, its extreme mobility, its having become both omnipresent and banal, a part of the furniture. The image that passes through the audiovisual circuit, according to Marc Chevrie, 'is no longer an image of something, it is the image for itself, pure exchange-value, definitively stripped of transparence, which neither dissimulates nor represents anything but another image.'[5] 'Why is there such fierce resistance to the linking of culture and technology' Armand Mattelart asked in 1984 and in doing so suggested a link between the exhibition, its critical assumptions and the changing audiovisual environment. 'Why have intellectuals so long been reticent not only in analysing the apparatus of cultural massification but above all in posing, other than in terms of sheer indifference or elitism, the problem of their own relations with the media?'[6] 'Passages de l'image' attempted to respond to this question, especially through the contribution of Raymond Bellour whose writing in the 1980s increasingly saw photography, cinema and video as functions of one another and inextricably linked.

The critical work undertaken in France during the 1980s and early 1990s constantly refers back to the modernist auteur-cinema as an ideal as, to use Bellour's words, an example of 'cinema as an ideal point located in the past … this nostalgic point'.[7] It is the 'inbetween-ness' of images that Bellour's writing emphasises. More than any other critic of the period his work accepts that cinema is no longer identical with itself, that it has lost its autonomy and is now one more station through which the image circulates. This acceptance is by no means simple. It has first to be preceded by the acknowledgement that relates to three media and one, infinitely divisible, consequence: 'the mixing, the contamination, the passage or movements between images that have accumulated at the convergence of three techniques and three arts: photography, cinema and video'.[8] The significance that Bellour invests in video is by virtue of its being 'the agent of all these passages between images'. Bellour's work has been largely concerned with providing a genealogy of the image-in-transit and, as such, comes closest of all the work in this period to providing the vestiges of a theoretical model. Its influence can be seen in a number of the essays that follow, especially those that either interpret the presence of the video-image in cinema or that deal with the surveillance image.

If cinema was an invention 'without a future', then video-art is one without a history. Self-electedly so, it appears. It's almost as though the form had internalised the conditions of its own technology, its memory being determined by its means of production, rewinding and erasing the multifarious pasts that make up its 40 year history. This has had a curious effect over the last decade in the UK, where a new generation of artists has elected to work with video and, in so doing, has frequently aped the work of innovators in the form such as Vito Acconci, Bruce Nauman and Marina Abramovic almost as though they had never existed. In fact, it took two exhi-bitions in the UK to bring to light the extent to which this 'young' generation was, in fact, slightly older than it appeared.[9] The major difference between the 'old' and the 'new' video art was that, where previously video had been very much outside the gallery – frequently antagonistic towards its institutionalised space, as it had been towards the institutionalised time of television – the moving image has now become fully installed within the gallery. In fact, the moving image has become installed just about everywhere else as well. So the 40-year history of video-art is one that runs parallel with the multiple mutations of the moving image: the waning and fragmenta-tion of cinema, the growth and tyranny of television, the arrival of new digital image-toys.

READY-MADE, RE-MAKE, RE-MIX: CINEMA REMEMBERED

'Cinema is young, only a hundred years old, but for us it's already dead. We've grown up with the video-recorder, perhaps it's as simple as that.'
 – Douglas Gordon[10]

The 1990s saw us size up to an excess of endtimes – centennial, millennial and digi-tal. There was a stopwatch certainty in the air, the weight of the centuries condensed to a matter of minutes, to countdown-time. As the ticking of history got progres-sively louder the art gallery became a combination of autopsy room and laboratory in which artists undertook a pathological dissection of film grammar and cinema his-tory. Steve McQueen and Sam Taylor-Wood, Gillian Wearing and Douglas Gordon all seem to have been working with 'cinema' as their material while using video and film as tools to engage with their own individual fragments of the collective memory of cinema. What can we call this sort of work? Filmic ready-mades or conceptualist remakes? Re-film, re-mix, re-stage; it was all to do with remembering. And nowhere was this more evident than in the work on Hitchcock (with Hitchcock? through Hitchcock?) that became a defining feature of contemporary art's relationship with cinema. To the extent that, by the end of 1999, a collection of such work, 'Notorious:

Alfred Hitchcock and Contemporary Art', showed in Oxford and Sydney, Australia. Why Hitchcock? It was as if the pieces collected in this exhibition wished to reveal the interior workings of the films, to show the hand of Hitchcock at work within our cinematic memories and to sink further into the films' self-reflexive embrace. The most celebrated of them, Douglas Gordon's *24 Hour Psycho* (1993), ticked out its frames, a slow-motion video flick-book of memory. It might have been shaped to the size of the hole through which Norman Bates spied on Marion Crane, but instead was a monumental screen-installation on which a decelerated video-projection of Hitchcock's masterpiece edged its way, slowly, obsessively and inexorably through eternity and a day.[11]

'Should we so readily applaud the blurring of boundaries between the artist's studio and the film studio?' an art critic asked, surveying a number of the major art and film shows that were being staged in the run-up to the centenary of cinema. 'The Italian Futurist Marinetti once called the museum a sepulchre and an ossuary for dead art. The worst cases of this crossover phenomenon conform to this model by deploying a blatant nostalgia for a culture of film – both commercial and experimental – that may no longer exist. It's this question of the potential death of cinema as an art form that underlies all these exhibitions and which is foregrounded in MoCA's [Los Angeles Museum of Contemporary Art] question 'what is – or was – the cinema?'[12] A few years on from these centennial shows, what has become evident is how they announced the desire of artists to work with cinema both as raw material and as a language. My insistence on the importance of video in the development of this genre of work is that it had not only established the presence of the moving image in the gallery but had also developed a repertoire of installation and environmental spaces by which to stage such images. However, those works that take pre-existing films as their material invariably confront their spectators with general questions about cinema that arise from the particularities of the films that the works re-contextualise. Writing about *24 Hour Psycho*, Stephane Delorme has suggested that 'Douglas Gordon's work re-orients the problem of the [filmic] work towards its reception: towards perception, memory, imagination or, in this case, the gesture of analysis (and not the method, nor the content)'.[13] Delorme usefully contrasts the current style of 'gallery-films' to the earlier deconstructive impulse of experimental films – in which individual fragments of cinema were treated and examined as 'found footage', or where the very apparatus of the cinematic experience was broken down into fragments – and concludes that the 'gallery-film' approaches cinema from a 'conceptual' rather than a 'plastic' point-of-view. Even while some of the tropes and processes of experimental film are visible in such work, the contact with the material of film that marked experimental cinema – consider how the direct intervention into the film material, a 'defacing' of the emulsion, bespeaks the characteristic 'anti-illusionist' gesture – is much less a feature of the gallery-film.

On one hand, cinema features in the gallery as a fetishised, found-footage fragment of its former self. As a spur to collective memory but equally as an element of filmic grammar, or what Michael Tarantino has called 'the grace notes' of a film, the tiny, almost imperceptible details, the peripheral elements or snatches of a scene which, when 'freed' from narrative, become memory-shards, elliptical moments.[14] In the gallery, where an orthodox conceptual art resistance to narrative holds sway, cinema's narrative imperative is replaced by an appeal to the spectator's memory. The film's story becomes less significant than our part in cinema's history. Again, the part and the whole. On the other hand, certain artists have chosen not simply to recontextualise pre-existing fragments of film but to re-stage and inhabit them – the re-make revisited. Pierre Huyghe and Mark Lewis have both explored this approach. Lewis has named his aesthetic the 'part-cinema', one that 'enjoys a dialectical relationship to the dramatic whole. These bits of cinema that I have been making are only possible because of the totalising dream of the traditional dramatic cinema.'[15] In approaching cinema as both a historical corpus of work and an industrial process, Lewis has detached and concentrated on industrial components such as the credit sequence (*Two Impossible Films* 1995–97) and the film pitch (*The Pitch* 1998) while also 're-making' classic moments from cinema's history, reprising the legendary seven-minute of mobile camera-work that opens Welles' *Touch of Evil* (1958), for example, but shooting it upside-down (*Upside Down Touch of Evil*, 1997) and remaking moments from Michael Powell's *Peeping Tom*. While I admit to finding Lewis's work curiously academic there is, nevertheless, something fascinating in the residual faith it betrays in what one might call the 'gestures' of film-making and in the desire to repeat the gestures of master-directors. Additionally, Lewis has made a statement that not only resonates across many of the 'gallery-films' but also informs essayistic films that deal explicitly with cinema and memory, when he admits 'My sense of most films is remembering a few great moments. A few interesting moments, that's all. Most film is story-telling. And perhaps story-telling is not the most interesting part of the cinema.'[16]

The phenomenon of the 're-make' executed as a conceptual exercise is one in which the exactness of the replicated gesture paradoxically speaks about the historical distance of the original's mastery and, at the same time, the wish to bring it closer. It is a phenomenon that has not been restricted to the rarified enclave of the gallery where a conceptual-art alibi comes into play around the process of recontextualising the filmic object and cinematic gesture. Gus Van Sant's re-make of *Psycho* (1998) can safely be considered as a conceptualist gesture precisely because it was made for the cinema and not the gallery. It is a feature film with a conceptualist sensibility to the extent that it acknowledges the impossibility inherent in all such remakes. While reassembling with pathological fidelity Hitchcock's shot-by-shot skeleton, the skin in which Van Sant adorns it can only make us think of the director as Norman Bates. This time round, the body (of work) in the cellar is mummified in celluloid. I can think of two other examples in 1990s cinema that have explicitly engaged in similar terms with the problem of what might be called 'the anxiety of influence' that the remake entails. In Michelangelo Antonioni's return to feature filmmaking, *Beyond the Clouds* (1995), there is an short linking episode shot by Wim Wenders where the elderly couple of Marcello Mastroianni and Jeanne Moreau, who had previously appeared together in Antonioni's *La Notte* (1961), act out what can only be seen as a meditation on Wenders' own cinéphilic discipleship. Wenders' self-acknowledged cinéphilia, cystallised in his relationship to directors such as Yasujiro Ozu, Sam Fuller, Nicholas Ray and, in *Beyond the Clouds*, Antonioni, takes the traditional form of the homage. Here it is diverted through the art of painting and the epochal encounter between Cezanne and the Mont Saint-Victoire. It is a moment that I imagine could cause hilarity among contemporary artists for its naïve faith in

the very idea of formal mastery and in the absurdity of even hoping that, by repeat-
ing the painterly and, by extension, the cinematic gesture, something of that mastery
can be rediscovered, almost by osmosis. Yet, the dialectic played out in this scene
– between cinema and painting, disciple and master, modernism and post-modern
mannerism – contains the elements that are present in the gallery-film-remake's
own relationship to cinema history.[17] In Olivier Assayas' *Irma Vep* (1996), a similar
fable is enacted in the story of René Vidal, a faded French auteur who has taken
on the task of re-making an episode of *Les Vampires* by the silent cinema pioneer
Louis Feuillade. For Vidal, the re-make is 'blasphemy', and not just because it is a piece
of TV hack-work, which results in the director committing an act of creative self-
destruction by turning in an eloquently defaced assembly of shots. Assayas' choice
of scratched, distressed footage is entirely in keeping with what Stéphane Delorme
decribes as the 'paradoxical elegy' visible in the rhetorical act of 'defiguring the
admired object, [which is] never as beautiful than when threatened with disappearance.'[18] Vidal's impossible project of a re-make becomes an experimental film-poem
to the eroticised anguish he experiences in being unable to summon forth the ghost
of *Irma Vep* from the very grain of his film-stock.

The material in 'Cinema Exploded' is not organised chronologically but, respecting
the hybrid and trans-media character of the images it examines, follows a roughly
thematic trajectory. So, we progress from the moving-image in the gallery, through
video-art to video-in-film, found-footage film and essay films.

NOTES

1   Bellour, Raymond (2000) 'D'un autre cinema' in *Trafic*, Spring, 7.
2   Youngblood, Gene (1970) *Expanded Cinema* EP Dutton, New York.
3   Bellour, Raymond, Catherine David, et Christine Van Assche (1991)
        Passages de l'image. Editions Centre Pompidou, Paris; Bellour, Raymond
        (1990) *L'Entre-Images: Photo. Cinéma. Vidéo* Editions La Difference, Paris;
        Bellour, Raymond (1999) *L'Entre-Images 2: Mots, Images* Editions
        POL, Paris. English-language translations of certain key essays appear
        in *Camera Obscura* Number 24, September 1990. See also Bellour,
        Raymond and Mary Lea Bandy (1992) *Jean-Luc Godard: Son & Image
        1974-1991* Museum of Modern Art, New York.
4   *Passages de l'image*, 6
5   Chevrie, Marc, 'Le cinema contre l'image: la valeur-image', *Cahiers du
        cinéma* May 1987, 395/6, 29
6   Mattelart, Armand, Xavier Delcourt and Michelle Mattelart (1984)
        International Image Markets: In Search of an Alternative Perspective
        Comedia, London, 15.
7   From the Raymond Bellour lecture at the National Film Theatre, London,
        1 February 1991.
8   Bellour, Raymond (1991) 'The Power of Words, The Power of Images',
        Camera Obscura, 24, 7.
9   The shows in question were 'Acting Out. The Body in Video: Then and

Now', Royal College of Art, London; MA in Curating Degree Show, 1995; 'Bruce Nauman', Hayward Gallery, London, 16 July-6 September 1998. On the issue of video as a technology and as an artform with a 'forgotten' history see Ian Hunt 'Vide Video', Art Monthly, May1996,196, 3-7 and Catherine Elwes 'Videoscan', Art Monthly May, 1996, 196, 8-11. Also informative on the art/film overlap with an emphasis on the role of video is Catherine Elwes 'The Big Screen', Art Monthly, September 1996, 199, 11-16 and Michael O'Pray 'Movie Wannabes', Art Monthly, October 1997, 10, 1-6.

10   Cited in *L'Entre-Images* 2, 268

11   A.L. Rees compares *24 Hour Psycho* to 'a distant and presumably unrecog nised ancestor', Michael Snow's *Two Sides to Every Story* (1974). His contrasting of the two works' formal procedures and their interpel lation of the spectator provides valuable insights into the ways in which strategies from the filmic avant-garde have been passed along and trans- formed in the quarter-century separating the two works. See A *History of Experimental Film and Video: From the Canonical Avant-Garde to Contempo rary British Practice* , BFI Publishing, (1999),109.

12   Fogle, Douglas (1996) 'Cinema is Dead, Long Live Cinema', *Frieze*, 29, 32.

13   Delorme, Stephane (2000) 'Found Footage: mode d'emploi' *Cahiers du cinéma*, Hors-serie, May 1992.

14   'How He Does It or The Case of The Missing Gloves': Michael Tarantino in 'Notorious: Alfred Hitchcock and Contemporary Art', Curated by Kerry Brougher, Michael Tarantino and Astrid Bowron, MOMA, Oxford, 11 July-3 October 1999. Ps 22-32.

15   Mark Lewis in conversation with Jeff Wall, *Transcript*, 3, 3

16   Ibid.

17   For discussion of French critical debates around cinema and painting see Elsaesser,Thomas, 'Rivette and the end of cinema': *Sight and Sound*, April 1992 and Chris Darke 'Rupture, Continuity and Diversification: *Cahiers du cinéma* in the 1980s': *Screen*, 34, 4, Winter1993.

18   Delorme, 91.

ART AND FILM:
ON SPELLBOUND (HAYWARD GALLERY, LONDON,
FEBRUARY–MAY 1996) AND PANDAEMONIUM (INSTITUTE
OF CONTEMPORARY ARTS, LONDON, MARCH–APRIL 1996)

ORIGINALLY PUBLISHED IN *ARTISTS NEWSLETTER* JUNE 1996

Louis Lumière who, with his brother Auguste, was one of cinema's pioneers, famously pronounced their invention to be 'an art without a future'. One hundred years on and it might seem like sophism to suggest that Louis was not entirely wrong. While all that has followed cinema – TV, video and the new digital media – has inevitably defined itself against the aesthetic influence of the medium, cinema itself has been absorbed by the brave new multimedia world. With such transformations in mind, 'Spellbound: Art and Film' at the Hayward Gallery and 'Pandaemonium: The London Festival of Moving Images' at the Institute of Contemporary Arts took the centenary as the opportunity to explore cinema's pervasiveness in our visual culture by way of its encounter with art. And from the evidence of the work on show, and to bowdlerise Lumière, cinema might be seen less as 'an art without a future' than 'the future of art'. The future of young British art, that is. Self-consciously, and with differing degrees of success, both 'Spellbound' and 'Pandaemonium' shared the same fertile moment, one informed by cinema's centenary and current tendencies in British contemporary art. The inclusion of young artists in both shows – Jaki Irvine, Gillian Wearing, Mark Wallinger, Michael Curran and Keith Tyson in 'Pandaemomnium'; Douglas Gordon, Fiona Banner and Steve McQueen in 'Spellbound' – looked like being a useful way of dealing with the potentially overwhelming weight of cinema's history, as well as promising an investigation of how these artists dealt with the influence of cinema. Young British artists have been strongly associated with work in film, video and installation formats, as 'General Release' – the British Pavillion Show at the 1995 Venice Biennale – demonstrated. But what does it mean to describe such work as 'cinematic'?

To answer this question requires a detour via video, as the medium that has most facilitated the introduction of time-based moving-image work into the gallery. Since Nam June Paik's Fluxus-influenced 1960s work with televisions, and with the work of artists such as Gary Hill and Bill Viola, video-art has come of age in both installation and single-screen formats. Video might be said to have become an orthodox practice for post-minimal, conceptual artists. The installation that engaged most with issues arising from the relationship between film and video was at 'Spellbound'; Douglas Gordon's *24 Hour Psycho* is just what its title says it is – Hitchcock's 1960 film projected at approximately two frames per second. Or rather, a video-tape of the film, slowed-down and projected at one-thirteenth of the film's normal speed. Gordon's work gives the images of Hitchcock's film (and, significantly, not its sounds) another life at another speed in another space. The other life he seeks to reveal is what he has called 'the film's unconscious', sought out by projecting the film images at extreme slow-motion. The other space is that of the gallery. This is a space outside of the cinema auditorium, where an institutionalised simultaneity of pleasure and constraint is bound up with the narrative imperative of mainstream film, and away from the domestic VCR. It is a space that demands different kinds of spectatorship and in Douglas' piece slow-motion is both a function of and expression of that difference. Although it could be argued that with the appeal to duration that is one of its features, 24 Hour Psycho takes its place within a long tradition of video-art where duration has been explored as a specific technological and aesthetic quality of the medium. Alternatively, 24 Hour Psycho might also be seen as a joke on this much vaunted 'specificity' of video, its instantaneous delivery of a 'real-time' image, one without a delay. It is precisely the 'delay' of an initially agonising, slowly entrancing quality that the video-support allows for in the slowing-down of Hitchcock's film.

If Douglas's work is 'cinematic' in the sense of taking the fascination of cinema as its subject and a classic film (with no small debt to the filmic avant-garde itself, the shower sequence being an exercise in Eisensteinian montage par excellence) as the object of that fascination, Steve McQueen's Stage is cinematic in another, equally fascinating way. Stage is a film (insistently film, no video projection here, but a 16mm projector whirring fussily inside its booth) of a black man – McQueen himself – and a white woman – actor Margaret Kinnon – involved in an awkward, lurking ballet of desiring looks and ambiguous gestures set against a stark background of anonymous urban spaces. With its concentration on the black-and-white grain of its film-stock and the careful framings of its characters, Stage resembles a loving recreation of moments from Cassavetes' Shadows and Antonioni's L'Eclisse, classic art-cinema modernism reworked as the stage for a new black presence in those classic white spaces of cinema.

The installation space is one where the image exists as an object. But an object in time, as well as in space. The most interesting installations on show accommodated their spectators in ways that cinema can never do. In narrative cinema the spectator is stitched into film by virtue of montage. In installation work, the spectator is present, equally active as in a cinema but in a different fashion – they are called on to exercise a new skill, what one might call 'three-dimensional montage'. That said, at 'Blink: The Moving Image as Installation', a forum on the closing weekend of 'Pandaemonium', Raymond Bellour made the fascinating suggestion that the idea of the installation had in fact long been present in film sets, as dramatic and stylised environments 'installed' within a film's narrative space. Pieces such as Jaki Irvine's Losing Doris, Gillian Wearing's The Unholy Three and Michael Curran's Fistula (all exhibited in 'Pandaemonium') and Stage embodied their fractured, disembodied narratives in the environment of sounds, images and objects they create. Each piece put into play an articulation of selected cinematic elements – some attenuated, some recognisable, others deliberately absent – to call upon the spectator and the placing of that spectator to consider what it means to make a 'cinematic' spectacle of an image. Video installation might then be seen as a means of embodying the irreducible physicality of the moving image.

With its two seemingly still black and white photographs – one of a woman seated looking out at the observer and projected large-scale on a bare wall, the other taking up a small window frame – and its gently spoken text, Jaki Irvine's Losing Doris is a work about absence. An absence referred to in the title, in the perceived absence of movement in the images – one of which flutters tremulously for an instant, as if animated by a gust of wind or by the breeze of the spoken words – and an absence further highlighted by the missing protagonist. But this protagonist is present every time a spectator enters the space and is addressed as a character in a three dimensional shot/counter-shot exchange. The space in Irvine's piece is there to be filled, ready to accommodate its spectator/protagonist, but on its own terms. Gillian Wearing's *The Unholy Three* held its spectator at a vigilant distance, opening the space between its three screens and its seating as one of scrutiny. Each of the onscreen participants are real-life performers, characters in the private films of their own lives. Possibly more than any of the other works, Wearing's extends the tradition of video-and-performance into an engagement with television conventions of fly-on-the-wall voyeurism.

Alongside specially commissioned installation works, 'Pandaemonium' comprised associated screenings of almost two hundred single-screen video works and independently curated programmes that gave historical contexts to the other works shown. These included retrospectives of seminal work such as that of former scratch-video supremo now computer-artist George Barber, video-art pioneer Nam June Paik, historical summaries of the important experimental film work of the London Filmmakers' Co-op and found-footage work in film and video. It couldn't be faulted in terms of its desire to contextualise and to explore exactly how 'new' the 'now' work is. Sadly, 'Spellbound' did little in the way of giving such contextualising perspectives and ended up providing less of a opportunity for debate than a kind of hotch-potch of work. 'First there was Britpop. Now Britart and Britfilm are taking the world by storm.' Cultural flagwaving as the curator's last refuge? Perhaps, but indicative of the show's shortcomings, indebted as it was to the lure of celebrity with little visible concern for the resulting quality of the work. So, poster boys Ridley Scott and Damien Hirst were lined up to pull in the punters. Hirst's first film since the kitsch-fest of his promo video for Blur's *Country House* single certainly generated the column inches. *Hanging Around* explores the Hirstian obsession with death and features Keith Allen as Marcus, a duffle-coated angel of death, dispatching sudden, arbitrary and bloody retribution to those he encounters in an off-hand, almost unwitting fashion and for no apparent reason. Sadly, as a film, it's a non-event. Gordon Burn disengenuously claims in his catalogue essay that *Hanging Around* is 'a challenge to the usual notions and practices of the art film … no scratches or stains or multiple superimpositions …'. Rather, in the place of these shorthand cliches for the experimental film, Hirst has provided a professional-looking piece of TV-friendly drama. The Hirstian obsessions are there, as are his mates and some of his favourite art-objects (as well as some of his own objects), but the film's polish looks like the work of a tyro TV director who wants to show [1] that he knows how to work with a professional crew [2] that he can capably put a producer's money on screen and [3] can he have some more please. Now, if Steve McQueen had got the rumoured five-figure budget that Damien Hirst was allotted, that would have been interesting.

If Hirst's name is shorthand for the Britart-pop-film axis, then this no doubt did the job for 'Spellbound' in signalling the principal element of its 'nowness'. But the celebrity obsession that underwrote the show delivered the least diverting work: Ridley Scott's derisory contribution of rostrum-photographed stills, designs and video material from his films *Blade Runner* and *Alien*. What were really little more than sketches tossed down in seignurial fashion to a needy, trainspotting public were exhibited as if they were archive treasures, irritatingly displayed on roof-hung video-monitors which one had to look up to, as if in awed genuflection. It was the film folk who fared worst in the galley space – Hirst's celluloid foray, Scott's scraps and Peter

Greenaway's installation space *In The Dark*. Greenaway's was a nice idea; 'expanded cinema' in the sense of all the elements of the cinematic experience – audience, text, props, actors – being separated from one another and displayed for the gallery audience to recombine in any way they saw fit – a set for films yet to be made, Greenaway-by-numbers. But the idea's execution was a combination of *sturm und drang* lighting and sound effects audible throughout the Hayward. Greenaway's installation overshadowed Eduardo Paolozzi's *The Jesus Work* and *Store*: an attempt to describe an indescribable film, another would-be *wunderkammer* of cinematic artefacts, some of them with films projected on them and that couldn't really compete with Greenaway's overkill. In the 'attempts to describe films' category, Fiona Banner's graphomaniac canvas and book exhibits were highly successful. Using text in a way similar to Gordon's deployment of slow-motion, and concentrating on a whole genre of films (Vietnam war movies) rather than on a single film, Banner makes an image (of words) of the impossibility of fully describing the experience of a film; very much a case of moving pictures being worth a million words or more.

To return to Greenaway. His is an interesting case, a film-maker with a powerfully motivating grudge against his chosen medium, formerly a painter and longtime installation-practitioner, he represents a link with the British experimental film tradition that has long been working at the intersection of art practice and film-making. It was this tradition that 'Spellbound' sought to play down, if not to dismiss altogether. This seems a curious and short-sighted strategy that is probably explained by the show's focus on a combination of the fashionably young – Hirst, Gordon, Banner, McQueen – and prestigiously older – Paolozzi, Greenaway, Rego, Gilliam. But this hostility to the experimental tradition meant not only jettisoning a particular history of the art/film encounter, it also required that the place of video in this schema be ignored and hence the potential to explore the traces of this tradition in the work of artists such as McQueen and Gordon was not fulfilled. Despite the catalogue's polemical claims for British art and film's 'promiscuous', 'mongrel' nature and for Spellbound's own 'principled eclecticism' (which came across looking like a programmed exclusion), the show was a missed opportunity and did not match up to the polemic.

CHERYL DONEGAN
ORIGINALLY PUBLISHED IN 1995 BY *FILM AND VIDEO UMBRELLA*

In her tapes Cheryl Donegan comes across as the all-American bad girl who likes her music loud, puts plastic bags over her head, smears herself with paint, romps about in bra and panties and displays her child-woman's body with look-but-don't-touch nonchalance. Is this overstating the provocative boy-toy aspect of Donegan's persona? Perhaps, but it's for precisely this reason that *Head* (1994) causes the hairs on so many necks to stand on end. Featuring Donegan as a polymorphously desirable sex-worker whose energetic exertions give the impression of this not being work to her at all, *Head* captures Donegan at her most overt. But, as Collier Schorr pointed out in *Artforum, Head* is above all about 'the simulation of total abandon', the image of someone faking it for real, a send-up of pornography's libidinal free-for-all that is enhanced by the tape's concision and control.

Donegan is part of a new generation of artists whose work with video-and-performance integrates formal strategies associated with the inaugural experiments of the 1970s. Exemplified by the tapes of Vito Acconci and Bruce Nauman, the emphasis of early video-performance pieces was on process, duration and repetition, and the single-take use of low-tech video. Donegan's use of these elements is marked, however, by its ironic engagement with cultural forms that have emerged in the interim, notably pornography and MTV. *Head* works as an exemplary piece of post-MTV neo-porn because of the tight temporal frame that is both asserted and enhanced through its appeal to 'the tradition' (in the static camera's unblinking observation of process) and the contemporary (in the tension-and-release logic of climax that the pop-promo format has built into it). This juxtaposition of idioms is ironically double-edged. They call attention to themselves as available, influential forms while simultaneously having their conventions undercut and re-routed, being made-strange in all their familiarity. In tapes such as *Head* and *GracefulPhatSheba*, the proto-pop-promo format doubly mediates the body and its representation. This is 'hot' material 'coolly' framed. In *Gag*(1993), a baguette is wedged erect between Donegan's thighs; with hands tied behind her back and mouth full she laboriously gnaws it down to a stub. *Gag* is straightforward to the point of being almost didactic in its focus; a *Head*-sketch, as it were, but without that tape's satirically libidinous element. Although different in their erotic atmospherics, *Head* and *GracefulPhatSheba* (Donegan doing a languid Dance of the Seven Veils) both replace the too-blatant phallic symbolism of *Gag* with the comic bathos of a squat plastic jug; obscure domestic object of desire or cheap and cheerful five 'n' dime phallus?

Banal objects crop up throughout the tapes; plastic jugs, wash bottles of paint and clear plastic sheeting that Donegan handles as if it were a membrane peeled from the inside of the monitor screen. Toys, tools and symbolic appendages all at the same time, they are put to use particularly in the painting tapes. To a dreamy acoustic accompaniment, *MakeDream* (1993) sees Donegan deliver her take on feminised action-painting in a piece whose bump-and-spray gyrations play with issues of artistic control. This is painting-as-performance, but also painting-as-dance, where the element of control is raised through the gestural element of the work and Donegan's use of a guiding music track to supply mood and rhythm for a splatter work-out.

Body-painting, yes, but painting from the body as well as on and with it. *MakeDream* crystallises elements that inform all her work; art as 'excess', an expression, like music and dance, of libidinal energies. The painting-tapes certainly have the aspect of an irreverent, post-feminist Grand Tour through art history; *Sunflower* (1993) especially, as the Life, Art and Death of Van Gogh made manageable for the MTV generation, but also in *MakeDream's* skit on American Abstract Expressionist machismo and *Practisse's* (1994) glancingly narcissistic homage to Impressionism.

But there is more to *MakeDream* than this. The music and performance completed, the tape continues to a coda; the camera slowly zooming in to make an unfocused image, washing out Donegan's figure and giving the splashes of blue a further abstracted colour-field quality. If Donegan's dance is the act of painting, then the final, still video-image transforms its residual marks to become a canvas. *MakeDream* then, is also concerned, in a surprisingly self-effacing fashion, with creating the effects of painting through the means of video. *Practisse* reverses the equation. Painting here takes place on and with the body. Placing a plastic bag over her head, finger-painting around her features and pressing her face to a transparent plastic surface, Donegan uses her body as surface and medium. Alongside this strategy is the same finger-painting technique, but applied to the monitor surface on which a video-still of Donegan's face receives broad Impressionist portrait strokes. In both scenarios the paint is further abstracted by being smeared and sprayed with water. One might speak of these effects as 'wipes' and 'dissolves' achieved physically, the result being a beguiling kind of painted video-portraiture, the effects of video achieved through painting. The painterly concerns evident in these and other tapes, including *Kiss My Royal Irish Ass*(1992), *Clarity* (1994) and *Rehearsal*(1994), shift Donegan's work beyond the defiantly throwaway character it cultivates into an engagement with art history and the practice of art itself.

In her seminal 1971 essay, 'Video: The Aesthetics of Narcissism', Rosalind Krauss wrote of 'a narcissism so endemic to works of video that I find myself wanting to generalise it as the condition of the entire genre'. It seems fitting that Krauss should have extrapolated this insight from a work by Vito Aconci (*Centers*, 1971), but given the evident lineage that binds the 1990s generation of video/performance artists to those of the 1970s, would it be fair to suggest that the narcissism Krauss identified over twenty years ago remains the condition of the work? Yes and no. Donegan's work is interesting for the way it can be seen to represent and negotiate just this question, posing the 'narcissistic' relationship to self present in video-and-performance by extending its terms.

Video/performance work has always played on the notion of presence that accompanies the individual-as-performer and the resulting emphasis on the body. In drawing from strategies associated with both dominant and marginal pop forms, Donegan spits them back out at a tangent to their mainstream incarnations. For her, narcissism is interesting only if addressed in the terms proposed by pop culture, where the cult of personality and the culture of celebrity position the spectator in a demanding marriage of convenience, both as consumer and ideal-ego introjector. In placing herself squarely in her work as performer, personality and parodist, Donegan brings to mind artists such as Acconci, but also Warhol's fetishisation of celebrity, as well as Madonna, that most conspicuous of post-Warhol shape-shifters. Cheryl Donegan, superstar? It is to be hoped that her fifteen minutes are not yet up.

DANIEL REEVES
ORIGINALLY PUBLISHED BY *FILM AND VIDEO UMBRELLA* 1996

Daniel Reeves' *Obsessive Becoming* opens with the camera closing in on images of family and violence. A search is on. Images morph one into the other, each an element in a larger picture characterised by strife and combat. Here is a climate of endemic violence that extends from the home to the war-zone, an association made explicit in the image of wholesome crew-cut schoolboys marching against a backdrop of raining bombs. For Reeves, the child is both agent and victim of a brutality that has been bred in the bone. It is this chillingly cyclical transition from a culture to a nature of violence (and back again; a closed and brutalising circuit) that *Obsessive Becoming* sets out to explore and that has its roots in secrets and lies, in the self-perpetuating sources of misery that blighted the artist's childhood, later jeopardising his adult life. 'The secrets in this family were immense. The secrets in this world are immense,' runs Reeves' whispered voice-over at one point. But the family and the world are seen as inextricably linked. One begets the other; childhood trauma leads directly to the savage epiphany of the Vietnam War which, in turn, sheds a harsh retrospective light on the no-man's land between these two points – one made dark by the deceits and delusions perpetuated by family, states and self. *Obsessive Becoming*, then, is the process of Reeves trying to name 'the lies, the secrets' – a process of catharsis and therapy, of necessary purgation.

In terms of themes and technique, *Obsessive Becoming* is a summation of Reeves' single-screen video works since the 1970s. As in *Smothering Dreams* (1981), the after-effects of his own combat experiences in the Vietnam War are extended into a general meditation on the human capacity for destruction that is seen as omnipresent. The specific personal detail of *Smothering Dreams* – Reeves' survival of an ambush while on patrol in North Vietnam in January 1969 – is subsumed within a deeper exploration of damage, both psychic and emotional, individual and global. *Obsessive Becoming* is both unashamedly autobiographical, a reckoning and exorcism whose first-person trajectory looks to pasts both ancestral – the branches of the errant Reeves family – and historical, to forge a humanist settling of accounts with a violence that Reeves clearly feels has forged him, and out of whose crucible he hauls himself.

The project's thematic ambition extends to its form. Reeves' videos combine a documentarist's eye for telling detail with a poetic sense of structure, a flair for virtuoso visuals and an overall formal control crucial to the emotional force of the piece. His facility for the kaleidoscopic possibilities of video-mixing, keying and montage is clear in *A Mosaic for the Kali Yuga* (1986). One of the most formally achieved treatments of a favourite theme in video-art – media overload – the piece manages to express visually what the postmodern image-storm feels like to inhabit. *A Mosaic for the Kali Yuga* looks to Eastern and Indian mystical traditions as models for spiritual solace. The formal techniques and philosophical positions characteristic of Reeves' work are further refined and explored in *Obsessive Becoming* but are structured around the tape's set of changes in emotional tone. One might say that the work moves through consecutive stages of remembrance and pain; rage and mourning; reconciliation, forgiveness and peace. Each of these stages of 'becoming' has a concomitant section that, in turn, has an emblematic centrepiece image from which Reeves' meditations, communicated through a combination of scrolling on-screen text and poetic voice-over depart.

The first part of Reeves' personal odyssey firmly establishes the central focus of the work, the family as a snakepit of lies and abuse, as well as its representative image. Again, it is an image of brutality, his step-father pushing Reeves' brother to the ground. Repeated, returned to and re-interrogated, this piece of family history on Super 8mm film takes on a textural density through its digital treatment that corresponds to the emotional density that gradually accrues around, behind and within the seemingly inconsequential act of casual paternal violence. The emphasis in this section is very much on the pain of recollection, but also on the illumination of the family history before that of Reeves' own childhood – a history of petty crime, state-sanctioned maltreatment, intimidation, unknown and absent fathers. Alongside the central image it is significant that the visual trope here should be that of a ripple, a spreading tremor visible in the images themselves. This ripple-effect speaks both of the distressing realities stirring beneath the innocuous surface of these home-movie images, as well as itself being an image of a chain-reaction, of the generations of pain whose birthright of resentment and confusion must be confronted before being shed.

The tape's second section takes the calculated risk of widening its focus on pain and brutality in an eloquent and sorrowing montage of Twentieth Century horrors. From the Holocaust through Vietnam to the Gulf War, Reeves' itinerary of harrowing images reminds us that this was a century of such despicable darkness that the abuse of a single child might seem inconsequential. It can be argued that this is a dangerously inclusive and generalised approach, one that lends as much to mute sentimentality as to the consideration of political specifics. While there is a lot in the argument against what might be seen as the parading of images that have become almost iconically horrific, there is no doubt that Reeves is insisting that the force of such images is their personal dimension, that such suffering is always a matter of individual pain. In a century that has excelled in genocide and mass destruction, as well as in generating parallel industries of guilt and celebrity compassion, it is, Reeves asserts, the names of the dead and not the numbers of how many died, that should be remembered. Again, there is a central image – two starving sisters in the Warsaw Ghetto, one tearfully comforting her dying twin – that is almost unbearably painful to look at in its depiction of tenderness and cruelty. Can we bear to look at such an image? If we can then it is already too late, for this means we cannot see the central truth it tells us about the sickness of the Twentieth Century.

That Reeves confronts this image, and asks us to as well, rescues the tape from the air of moral relativism that lingers around this section, delivering instead a commitment to the individual's duty to overcome horror by facing it raw. And to never forget. The tape's third and final phase looks to this state of individual compassion and tenderness, the little victories of love in the face of overwhelming cruelty and Reeves' own experiences of sexual abuse by a parental figure. The footage that speaks most clearly here of this closing mood of reconciliation is, again, documentary: Reeves himself pitching a revolver into a lake and of an old woman, close to death, being lovingly tended to and fed. Over this latter image is the voice-over reminiscence of an Asian friend of Reeves' who recounts how he 'imagined his mother as a little girl' and arrived at a feeling of deep love, compassion and care. This section's central image is one born in the mind of the individual viewer, and called forth by the combination of the spoken words and the on-screen image, by the injunction to 'imagine the adult as the child, and then imagine the child as an adult'. The cycle of brutalism is broken, culminating in a peace that is far from quietist and that has been accomplished through courageous struggle.

GANG WARFARE:
INDEPENDENT ART SPACE, LONDON
19 OCTOBER–16 DECEMBER 1995
ORIGINALLY PUBLISHED IN *FRIEZE* 26 JANUARY/FEBRUARY 1996

'Gang Warfare' comprised six viewing stations, each consisting of a wooden trestle table, a VCR and a monitor. Fading flowers on each table added a wilting touch of domesticity to the white cube of IAS. The sixteen hours of video material in the exhibition was thus presented in a way hardly calculated to seduce prospective viewers. Curated by Michael Corris, each compilation tape represented, in its allotted space, one of the show's six 'possible worlds' – each a snapshot of current video-art practice. However, as Corris notes in his catalogue essay, 'video-art', with its implications of artistic specificity – may itself be anomalous. As Corris sees it, video is ubiquitous: 'The social context of video – its field of struggle, if you like – is not only television and film, but all visual culture.' This is a bit like having your tape and eating it. For Corris's purposes, it is the element of what one might call 'private languages' at work within and across the tapes that intrigues him. Much is made of this in the idea of the show; the 'gang warfare' of the title being as much concerned with the semiotics of cliques and art gangs, as with South Central LA-style face-offs.

What do these private languages speak of? Sex and singing, by and large. There's a significant emphasis in work, predominantly by young women artists, on porn clichés: three 'Heads' (Cheryl Donegan, Jemima Brown, Jake and Dinos Chapman), one 'Suck' – Karen McGarry – and a Sarah Lucas, sausage included. All these pieces insist on the real-time qualities of low-tech video which links the works to a founding tradition of video and performance personified in the 1970s by luminaries such as Vito Acconci and Marina Abramovic. Donegan's *Head* (1993) features the artist as a polymorphously desirable sex-worker whose energetic exertions give the impression that this is not work for her at all; of the porn parodies it's by far the best. Although Jake and Dinos Chapman's *Bring me the Head of ...* (1995) is featured in the catalogue as part of the show, it was not available for viewing. Interestingly, the thin line separating playing with the codes of pornography from actual pornography seems to have been overstepped in this work.

If these pieces are about extreme performances that become banal through generic repetition, then the 'singing' tapes are a part of a more homely subjectivity. Here, the video camera is equivalent to the bedroom or bathroom mirror in which the artist perform defiantly unstarry takes on musical numbers. Max Wigram's *Hey Girl* (1995) is like a bad dream of Bryan Ferry, the lounge lizard laid bare. Yan Duyvendak's *Songs 94–95* (1995) becomes cumulatively bizarre through its performer's strenuous muggings: without a music track, one studies the face for clues to the emotional atmosphere of a song. Two tapes stand out. Nicholas Bolton's *Singing* (1994) uses the same low-tech strategies as others but achieves the most acutely charged atmosphere. The image is like that of a surveillance camera set in the ceiling, cruelly and anonymously objectifying its subject while the mumbling and cracked singing is uncomfortably personal and intimate. If Stanley Kubrick had been a video-artist, he'd make tapes like Bolton's. Less of a performance piece, *Das Audere Universum des Klaus Beyer* (1994) is a documentary study of provincial German Beatles-obsessive and experimental film-maker Klaus Beyer. It starts out looking like voyeuristic TV anthropology but becomes an utterly fascinating examination of the amateur in his own habitat.

Judd Herrer's *Non Existent Hero* (1995) and Franz Staffenberg and Christopher Roth's *Happy Days* (1993) are representative of 'found footage' pieces that suffer from the symptoms of media overload they clearly wish to critique. Working from the angle of analytical montage, they ignore the dialectical possibilities available in paying equal attention to the soundtrack (such as one finds in video-montage by Godard, Chris Marker or Haroun Farocki), and almost fall into TV seductiveness through their look. In fact, TV formats make a strong showing through the inclusion of four ZAPP magazine compilations and Tony Kaye's advertising work. The Kaye material, the present *ne plus ultra* of the advertising image's sheer surface, is proof that advertising imagery in the hands of a director like Kaye is simply the most public of private languages. At the other end of the spectrum though, is Sarah Mallock's *A Return to Warwick Avenue* (1995), an excellent – if overlong – example of abstract video. The camera trails through the London Underground at chest height: the image is tremendously decelerated and colours bleed into one another while the motion lags as though underwater. Mallock does for metropolitan depths what Bill Viola did for downtown Tokyo in *Hatsu-Yume (First Dream)*. One of the most unwittingly astute comments on the almost gnomic quality of some of these private languages is contained in Max Wigram's *Joint Roll* (1995), a real-time lingering on spliff construction. Wigram is clearly on to one of the best ways to allow these languages to make sense.

TERMINAL FUTURES:
INSTITUTE OF CONTEMPORARY ARTS, LONDON
OCTOBER 1994
ORIGINALLY PUBLISHED IN *FRIEZE 19* NOVEMBER/DECEMBER 1994

Whenever I hear the word cyberpunk I reach for my anorak repellent. Given the choice between J. G. Ballard and William Gibson, I opt for the former every time. My technological armoury consists exclusively of a steam-driven PC used as a glorified typewriter. So what was I doing at 'Terminal Futures'? The ICA weekend event aimed to explore 'the hype and the hope' of new electronic media, promising a concentrated snapshot of how this field constructs itself. What is its jargon, its philosophical moves? What music does it listen to? How quickly would I develop a virtual attention span (i.e. nod off)? 'Terminal Futures' consisted of ten symposia over two days including presentations by Australian cyber-feminists VNS Matrix; American techno-activists Critical Art Ensemble; and European representations by, amongst others, Milan's Decoder Group and Miss Akira from Amsterdam's pirate radio station, Radio Patapoe.

During the weekend it transpired that activists and aesthetes alike shared the same set of philosophical reference points – Deleuze, Bataille, Foucault, Baudrillard *et al* – out of which mostly came cyberbabble. For lucidity and an unusual absence of the evangelism that so often accompanies techno-activists, I listened to Steve Kurtz from Critical Art Ensemble. His was the best of the papers concerning strategies for maximising the communicative potential of new technology through wresting control from the State or proprietary culture. What was most interesting about Kurtz was the straightforward modernist romanticism in his declaration of faith in a new avant-garde, corresponding to late-nineteenth/early-twentieth-century models. Inter-war Futurism is the ideal model here – the same fetishisation of the machine, the same potential for overheated libertarian rhetoric. Given the institutional location of CAE at Carnegie-Mellon University, where the 'smart weaponry' deployed in the Gulf War was developed, the romantic-modernist approach made some kind of sense.

Surveying the field as represented by 'Terminal Futures' it became increasingly clear that the most astute and interesting of the practitioners and pundits shared this appeal, if not to modernism *per se*, then to the nineteenth century, for their references and inspirations. In his presentation on pioneering work in computer art and music, Stephen Holzman demonstrated how the formulae of Kandinsky and Schoenberg have been used as software models for modern experiments. Likewise, the three most singular artists exhibiting here, Stan Douglas, Graham Weinbren and Toshio Iwai, were also looking backwards to look forward. References to early cinema and pre-cinematic vision machines united all three. Douglas's *Ruskin BC: Pursuit, Fear, Catastrophe* (1993) takes Schoenberg and silent cinema as its points of departure in its politicised deconstruction of processes of cinematic signification. In *Sonata* (1994), Weinbren has forged the most intellectually ambitious of the 'interactive cinema' works at the event. He understood the notion of 'interactivity' as not in itself new, nor necessarily intellectually lightweight. Rather, it can be used as a flexible tool in the process of perception. In its reading of Tolstoy's *The Kreutzer Sonata* via Freud's case study *The Wolfman*, *Sonata* combines cinematic technique with computer interactivity to allow the spectator to organise his or her own way through a labyrinthine proliferation of associations. With its unashamedly high-brow reference points, *Sonata* stood defiantly apart from the other experiments in interactive cinema present, in that it had ambitions beyond the desire to relive one's first experience of *Blade Runner*. *Burn: Cycle* (1994), the 'interactive action movie' by London's Trip Media for Phillips' CD-I stands as the current paradigm of this tendency. Real toys-for-the-boys stuff, its aspirations are visibly caught between the headlong narrative thrust of the action movie and the delirium of Japanese *manga*.

If Weinbren is interactivity's Einstein – to overwork the modernist analogy a little – then Toshio Iwai is its Disney (remembering that Sergei was a big fan of Walt). Iwai's presentation of his work was a revelation. It is consistently remarkable in its lucid and simple execution of strong ideas; he has the complete command of multimedia that a virtuoso has of their instrument. Starting with flip-book animation, Iwai has since gone on to use pre-cinematic machines such as the Phenakistoscope and the Zoetrope as if cinema had never been invented. He creates hallucinatory interactive video installations for public and gallery spaces, and his TV work in Japan has made him a cult figure. His most recent piece of interactive work, 'Music Insects', has the remarkable ability to make visible the act of musical composition and is currently being adapted for the Super Nintendo Entertainment System. The Disney analogy is not entirely fanciful: the reaction of the ICA audience to his work was akin to what one imagines of the first Disney audiences – laughter, delight and wonder. It was illuminating to see this recourse to early modernism and pre-cinematic techniques as a vital defence mechanism in the face of the largely uncritical enthusiasm towards the whole cyberpunk/apocalypse chic.

GARY HILL: IN THE LIGHT OF THE OTHER
OXFORD MUSEUM OF MODERN ART
7 NOVEMBER 1993–9 JANUARY 1994
ORIGINALLY PUBLISHED IN *FRIEZE 14* JANUARY/FEBRUARY 1994

To inaugurate the first British exhibition of Gary Hill's recent video installations, the Oxford Museum of Modern Art held a day seminar that, on paper, seemed like a good idea. The Human Anatomy Lecture Theatre was well-chosen for discussion of Hill who, in his work, often documents and dismembers images of the human form. The speakers, including Lynne Cooke and Raymond Bellour, looked promising and we were to prepare for a 'performance/intervention' by Hill himself with his poet collaborators George Quasha and Charles Stein. The theme was to be the influence on Hill's work of the French writer and literary critic, Maurice Blanchot. What prevailed had far more to do with Blanchot than Hill: continental literary theory was privileged over any examination of what Hill's place might be in the contemporary video art firmament. While this no doubt kept the Blanchot devotees happy – a large contingent, judging from audience questions – there was an equally sizeable group that, at the end of the seminar, expressed the feeling that the Blanchot angle had produced more heat than light. So, when it came time for the promised 'intervention' – a back-lit body behind surgical screens, a micro video-camera scanning pages of a book in close-up with the images relayed onto auditorium monitors, and a polyphony of voices speaking in language clear and unrecognisable – it took on, for a moment, a character which seemed to parody the language of academic obfuscation that had dominated the day thus far.

From which it would be tempting to conclude that as yet, the British don't know how to talk about video-art. We had better learn, and fast. The arrival in this country of major exhibitions of work by Hill and Bill Viola, among others, provides a relatively sustained opportunity to get to grips with an art in constant mutation, one that has transformed well beyond the critical paradigms provided by such critics as Rosalind Krauss. It was a pity, then that Bellour (whose seminal study of the moving image *L'entre-images: Photo, Cinéma, Vidéo* remains shamefully unavailable in English) was bottom of the bill – by which time everyone was flagging – and delivered a very generalised paper. It was a salutary experience, after the seminar, to allow Hill's work to speak for itself. Or, rather, to speak to itself. Two of the multiple-monitor pieces indicate the advanced stage Hill has reached in integrating sound and image in order to establish video as a tangibly physical experience: working with the body, these pieces act on our bodies. *Inasmuch as it is Already Taking Place* (1990) compels us to approach its sixteen uncased monitors of widely differing sizes, featuring close-up fragments of the male body, and asks us to listen to sounds of subdued scrapings of a finger on a page (the detail staged and magnified in Hill's intervention), quiet, incantatory murmurings and the rubbing of hands.

Where *Inasmuch* … beckons, *Between 1 & 0* (1993) keeps us at a physical distance. Thirteen fourteen-inch monitors forming a Greek cross on the wall flash extreme close-up images of body details in extended linear flurries across its limbs. The sense of a body coming into being as an image, but never achieving its complete form, is matched and enhanced by the sound of the manic scribble of graphite. The quasi-pornographic address of its imagery positions us as voyeurs, but the images and sounds come in irregular, intermittent blizzards – the viewer is stunned but enticed. But it is the now legendary *Tall Ships* (1992) that stands out – both as a departure from, and a development of, elements in other works. A departure in formal terms; here, unlike elsewhere in the installations, we are presented with complete figures, this time silent, and with the monitor (so insistently foregrounded in the other 'body' pieces) significantly absent. Instead, we have sixteen black and white images of people projected onto the walls of a deep, almost entirely unlit corridor-like space. The movements of the figures are triggered by the spectator's own passage through the space, courtesy of a computer-controlled interactive system. The incorporation of the element of regulated chance in *Tall Ships* means no two experiences of the works are exactly the same, but the silence of these sepulchral figures as they approach, pause and turn away from us makes the sensation one of simultaneous distance and intimacy. It is this work that finally reveals the poverty of the appeals to Blanchot and the theorists' inability to account for the complex physicality of the spectator's response.

BILL VIOLA: LANDSCAPES OF THE MIND
ORIGINALLY PUBLISHED BY *FILM AND VIDEO UMBRELLA* 1997

Bill Viola has stated that 'the natural landscape is the raw material of the human psyche'. Indeed, landscape and its transformations are dominant themes on which his work has played a series of subtle variations. From the heat-haze mirages of the Tunisian Sahara in *Chott-el-Djerid (A Portrait in Light and Heat)* (1979) to the kaleido-scopic rainstorms of downtown Tokyo in *Hatsu Yume (First Dream)* (1981), Viola's landscapes are both natural and man-made. Viola looks for the residual human pres-ence in the vast expanses of nature, just as he does the residue of nature in the urban non-places of edge-cities and parking lots. Nature and Civilisation are not essentialist oppositions to be faced off, one against the other, in predictable bouts of binary logic. Rather, his work suggests that one is contained within the other, sometimes in vestigial traces, sometimes hidden. Landscape, therefore, conceals as much as it shows.

In *Déserts* (1995), the wilderness is not only arid and adamantine but is also the topography of a desolate human landscaping. *The Passing* (1991), from which *Déserts* draws key visual motifs, holds the master-image of an unresolved tension between vying landscapes – a truck and a mobile home sunk in sand and water, half-visible, half-submerged. The image marks a kind of frontier, a borderline between two states – the paraphernalia of civilisation gradually succumbing to creeping erosion. Has civilisation emerged from ancient waters or is it sinking back into centuries of sand? The desert, then, is a kind of memento mori, a reminder of impermanence and the presence of death in life. It is a crucial image for what it reveals of Viola's conception of landscape – a means by which transitions from one state to another can take place.

Viola's treatment of landscape is encapsulated by the artist's own equation: 'perception over time equals thought'. Each work explores the consequences of duration on perception, what Viola calls 'unrelenting vision, heralding a shift in con-sciousness'. It has often been noted that this approach sets Viola's work definitively apart from the fast-cutting fury of the contemporary image-storm within which the video aesthetic is thoroughly embroiled. Viola's insistence on stasis, on a kind of visual 'silence' in his work, has affinities with ascetic and meditational practices, reinforced when one considers that Viola's *via negativa* is often represented by desert land-scapes of one kind or another.

From this durational approach emerges an exploration of perceptual confu-sion. *The Reflecting Pool* (1977) introduces the ambiguity of vision as a theme to be explored through an emphasis on temporal duration and in relation to landscape. The image's static frame, here divided into upper and lower halves, undergoes subtle yet startling transformations. Viola's body is suspended in mid-leap above a wood-land pool. By the time the image of his body has gradually dematerialised, one's attention has become so engrossed in the turbulence of the pool's surface that this slow erasure comes as a surprise. The hallucinatory visual flux of *The Reflecting Pool* was obtained through sophisticated post-production techniques; the image remains spatially unified and coherent, it is one space, but the time of the image is multiple, consisting of real-time, still and time-lapse effects. Viola has admitted that many of his tapes throughout the 1970s were 'structural' in approach, concerned with deconstructing the nature and qualities of the medium. *The Reflecting Pool* can be seen as a transitional work. It maintains some of the formal characteristics of the preceding period (the surface of the pool might be read as a screen within the screen, a watery *mise-en-abyme*) while anticipating the forthcoming fascination with the phenomenological reality of landscapes and a corresponding real-time approach to their representation. In later works, the effect of temporal transformation gives way to a meditation on space and location.

Duration is a constant throughout the tapes, both in the filming and in the real-time physicality of the spectator's experience of them. In fact, *Chott el-Djerid* and *Hatsu Yume* approach an almost elemental temporality, something made explicit in Viola's own statement on how, in *Hatsu Yume*, he thought 'it would be interesting to show a rock in slow-motion'. The emphasis on finding another perceptual wavelength (one dictated by landscape to best reveal the environment-as-sensorium) is closely allied to Viola's thoughts on the limitations of human perception, and in particular the inadequacy of the eye. In *Chott el-Djerid*, for example, the desert becomes a hallucinatory dreamscape of shimmering heat images. One's eyes work to discern substantial figures amidst the optical flux of a visual field lacking any organising perspective. *Chott el-Djerid* could well stand as a paradigm of Viola's approach to the ways in which certain landscapes induce visual uncertainty, one that emphasises 'field perception' rather than 'object perception'. The studies in human perception that Viola undertook early in his career are further elaborated upon in his work's treatment of landscape, where 'The visual is always subservient to the field, the total system of perception/cognition at work ... the awareness or sensing of an entire space at once.' This idea itself departs from and explores Viola's contention that video as a technology – and hence as an aesthetic/perceptual experience - has stronger but less commonly acknowledged affinities with human sound perception than with visual perception. We receive sound more passively than we do images. Our eyes are constantly filtering information from a field that is automatically less extensive than the auditory field by which we are surrounded. Viola explores the model of human sound perception as a way of producing the sense of perceptual immersion that is one of the strongest and most enduring features of his tapes. One senses acutely that the field of Viola's tapes extends infinitely around, behind and beyond his camera; the image is only a fraction of the landscape. In *The Reflecting Pool*, as in the closing moments of *Déserts* (itself a response to the atonal soundscapes of Edgar Varèse inspired by the desert), the figure of a body plunging into water might be read as a literal image of the immersive perceptual experience that the tapes seek to create in the spectator. If the landscapes of *Chott el-Djerid* and Deserts are macrocosms of the this perceptual field, then in *Hatsu Yume* it is treated in microscosm: specifically in the sequence when the lights of a Tokyo street are filtered though rain on a car windscreen and shot in a combination of slow-motion and extreme close-up.

Lanscape as artistic subject matter has been informed by numerous influences and its association with transcendentalism, revelation and the sublime goes back to Kant and *The Critique of Practical Reason*. In Viola's work one inevitably finds echoes of nineteenth-century Romantic painting from Caspar David Friedrich to Turner as well as of the visionary pantheism of Wordsworth and Walt Whitman. This association between landscape and the human psyche is one that Viola excavates as a means of linking inner and outer worlds. True to the Romantic paradigm, landscape is viewed as a Way Within, a vista onto which the interior can be projected and by which archetypal themes are illuminated, just as Viola's work itself demands an analogous return to first principles - those of 'being'. In this respect, it is noticeable how Viola's unapologetic 'mysticism', expressed in his fascination with Indian and Oriental phi-losophies, clearly unsettles Anglo-Saxon critics, many of whom are all too ready to lump him in with other exemplars of the New Age zeitgiest. In fact, it makes more sense to think of Viola as a direct descendent of the American filmic avant-garde and of John Cage and the Black Mountain College ethos of what might be called 'Transcendental American Modernism'. The issues relating to the life of the spirit that Viola's work raises - whether expressed in metaphysical, religious or mystical terms - should not be dismissed as either abstract or arcane in nature but are of pressing concern right now. Viola's tapes are a series of reports from the edge of perception that extend the visionary artistic tradition into a modern technological medium.

FEELINGS ALONG THE BODY: INTERVIEW WITH BILL VIOLA
ORIGINALLY PUBLISHED IN *SIGHT AND SOUND* JANUARY 1994

The arrival on the market in 1965 of the first portable video camera, the Sony Portapak, is often cited as the decisive moment in the origin of video art. In the intervening thirty years, three names have come to represent the artform: Nam June Paik, Gary Hill and Bill Viola. Each has produced work in the formats of single-screen tapes and video installations, and each has developed an individual signature: Paik's ironic and playful confrontations of television with the spectacle of itself, Hill's austere dislocations of objects and bodies in space, and Viola's exploration of video as a visionary medium. The characterisation of Viola as a video visionary has become a glib way into twenty years' worth of work whose consistency and strength emerge from a seemingly paradoxical combination of technical sophistication and a defiantly mystical purpose. The arrival in London of Viola's most recent installation works is a splendid opportunity to test his art against the morass of clichés with which critics too proud of their own powers of rationalisation have surrounded it.

'Unseen Images' (Whitechapel Gallery, 10 December 1993–13 February 1994) features seven installation works which together illustrate the dominant themes and techniques of Viola's work in video since the late 1970s. Before the benchmark tapes *Chott El-Djerid (A Portrait in Light and Heat)* (1979) and *The Reflecting Pool – Collected Works: 1977–1980*, Viola's work was marked by the structural tendency of the American film-making avant-garde of the late 1960s and 1970s, concentrating on either the mechanics of perception or the properties of the medium itself. From the early 1980s Viola's work increasingly incorporated the artist's interest in ancient Oriental and Middle-Eastern cultures, barren 'empty' landscapes and the possibilities for revelation provided by the image's extended duration. From these preoccupations developed the recurring cycles of images that characterise both the installations at the Whitechapel and the most recent of Viola's tapes, *The Passing* (1991).

The Passing collapses life and death, light and dark, the transitory and the eternal into a 54-minute dream narrative provoked by the death of the artist's mother in 1991 and the birth of his second son nine months later. But while the impetus for his work may be personal, its language is never private: Viola insists on finding connections between inner and outer landscapes. *Hatsu Yume (First Dream)* (1981) was filmed in Japan, *Chott El-Djerid* in the Tunisian Sahara and *The Passing* in the desert of the American south-west. All these works are in part meditations on the states – mental, physical and, by extension, spiritual – provoked by prolonged exposure to such spaces.

Seeing *The Passing* recently I was struck by a comment a friend made about the experience: that it was a work she would 'remember with my body'. The way Viola's use of time makes the viewing experience physical, something to be felt, is a key feature of his work. While often visually ravishing, his tapes have systematically avoided the seductive special effects so readily available in video post-production, an aesthetic chasteness that reaches its apogee with the decision to shoot *The Passing* in black and white.

'The obscenity of colour can so easily be misused in places such as the American south-west – I mean all those colour photographic shots of red sandstone rocks against a deep blue sky. I had been to those places and I couldn't imagine going out there with a colour camera – especially a colour video camera, which has a kind of electronic colour that's less subtle than film. So it had to be black and white. The decision was compounded by the fact that I wanted to record a lot of it at night. I had special low-light cameras which were black and white, and there's not a lot of colour at night anyway.

BV: For me this medium has always been physical. The first time I used a video camera I signed it out of the university media centre and an hour later, I slipped and fell on it, crushing it into tiny pieces. It was a good way to start – I figured that if you could sit on it and break it, you shouldn't be afraid of it! But that kind of physical experience apart, I think cinema is a physical medium. Sitting in a darkened room hearing sound and watching movement and light is a very physical experience. Working with video, I found I started to connect intuitively with the body. And then when I began to work with installations, putting images in rooms and having the whole room be part of the piece, the physical presence of the viewer became part of the way the work functioned and I realised I had to study our bodies.

Viola has said that 'video treats light like water,' and certainly images of water recur throughout his works. In *The Passing* the central image if of a man submerged, combining connotations of death by drowning with the pre-conscious state of amniotic suspension. A similar image stands at the centre of the *Nantes Triptych* installation (1992), flanked by those of a young woman giving birth and an old woman dying. If Viola's work explores conventional water symbolism, it has equally employed it to formal ends. *Hatsu Yume* approaches water as a refracting, rather than reflecting, medium. The lights of a Tokyo street are filtered through the rain on a car windscreen. Extreme close-ups from macro-lens cameras document, in the everyday occurrence of a city rainstorm, a kaleidoscope of abstract patterns and sumptuous colour.

BV: I've always been drawn to water. I had a near-death experience when I was about ten years old – I fell into the water and almost drowned. I remember clearly that I wasn't frightened at all – it was a beautiful experience: the deep, blue-green colour and the little plants waving on the bottom of the lake bed and a few fish. It was fascinating, then this big arm came down and abruptly pulled me out of that incredible world. Then I started to cry. I've been interested for the last twenty years in the work of a Sufi writer and artist from thirteenth-century Persia called Rumi. In one of his works he describes us as being like bowls floating on the surface of a great ocean. As we go through life, the bowl slowly fills up with water, and when the water reaches the top the water within merges with the water outside and we don't need the bowl any more, it slips slowly away beneath the surface. It's a very beautiful image.

Viola opted out of art classes to work with video while a student at Syracuse University in the 1970s. At this time he was also involved in experiments with sound and electronic music. The investigation into the relation of sound and image has been an enduring feature of his work. Relying rarely on the spoken word or music, the sound on Viola's tapes conveys the sense of a perceptual field that completes the viewer's experience of the image rather than simply illustrating it. As Gene Youngblood has put it, it is 'a kind of *musique concrète* which suggests that time has a sound'.

BV: Sound gave me another one of my models. Vision is very selective and focused, whereas sound exists all around you; it is much more diffuse. It is analogous to a perceptual field, or field of being, which in essence is what we are. We're centred in our bodies, but our bodies are extended out through our memories, our past associations and the places we've been. This idea of the human being as a perceptual field gave me a way to approach images that helped me to get beyond the image's seductive power. The camera is a very misleading device because all you have to do is press the red record button and you generate an image. This image is complex and realistic, based on what you know to be there when you're shooting. It's coloured, there's sound in it, and you can think, 'Hey, that's pretty amazing! I did that!' Of course, that's just the first stages, similar to a child making a simple line on a piece of paper – you have to go beyond that. All the movies you've ever seen and all the television you've ever watched is in there when you pick up that camera. When I started working with a video camera, it was sound that informed the way I moved it. The way the camera moves in my 1976 piece, *The Space Between the Teeth*, shooting down the hallway at high speed through a series of fast cuts, came directly from thinking about sound. When I was setting up for that piece I was palpably experiencing the soundwaves going down that hallway: I could feel them travel down the hallway, bounce off the camera and come back again. I wanted to move my camera that way – it was an idea that came from an acoustical approach, not a visual one: what would it look like to be on the crest of that soundwave, riding it down the hall? That, plus the idea of the "undersound", gave me an important way to approach the image. I interpret what I call the "undersound" in my work as a deep rumble, the sound of wind, of heavy machinery, a continual sound that I think of as being in the basement of our lives. One of the reasons I feel so comfortable about working with video is the fact that a video recorder is a magnetic tape recorder: it is electromagnetic and is based on the audio tape recorder, as opposed to film, which is based on emulsion on acetate. In film, sound is an add-on, a physically separate system; with video, the sound is recorded on the tape with the image and the image is integral to the sound. Of course, that's also the case with the human body: we don't, unless we're unfortunately handicapped, get images without sound.

It could be said that Viola uses video against the grain. In the storm of images that today incorporates both MTV and surveillance technology, his video work occupies a privileged place – in the eye of the storm, if you like. It is a space where a decelerated, more meditative use of video takes place.

BV: When I was younger I tended to react more viscerally and adversarially to things. The video equipment I was using defined itself in opposition to the larger culture and the powers that be, which we were all fighting against and trying to reform. Video was an important part of the counter-culture movement of the late 1960s. *The Space Between the Teeth* was the first time I worked with computer editing systems where I could address an individual frame and cut on it. There was a series of fast, montage-like cuts in the tape, and when I showed it I remember that some of the video community, particularly the video purists, criticised it because they thought that this was a film technique; video didn't do that. Then, years later, MTV came along and suddenly everybody is cutting like that; it has now become a video technique. One of the things that's fascinating about working in this medium for twenty years is that what I'm working with now is not the same as when I started. It's a medium in transition and it looks as though it will continue to transform itself in the future. I think that the idea of slowing things down came from my personal experiences, from visiting the desert when I was living in New York and experiencing how not only the visual environment changes, but how time changes as well. When a car is coming at you at fifty miles an hour when you can see 700 miles clear straight ahead, the car is going to take over an hour to get to you. time is modified by different places.

Art and technology converge in video art. In Viola's work, this meeting is made particularly interesting through the attempt to reconcile formal aspects of the western high-art tradition with high-tech modernity, as in the triptych framing device of the *Nantes Triptych*. But far from being post-modern parody or avant-garde gesture, the hybrid, multi-media and transcultural nature of Viola's work testifies to the artist's own re-readings of art history and to the questions posed about the nature of the relationship between the artist working in mass-media technology and the spectator.

BV: I belong to a generation that stands possibly at the end of a 150-year-old model of art-making, which was evolved in France and which we call the 'avant-garde'. The avant-garde – originally the idea of breaking with the academy and neo-classical art – was an adversarial role. I think that now we're seeing the later stages of that model being played out, and in these stages we're seeing some of the problems that arise, one of which is the isolation of artists from the community they're working in. We have this thing called the "art world", which has a very rarefied atmosphere, much like academia, and which stands in isolation from the community at large. Artists of my generation who have picked up one of the dominant tools of communication – television – and attempted to make art with it have taken a radical step which we haven't seen since the Renaissance or possibly the baroque period. In 1975, my first work to be broadcast on television was seen by half a million people. That creates an incredible opportunity. I don't know if I can use the word 'responsibility', but it certainly necessitates a contact with people that is going to bring into focus all the issues of the avant-garde position. After I made my peace with art history, having had it ruined for me at art school and then studying it on my own later, I saw the connections from the point of view of the artist, which is what they don't teach you. They teach you art history from the point of view of the scholars and researchers, from an external spectator, educated observer point of view. I came in through the back door when I started to develop my own artistic practice and started to realise what it means to be an artist, to be doing this work. I think what drove me was the realisation that, to take the example of the triptych, the form of the triptych is not only a form in art history and therefore a familiar form to the western eye in particular, but is also part of the structure of consciousness. The tripartite structure of the universe is a basic element in the Christian tradition – earth, heaven and hell.

When one works with that form, besides making connections with the specific form of the triptych altarpiece, one is also working with a latent structure of consciousness.

Georges Méliès saw cinema as an art form that was capable of recording images hitherto undocumented, such as the wind in the leaves of a tree. In its insistence on perceptual duration and its attentiveness to landscape and the possibilities for abstraction in the play of light on water and land, Viola's work might be seen as having developed precisely what Méliès identified as cinema's first vocation. Because of its narrative imperative, cinema has largely relinquished this idea. Has video, in the work of an artist like Viola, taken it up?

BV: I think cinema is capable of producing this kind of image, and even in banal Hollywood movies, if you can detach yourself from the dramatic story line, you have moments – through a cut or a camera angle or a point of view – of this other side of cinema. It's fascinating to see how this visual emphasis, which was strongly evident in the work of the early film-makers – Méliès, Vertov and so on – has played itself out alongside literary-dramatic lines. All that reviews of movies talk about today is storyline – so-and-so meets so-and-so and then they get divorced. They don't talk about light and image and sound any more. Obviously approaching this as an artist, and being influenced by the work of the American avant-garde of the 1960s – Stan Brakhage, Hollis Frampton, Paul Sharits – made me realise that you could do things with this medium other than what I was seeing on television, which in my childhood included a lot of old movies. A camera, as blunt and passive a device as it is, basically records the light that comes into it in a mechanical way. But when you turn that instrument on and the wind blows through the grass, what you capture is more than just a visual image. If you lay the film strip out in front of you, you see a series of still shots of grass. But when you project it, all of a sudden these blades of grass are moving! I still share an almost medieval fascination with the magic of these things. I think the narrative imperative has modified the agenda of working with the moving image; there's a gravitational pull that the force of the story exerts. At the close of the twentieth century, with things like MTV and the most different departure from this traditional narrative line, the television commercial, forms are beginning to open up to the point where if we jump ahead a hundred years, I think we'll look back at many of the things done in this century as p being primitive in much the same way as we look on medieval painting that didn't use Brunelleschi's system of perspective as being childlike.

André Bazin identified two types of film director – those with 'a faith in reality' and those with 'a faith in the image'. It may appear paradoxical in the age of video, where image and reality are collapsed in the idea of the simulacrum, that Viola implicitly revives a kind of Bazinian 'faith' in attributing to the image an ontological status that has been fatally compromised.

BV: I've never lost my faith in the image. To take an example: there are thousands of images of the Grand Canyon. Within this phenomenon that a lot of current theorists are fascinated by – this rush of banal images – the image of the Grand Canyon has taken on its own life. But when you're standing at the edge of the canyon, whether you've seen a million photographs or you've seen one, it doesn't matter. There's this incredible presence which wipes away all the clichés and you begin to see the real thing beneath the pale reflections we are trying to capture.

SOMEONE TO WATCH OVER YOU:
ON SOPHIE CALLE'S DOUBLE BLIND (USA 1993) AND
MICHAEL KLIER'S DER REISE (THE GIANT) (GERMANY 1984)
ORIGINALLY PUBLISHED BY *FILM AND VIDEO UMBRELLA* 1994

We call it 'video-culture'. Or we might know it as the Situationists' 'Society of the Spectacle' or Baudrillard's 'simulacrum'. Or, simply, as a permanent state of surveillance. From shopping mall to satellite, encompassing the local and the global, the public and the private alike, the video-camera and its images are increasingly ubiquitous. Yet as widespread as these vision machines have become, their imagery is paradoxically marginal; at least within a visual culture defined by television and cinema. Two video pieces, Sophie Calle's *Double Blind* and Michael Klier's *Der Reise (The Giant)* put precisely such marginal imagery, from extreme ends of video-culture, to powerful and provocative use and call forth an array of questions about our place as individuals in the modern mediascape. Furthermore, as video works, both tapes depart decisively from the positions discernible in cinema and TV.

It is true to say that cinema has proved in equal parts fascinated by and defensive towards the arriviste technology of video. While innovators like Jean-Luc Godard, Atom Egoyan, Wim Wenders and Chris Marker have incorporated it as a formal element that allows for a self-reflexive space to be installed within cinema. More mainstream movies – from *sex, lies and videotape* to *Sliver* – have tended to appropriate video into a limited repertoire of narrative and generic gestures toward Hitchcockian voyeurism and Langian paranoia. In all of this (steadily growing) number of films, the presence of video is both functional – in that it adds a (semipornographic) hint of the explicit to the narrative concerns of sex, voyeurism and deceit – and symbolic – in that, even within such narratives, video points to a whole other image-world beyond cinema; one that if it hasn't actually usurped cinema, has simply absorbed it within itself.

At the same time, TV series such as *You've Been Framed* and *Video Nation* clearly indicate that, at some fundamental level of cultural understanding, the video image has assumed the mark of a zero-degree realism formerly attributed to Super 8mm/home-movie film. One of the chief reasons for this perception of video as the iconic realist image is through its recognition as an instant image, its technological capacities inflecting the cultural identity it possesses. One only need consider the vogue for 'reality programming' imported from the US and evinced in shows like *Crimewatch UK* which either reprocess surveillance camera footage or feature 'eyewitness' video, as it were, straight from the scene of the event. The video/surveillance camera here becomes a sort of optical prosthesis to TV, a hyper-vigilant supplement to the outside broadcast. In its very immediacy, the surveillance image is a paradigm of video, what Raymond Bellour has called its 'pure and atrocious image. Invisible by being everywhere, blind by virtue of being all-seeing ... the neutral and negative version of Christ Pantocrator.'

While it is interesting to reflect on the fact that there are, at this moment, probably millions of surveillance cameras patrolling their own small square of ground, unblinkingly, for interminable periods of time, most of the images they capture will rarely deviate from the merely functional or utterly banal. But if one considers those surveillance images that have acquired troublingly iconic status – the images of the abduction of James Bulger, the assault on Rodney King, the Gulf War – one understands that all share similar narratives of horror, abjection and destruction. Such images call for an excess of commentary, a supplement of narrative to which they can be attached. These narratives, combined with the realist 'grain' of the video-image itself, incarnate the surveillance image as evidence. By virtue of such narrativisation, the facts of the image are laid open to interpretation and from there to the possibility of fictionalisation.

Michael Klier's *Der Reise*, on the other hand, presides over what might almost be described as a carnival of 'raw surveillance'. Seemingly grounded in a stubborn refusal to make the customary selection of the telling image, Klier's piece in fact has the opposite effect of allowing that process of selection freer rein. In preserving the surveillance camera's slow saccadic movements, its scanning of the surface of the world, the piece reproduces – albeit at a technological remove – the action of the spectator's own eyes in the Gestalt search for patterns and correspondances; our urge to summon meaning and event from what are, to all intents and purposes, unremarkable, 'uneventful' scenes. In this, *Der Reise* has close cinematic equivalences to other experiments with perception: Michael Snow's *La Région Centrale* and Michelangelo Antonioni's *Blow Up* spring to mind. As does the pioneering work of the Lumière Brothers and Dziga Vertov, whose euphoric experimentation was inseperable from their desire to document the everyday life of the metropolis. Perhaps Klier's tape will have a lingering resonance as an end-of-the-century, end-of-cinema *Man with a Movie Camera*; the human agency predictably removed and the euphoria having evaporated, what remains are the disembodied images of everyday life on another planet.

Double Blind, too, makes deliberate play on the sense of dissociation and detachment that has been such a common motif in video. Where the surveillance image has its own terrain, that of public space, the camcorder's parallel incursions into the personal and private elicit analogous feelings of confession and voyeurism. And what is video-voyeurism, after all, but a kind of intimate surveillance? Documenting the state of being-alone-together that pervades the authors' burgeoning but distinctly uncommitted relationship, *Double Blind* is especially interesting for the extent to which it engages with these formal questions to a sophisticated and affecting narrative end. Examining, and often parodying video's solipsistic nature, while neatly avoiding the narcissistic culs-de-sacs that bedevilled the video-art of the 1970s, the tape's judicious use of fades and dissolves , of voice-over narration and diary structure, of real-time footage and video stills, suggests a kinship with films like Egoyan's *Calendar* and, more explicitly, Chris Marker's *La Jetée* while, at the same time, marking out a style and direction totally its own.

What do Klier and Calle suggest about a life lived under the lens? That it's lonely out there among all those images. That we are isolated from others and endlessly self-observing. Perhaps having the capacity to make the images oneself might allow for a little extra lucidity, might make it easier to bear. But that's no promise.

CINEMA AND VIDEO AT WAR
ORIGINALLY PUBLISHED IN *SIGHT AND SOUND* JULY 1993

Towards the end of the documentary *Hearts of Darkness: A Filmmaker's Apocalypse*, Francis Ford Coppola enthusiastically imagines 'some little fat girl from Ohio making a beautiful film with her dad's video camera.' In Coppola's scenario, film will be re-established as an art at the expense of cinema as a business. Queer avant-garde video-diarist Sadie Benning could well be Coppola's dreamgirl, with the camera in question being the lowest of low audio-visual technologies: the $200 Pixelvision video camera manufactured for children (and now discontinued) by the corporate big daddy Fisher-Price. In Benning's 1992 tape *It Wasn't Love*, she parallels her use of this low-end technoloy with an appropriation of Hollywood archetypes – the vamp, gangster, crooner and thug among others – in a strategy of neo-punk DIY. This is perfectly expressed in he declaration, 'We didn't need Hollywood, we were Hollywood.'

Coppola and Benning: the mainstream and the margins. Cinema and Video: Cain and Abel, as Jean-Luc Godard put it. With film increasingly incorporating video, the traditional face-of that so often pits the two technologies against one another – the 'direct' light of film versus the 'indirect' light of video – seems finally to have dissolved. Or has it simply been replaced by a derivation of this same opposition – one that currently expresses itself in a cinematic fear and loathing of the video image, which is employed to characterise a nightmarish gamut of *fin-de-siècle* anxieties? The video image as a symbol of the end of the century? But whose century? Cinema's, of course.

In June 1982 the American journal *Film Comment* ran a special supplement on video that included reports on the cable boom, MTV and video-art. But nothing on video-in-film. Certainly, there was a lengthy assessment of Coppola's then state-of-the-art Zoetrope experiments in 'electronic cinema', but from the angle of it being an interesting, if exceptional, hybrid of the two media, a film-into-video cross-pollination. Perhaps this oversight was due to a desire to negotiate, or simply to avoid the familiarity reductive *parti-pris* – for film, *ergo* against video.

In the same issue J.Hoberman rendered the tenor of the times with his admirably inclusive, though somewhat disingenuous, statement that 'Movies and video are two kinds of Cinema.' Much appears to have changed in the intervening eleven years. Cinema, to bowdlerise somewhat from the Godard quotebook, has since become occupied territory – the video image is now ubiquitous. But anyone could have told you that, anyone who'd seen *Videodrome*. *sex, lies and videotape*, *Henry: Portrait of a Serial Killer*, anything by Atom Egoyan, *Patriot Games*, Walter Hill's *Trespass* – to list a few disparate but key films. Far more interesting are the terms of video's ubiquity. Or, put another way, what has video-in-film come to mean?

Video-in-film allows cinema to access images from its margins – from amateur video, high and low-tech surveillance equipment, pornography – and resituate them. Often employed in film in order to implicate the spectator as consumer and voyeur of such images, video might also be seen as cinema's means of responding to media massification and to its own loss of sovereignty in the process. Yet even as video is made up of this variety of forms, it has a limited repertoire of functions, all of which hinge on video being seen as cinema's other. To gauge how homogenous the connotations of video-in-film have become, it is revealing to look back to an early example (probably not the earliest, but indicative nonetheless): Paul Mazursky's *Down and Out in Beverley Hills* (1986). What is striking from this distance is how archaic the video images seem, almost quaint but also euphoric. This film doesn't have any problems with video; it appropriates the visual styles of MTV and 'scratch video' (remember 'scratch video'?) and puts them to work to add a little post-modern noise to an adaptation of Renoir's *Boudu sauve des eaux*. The euphoria comes from the fact that the film features a new cinematic figure – the kid with the camcorder – who is grounded in an almost prelapsarian vision of video culture. This is before the Gulf War, before the Broadgate bombing and before video had come to be identified as witness to real horrors that would otherwise have remained invisible – the abuction of Jamie Bulger, the assault of Rodney King, the repeated sex crimes (recorded by their perpetrator on security video) of Algerian police chief Mustapha Tabet.

Mazursky's kid has not aged gracefully – something happened to him in that Beverley Hills bedroom to produce a troupe of characters whose relationship to video is seen almost exclusively in terms of a problematised masculinity. And in films populated by these human adjuncts to video technology, the Godardian vision of the camera as 'communication in a solid state' is transformed. The camcorder becomes alienation in a solid state. Video gets in the spaces between people, materialises the desires that reside there – especially the guilty, transgressive desires – and makes that space thick with images, insuperable. Fast-forward, rewind, freeze: these vital attributes of video are germane to all manner of fetishistic desires (*pace* the homicidal Henry and Otis in *Henry: Portrait of a Serial Killer*, the impotent Graham in *sex, lies and videotape*). At one level, video-in-film is a character in itself, both the expression and materialisation of fetishistic drives, locked into a double-bind of symptom and cause with its user and its user's desire.

Alongside this (already somewhat hackneyed) expressive presence, video-in-film opens up equally important formal possibilities. It is immediately reflexive and mediating, installing another image-time within the time of the film and allowing modernists *manques* such as Wenders in *Notebook on Cities and Clothes* and Egoyan in *Family Viewing* to create *trompe l'oeil* effects that fragment both the narrative and the image on the screen. Likewise, in Bertrand Tavernier's *L.627*, precisely because the film wears its realist aspirations so visibly, it must also acknowledge its usurper in the realism stakes by accommodating video, with its 'extra quantity of analogy', to quote French critic Raymond Bellour. Bellour suggests that in the successive histories of the mechanical reproduction of the world, photography produced the first image to be invested with a 'quantity of analogy', a basic realism to which cinema adds the analogy of movement. Video supplements this with 'a new analogy, that of an image without any delay.' As a simultaneously degraded and clinical presence within the well-mastered film image, the video-image has come to replace the grain of 8mm and newsreel with its own zero-degree realism. That (film) was then, this (video) is now.

In *L.627* Lulu (Didier Bezace), an officer in the Paris drugs squad, moonlights as an of-duty video-maker. This would-be film-maker turned cop (Lulu failed the entrance exams for IDHEC, the French film school) hits on the idea of taking to work the camera which, until then, he has used solely to film weddings (or in a playfully half-hearted but nonetheless telling attempt to cajole his wife into a little home-video eroticism). Having been the recorder of intimate images, Lulu's camera becomes an instrument of surveillance.

The implication is that surveillance is always already a function of video – whether at the manned, local level of Lulu's usage or in the form of the seemingly autonomous 'eye-in-the-sky' of Philip Noyce's *Patriot Games*. Noyce's film, which self-consciously plays with hybrid images of satellite surveillance, is a showcase for state-of-the-art imaging equipment. (Noyce further explores this theme in the Sharon Stone thriller, *Sliver* whose narrative concerns an apartment block owner who may or may not be using surveillance cameras to spy in his tenants.) Yet while the video image undoubtedly functions as an ultramodern tic, there is more at work here than a simple high-tech spicing of generic leftovers. These images announce that there is no longer any circumstances in which everything cannot be seen.

Such an overwhelming mediation of reality was the subject of *The Society of the Spectacle*, a text written over thirty years ago by the French Situationist critic Guy Debord. And though the Situationist International has tended to be sidelined as a prankish aberration, the surrealistic sloganeers of May '68, it was Debord's work – dour, epigrammatic but prophetic – that made possible Baudrillard's notion of the simulacrum. For Debord, the spectacle was late capitalism's crowning glory, alienation extended beyond its Marxist materialist base to a near-metaphysical state of being where reality is separated from itself in an image. 'But the critique that reaches the truth of the spectacle' he wrote, 'exposes it as the *visible* negation of life, as the nega-tion of life that has become visible.' It is no surprise, then, that certain film-makers should themselves undertake something approaching Debord's critique, aware of their medium's complicity but spurred on by a desire to distinguish cinema as some-how different from the extended reach of the spectacle incarnated in what we now call video-culture.

Noyce is no such director. The video-images in *Patriot Games* start from and call upon images attached to specific events, or rather images that have become events in themselves: the electronic warfare images of Operation Desert Storm. The film is haunted by these event images and its video images are their ghosts. These are images of war which, as a state of permanent emergency, extends into the living room via television and video. The spectacle has its own home front.

Aside from the fact that both films share an opening screen-engulfing squall of video static that rapidly resolves itself into camcorder images of a mob slaying and a farmyard slaughter respectively, Walter Hill's *Trespass* (1992) and Michael Haneke's *Benny's Video* (1992) beg to be considered as the recto and the verso of the con-temporary spectacle. In *Trespass* Hill plays with 'accidental' surveillance-by-camcorder (that descends directly from the George Holliday footage of Rodney King's assault) and turns a battle between two white treasure hunters and the drugs gang onto whose patch they have strayed into a fable of the entropic consequences of racial conflict. Claustrophobically staged in a warehouse on the point of collapse – an urban America in microcosm – the film has the tail-chasing energy of a farce which, if the video images didn't carry with them such grave connotations, might be funny.

The narrative is set in motion by the camcorder images of the killing of one of the gang by a rival dealer on whom they seek revenge. The images are captured by a young blood called 'Video', whose camcorder shots punctuate the film and serve a variety of functions. The principal of these is video-as-documentary-evidence, as the proof on which to base a slaying (or, by inference, a courtcase, an acquittal, a race riot, a retrial …). 'Video never lies,' says the black street kid with the camcorder, but the ghostly resonance of the images is contained by parallel deployments that accommodate the to-camera lip-synch peformance style of the promo-video and hence capitalise on the status of Ice Cube and Ice-T as rap icons. As *Cahiers du cinéma* pointed out, *Trespass* also signals 'the somewhat pretentious will to mix genre cinema with modernist cinema, to make as if, say, Raoul Walsh had seen a few Wim Wenders movies.' In this hybrid, the images of Rodney King in the hands of the LAPD (in their own way as epochal as the Zapruder frames of the Kennedy assassination) are called forth, but their iconic force is irretrievably compromised by Hill's concessions to the MTV aesthetic. Or could it be that the incorporation of a promo-video aesthetic, heralded by Mazursky's film, is problematised, Mazursky's innocent euphoria now haunted by the extra-cinematic images of the King video?

Set against the rap energy of *Trespass*, Haneke's film is a model of European art-cinema sobriety, shot through with a cultural pessimism that makes Wenders' habitual Ozu-invoking nostalgia appear celebratory. *Benny's Video* is the second of a projected trilogy of films, the first being *The Seventh Continent* (1988) and the third to be the story of a serial killer seen from the perspectives of his victims. They chart the director's account of 'the progressive emotional glaciation of my country'. Benny (Arno Frisch), a lonely Austrian adolescent left to his own devices by his well-to-do parents, shuts himself in his bedroom with his video equipment. The blinds permanently drawn, the outside world intruding only through a surveillance monitor on the wall, bookcases stacked with video cassettes, Benny views and re-views the tape that opens the film – a home video of a farmer's 'humane' killing of a pig with a shock-stick. Not a bloody death, only an overdose of electrical current; not a trace of the act's violence, just a squeal, then silence. Benny has stolen the instrument and, when he invites a girl of his own age back to his den to watch the tape, he tests the implement on her. With the first shot to her leg she collapses, screaming. A second shot to the head and silence. Benny's video has been recording throughout and it is these images that his parents see and to which they respond by covering up for their son, the mother taking him on holiday to Egypt while the father, unknown to Benny, disposes of the body.

'Video never lies' – but Benny's parents, faced with the evidence of their son's crimes, conceal the truth of his act from the law and the truth of their own act from their son. But Benny has them taped – this time aurally – and the film closes with a surveillance-camera image of the parents being arrested following Benny's confession. Benny's crime is the reflex action of an adolescent 'glaciated' by his immersion in the video-culture, and the film is as bleak and undemonstrative as Benny himself, this bourgeois European kid-with-a-camcorder, a video-somnambulist impassive as a Bressonian 'model'. If his sounds damning, Haneke intends it to be. For while in *Patriot Games* and *Trespass* video is the ghost of other images and other events, Haneke casts video as the very incarnation of the evil demon of images.

The numerous fascinations of *Benny's Video* stem from the cinematic values it counterposes as alternatives to the video culture and its discontents. For Haneke employs a deeply Bressonian 'cinematography' (a word used expressly in the director's statement), one marked by a refusal of spectacle, a concentration on gesture –

particularly in the exchange of money, highly reminiscent of *Pickpocket* and *L'Argent* – a mostly static camera and actors treated as 'models'. He also stages what must now be the paradigmatic Bressonian resolution, where the possibility of salvation comes only through imprisonment and the judgement of the law. Haneke's turning to Bresson says a lot about the director's own vision of cinematic values. It is as though Bresson provides the strategy necessary to exorcise the demon evoked by video as well as a model of cinematic restraint available to film-makers who cannot trust the audio-visual but wish fervently to demonstrate the special status of cinema within it, and somehow apart from it. From the opening images to the closing surveillance shots, the film reveals what it sees as the pernicious multiplicity of functions such technology makes possible – the camcorder that records the killing is also used to film mother and son's Egyptian holiday. While on one level it is a manifesto well in tune with current moral panics over video violence, and will no doubt be welcomed by those panicking as well as those propagating the panic, it also stands as a kind of limit-case of film's incorporation of video.

The surveillance camera represents the *ultima ratio* of the spectacle as defined by Debord, and cinema's incorporation of it has grown in parallel with its developments in scope and scale. From Lang's vision of domestic surveillance in *The Thousand Eyes of Dr Mabuse* (1960) to the interface between Hollywood and the Pentagon's 3Ci (control, command, communications, intelligence) operations portrayed in *Patriot Games*, surveillance has become the culminating state of the image, an essentially pornographic *mise-en-scène* in which we are both actors and, thanks to the camcorder, directors. The pornographic is understood here as the reflex response of voyeuristic participation that surveillance entails and whose founding example is pornography itself. Or, as Frederic Jameson has put it: 'Pornographic films are only the potentiation of films in general, which ask us to stare at the world as if it were a naked body.' It only remains for a Cronenberg or an Egoyan to take the next technologically feasible step (and so fulfill the dreams of paranoid fantasists everywhere); that of making a film that incorporates the technology of fibre-optic cameras in a generic hybrid of body-horror and modernist cinemas to concoct a narrative of internal surveillance.

The vision of videophilia that *Benny's Video* presents is qualitatively different from the cinéphilia of a previous age, with Benny's room an electronic nightmare of Plato's Cave. The severity of this vision and the moralistic position that underwrites it refuse to countenance the liberating possibility of video. In Haneke's schema the engagement with video represented in the work of someone like Sadie Benning cannot be acknowledged; video enslaves rather than liberates. But Haneke's is only one of the spaces permitted to video-in-film and beyond the polarities of video as either ghostly or demonic lie the more experimental hybridisations of Egoyan, Wenders, Godard. And beyond these …? Keep watching these spaces.

FROM THE MILLENNIAL IMAGE-MILL:
ON JOHAN GRIMONPREZ'S DIAL H-I-S-T-O-R-Y (NETH./FR. 1997)
AND JOSH OPPENHEIMER'S THE ENTIRE HISTORY OF THE
LOUISIANA PURCHASE (USA 1997)
ORIGINALLY PUBLISHED IN *ENTROPY* SUMMER 1998

'Once upon a time there were the mass media, and they were wicked, of course, and there was a guilty party. Then there were the virtuous voices that accused the criminals. And Art (ah, what luck!) offered alternatives for those who were not prisoners of the mass media. Well, it's all over. We have to start again from the beginning, asking one another what's going on.'
– Umberto Eco, 'The Multiplication of the Media', from *Faith in Fakes: Essays.*

The image-storm has settled in. No longer a freak condition, it has become the eye's climate. The forecast is severe, promising that the storm will become denser still. And we will enter it as naturally, as uncomplainingly, as slipping between the sheets.

Such a half-step of semiological despair, derived in the first place from Baudrillard, has become a reflexive move among those half in love with the condition they effect to despise. the ultimate condition of voyeurism has been arrived at. If one considers the extent to which politics has become the province of canny media mind-games, and the profound confusion between celebratory and confessional urges in the culture, as well as the suspicion with which conventional and fly-on-the-wall documentary forms are now viewed, then the realisation breaks that we are utterly caught in what Don Delillo has christened 'the millennial image-mill'. Joshua Oppenheimer's *The Entire History of the Louisiana Purchase* and Johan Grimonprez's *Dial H-I-S-T-O-R-Y* can each be considered as accounts of what it's like to inhabit this over-imaged yet visually undernourishing condition. And if the 'millennial' seems too commonplace a symptom and qualification in what follows – too bad. We're not quite there yet and it seems worthwhile thinking about both films in millennial terms because to do otherwise is simply denial.

We know that the hory sociological idea of media massification has recently been re-christened 'convergence', but it retains the same idea at base – that everything solid will surely melt into the digital ether, that many more channels doesn't automatically mean any more choice, other than for home-shoppers and fans of armchair gardening. So taking stock of this profusion of images suggests that the 'return' of the found-footage film is both vital and timely. It's not hard to imagine traditional documentarists, with their remit of investigative journalism, being shocked at the 'irresponsibility' of these films. But this would be to miss the point of them, operating, as they do, more in the sphere of imaginative analysis that marks the avant-garde or experimental tradition of 'found-footage' films. According to the definition William C. Wees offers, such films 'seek to interrupt the endless recirculation and unreflective reception of mass-media images' (From 'The Art and Politics of Found-Footage Films', in *Recycled Images*). The two seminal examples from the 'classic avant-garde' would be *Tom, Tom, The Piper's Son* (Ken Jacobs, USA, 1969-1971) and *A Movie* (Bruce Conner, USA, 1958). In the former, there is a play with the processes of spectatorship and perception alike, in the sense that Jacobs works with the image –

in this case, a short film by Billy Bitzer from 1905 – treating it for texture and motion through optical printing processes.

The images in the films by Oppenheimer and Grimonprez are frequently weighted with history – their own and that which they represent. Their grain and texture radiate history and it's in this quality that they approach the more perceptually-oriented work of Jacobs, but don't fully engage with the possibilities of exploring the image 'from within'. This is not a criticism, for both films seem to be aiming more at describing the state of living within an image-world whose history is that of 'the spectacle'. That said, Chris Petit's video *Dead TV* plays with the textural aspect of TV imagery through digital re-photography and avid editing. Oppenheimer and Grimonprez likewise treat both video and film with careful attention to the abstract textural qualities that re-photography can provide, whereas Jacobs and others of a Structuralist/Materialist bent such as Kurt Kren have explored fragments of narrative cinema and found footage for their perceptual qualities, foregrounding rhythm and duration – crucially, elements of editing.

Perhaps because Grimonprez and Oppenheimer both construct narratives – personal, literary and unreliable in tone – they approach their found-footage with an eye for collage and compilation, with a knowing appropriation of images and their recontextualisation. The issue of context is important as regards *Dial H-I-S-T-O-R-Y*, which emerges from the European fine-art, gallery context and has a life as a single screen monitor installation. That it should have such a life is hardly surprising; the question of context is central to contemporary art-practice and Grimonprez is working on the increasingly active borders between video-art and experimental film.

Where Grimonprez' video in a sense relies on its Delillo-derived voice-over commentary for its poetically jaundiced tone, Oppenheimer's approach is different, preoccupied as much by fabulation and the strange hinterlands of the American cult imagination. ...*Louisiana Purchase* provocatively mixes documentary with fiction, reconstruction with straight interviews, poetic sequences with 1950's American educational films. The film is 'fake documentary' – but no more or less than Nick Broomfield's extremely problematic *Kurt and Courtney*, where documentary tics disguise the fact that what the film really requires is the discursive playfulness of an Oppenheimer or, in absolutely world-class terms, a Kiarostami. Oppenheimer uses his account of the story of Mary-Ann Ward – one of alien abduction and self-invention – as a jumping-off point for a kaleidoscopic tour of the popular American imagination. And the story, as a pretext, has the ring of an all-too-plausible falsehood.

It is this conceptual wager that the film is based around, the idea that Mary-Ann Ward, although entirely imagined, is 'true' enough as fiction, to have persuaded the various assorted fringe dwellers – militiamen, ufologists, religious hysterics – to participate in the film and offer their perspectives on the case. Oppenheimer treats the stories as one, vast and collectively-hallucinated – one that simply never stops proliferating and that, with viral adaptability, absorbs all its counter-arguments within it, feeding on them and becoming stronger and madder still.

Neither film is directly concerned with the documentary truth *per se* but more with the iconic after-life of the images that constitute their found footage. Grimonprez searches for meaning through juxtaposition. Sometimes it's a matter of laying almost indecently banal music over horrific images. For example, in the functional, anonymous no-space of an airport terminal awash with blood lies a woman's red boot, an ugly puncture just below the knee-line. Generic muzak seeps over the image. There emerges across the film a virtual history of the 'generations' of TV, in the sense that audio-visual technicians talk of copies taken from a master-tape as being of first and second 'generations'.

There is also another take on the word at work here, however – the idea that historical generations identify their iconic images in part through the property of their 'grain'. Roughly speaking, this would break down as 1960s and 1970s TV having used film, with the 1980s and 1990s seeing video becoming the standard. The continuity across these generations that Grimonprez identifies is the most disturbing aspect of the film, that of the mass-media's collusion with terrorism, and vice versa. In *Dial H-I-S-T-O-R-Y*'s account of airliner-hijacking, the media scrum set up their long lenses and train them on Revolution Airstrip in Jordan, waiting for the planes to explode, as though the event were another sudden-death penalty shoot-out or Grand Prix pile-up. By playing fast and loose between these generations of images and by explicitly focusing on the murderous reciprocity of the media/terrorist relationship, Grimonprez takes us further into the image-world where reality is inseparable from its image – 'Nothing happens until it's consumed' (Delillo again). And the place where these images nest is in the home. The living room has become the home front in the media war and, in many ways, for all its attempted irony, *Dial H-I-S-T-O-R-Y* secretes a sense of deep disturbance at this state of affairs. This, after all, is the world of the second-degree. And it burns the eyes.

ASYLUM
DIR: CHRIS PETIT & IAIN SINCLAIR UK 2000
ORIGINALLY PUBLISHED IN *FILM COMMENT* JULY/AUGUST 2000

When *Asylum* screens on British TV it'll either have viewers hammering at their sets and wondering if there's an electrical storm in their neighbourhood, or scratching their heads at the labyrinthine pseudo-sci fi narrative. Describing itself as 'a film about exile, memory, madness', *Asylum* is the third collaboration between the British film-maker/writer Chris Petit and the novelist, essayist and poet Iain Sinclair. Continuing their exploration of marginalised cultural figures, the duo has extended the distressed, multi-media textures of their previous collaboration, *The Falconer* (1999), to create a piece that, while conceived for British TV, pushes at the limits of what television currently deems to be aesthetically acceptable. Not for nothing does the film carry the subtitle *The Final Commission*. Working with a heavily textured, multi-layered tapestry of formats — re-filmed digital video, Super 8mm and multimedia graphic design (courtesy of graphic artist Dave McKean) and set against Bruce Gilbert's densely worked sound-design — *Asylum* is a paradoxical puzzle-film, an essay on cultural memory that looks to the future in its use of technology while expressing doubts about what Sinclair describes as 'the over imaged, over-informed wastelands opened up by the new information technology'.

The film opens at some nominal future date, 'Year Zero + 14'. A rampant virus has been created 'in the protein soup of bad television with the sole aim of destroying its own memory — the last cultural traces'. A researcher named Kaporal (voiced by Petit as though reciting a suicide note) is brought out of retirement to make sense of the remaining fragments of an abandoned, pre-viral project called 'The Perimeter Fence'. These scraps of footage detail an assignment on which a young female sound-recordist, Agent Matthews (Emma Matthews, the film's editor), is dispatched by a shadowy information-broker (Sinclair). Matthews is instructed to track down the writers Michael Moorcock, Ed Dorn and James Sallis, who Sinclair describes as 'a kind of illuminati, who hold on to the cultural memory of the race'. A previous project, erased from TV's memory files and known as 'The Falconer' (this isn't a film that's afraid to tread the fine line between self-reflexivity and solipsism) had led to the disappearance and presumed death of the previous researcher, a photographer named Françoise Lacroix. It transpires that Agent Matthews wants to track down Lacroix and reunite her with her twin — a course of action, Sinclair warns, that could result in time itself being thrown out of joint.

As an example of 'digital film-making', *Asylum* is light-years ahead of the Dogme 95 school of kinetic realism or the camcorder-horror of *The Blair Witch Project*. If it's close to anything recognizably generic then it's working away at the cracks between the ludic masquerades of fake documentary and the layered essayistic digressions of Chris Marker's *Sans Soleil* and *Level 5*. Call it 'discursive digital metafiction', if you like. *Asylum* is the closest British TV has come to producing a virally vital, circuit-burning piece of digital film-making which is as much about 'noise' as it is about 'signal'. Interference is the aesthetic here. The film-makers are working with the notion that TV transmission works in the collective unconscious in the same way as synapses do in the brain, transmitting signals across a void, and *Asylum* is out to scramble your synapses. In this respect Petit and Sinclair have taken the work of *The Falconer*, whose aesthetic owed much to the highly sophisticated image-text relationships of the graphic novel, and extended its reach into the television set itself – as a domestic object that's always 'on' even when it's 'off' and as a regulated flow of time, an eternal TV present-tense. This approach was evident in *negative space*, Petit's last video-essay for BBC2, where he was working with the space of the frame, frequently breaking it down into two juxtaposed polaroid-style squares within which was run re-filmed footage from classic films. *negative space* was equally concerned with memory – as incarnated by the key figures of Manny Farber and R. W. Fassbinder – and technology, chiefly video and film. But *Asylum* takes the formal approach further. It's as much about TV as it is about literature. TV as a machine for forgetting but also as an aquarium of memory, a mind-screen of repressed cultural consciousness that's given form in bubbling eruptions of sound and artifacted lags of digital imagery.

The look and structure of *Asylum* have been arrived at through the working methods that Petit and Sinclair have adopted since their first collaboration on *The Cardinal and the Corpse* (1992), a far more conventional TV piece, and have benefited from the metafictional strategy of overlapping real people with fictional surrogates. Theirs is almost a home-video aesthetic, with Petit and Sinclair filming (and refilming) when they can with Super 8 and domestic video outside of a strict professional schedule. For each film shot in this way – *camcorder-stylo* style – they generate a huge amount of footage that overlaps across projects. They don't shoot to fit a story but find the story in what they've shot, weaving *post-facto* metafictions into what effectively becomes 'found footage'. Hence the attention given to a labyrinthine narrative structure in which several tenses overlap, time shifts across cuts and stories vie, overlap and dissolve. In *The Falconer* the object that represented this metafictional method, its *mise-en-abyme*, was a mysterious whalebone box supposedly possessed of occult powers. It figured across the film as a shape-shifting fiction-detonator, a little bomb of story. In *Asylum* the same role is played by 'the virus'. The science fiction narrative in *Asylum* is an *X–Files* conceit that's also a nod to Moorcock, who was involved in writing and editing the influential science fiction magazine *New Worlds*, where he published James Sallis and J. G. Ballard, among others.

But the concern with TV and new technologies as 'viral' is productively paradoxical. It is 'the virus' that generates the film's narratives, just as it is the new technologies of digital video and Avid editing that makes *Asylum*'s aesthetic 'otherness' possible. Some of the most interesting examples of what one might loosely term recent 'multimedia' work have also been dealing with the issue of cultural memory. So Godard's *Histoire(s) du cinéma* series and Chris Marker's recent CD Rom *Immemory* are works that can legitimately be set alongside *Asylum*, as well as Petit's recent work. What's at stake in all this work is an engagement with a literary, cinéphile inheritance by artist film-makers who have, through age, temperament, circumstance or sheer exploratory zeal, chosen to work with technologies that enable their essayistic and analytical tendencies to be brought to bear on their own memory files.

There's more than a touch of JLG in Petit's recent work; the use of what one might call 'primary sources' – film excerpts in *negative space*, CCTV footage in his 1993 video-essay *Surveillance* – that are commented upon discursively and treated almost as jewels of 'found footage'. Equally, Petit has admitted to an interest in including the post-production process as part of the finished film. Given that *Asylum* – like much of Petit's recent work, extending back to his mordantly comic essay on the paranoid crime novel, *Thriller* (1994] – is a film that's truly been made in the editing suite, there is plenty of evidence of the Avid digital editing system being pushed for all its worth, until steam comes out of its circuitry.

As forward-looking as *Asylum* is in terms of form and technology, there's a moment when the limitations of its structure come up against the complexities of its subject matter. The poet Ed Dorn is shown railing against the Western military engagement with Serbia over the war in Kosovo. For Dorn, Madeleine Albright and Richard Holbroke's diplomatic mission was about erasing the Serb's sense of their history, seeking to put off-limit their will to escape 'the Muslim yoke' (Dorn's words). In Dorn's account, the Serbs were coerced into forgetting – '[they] don't get to remember the field of Kosovo'. He follows up by stating that 'the legitimate motives of the past [are] not being brought forward with the respect they deserve', a state-ment that the film-makers extract as a refrain for their film. This is a specious strat-egy that Petit and Sinclair should expect arguments about. It reduces the equally compelling counter-interpretation that the Serbian leadership (ditto the Croatians under Tudjman) actively sought to revitalise an ugly brand of nationalism by playing precisely on 'the cultural memory of the race'. This isn't solely a point about political details. Perhaps the argument that the film alludes to here – only alludes to, never addresses directly – is that, in a culture of short-term memory, the political objective correlative that often takes shape is a warped and blood-thirsty nationalism which seeks precisely to invoke 'the cultural memory of the race'. This sequence betokens opportunism on behalf of the film-makers and a political complacency that isn't made up for by the acuteness with which they address their 'other subject' of cultural memory-loss. But, of course, it isn't 'other' at all, cultural amnesia and political oppor-tunism are intimately linked. Here, Petit and Sinclair run the risk of replicating one of the features of the 'bad television' at which the film takes aim – the reductiveness of the soundbite-driven interview. That they do so is symptomatic of the limits of their approach. Visually poetic and polemical in intent, *Asylum* can't extend to accom-modate argument. And a subject like Balkan nationalism requires a greater discursive focus than this film can manage. Maybe the comparison with Marker is not entirely accurate after all. The wise old owl would have done history the service of arguing the other account as well.

PROFESSION: REPORTER
ON JOHN SERGEANT'S THE BLUE SUMMER (UK 1999)
ORIGINALLY PUBLISHED IN *COIL* 1998

'You deal in words and images. Fragile things.'
  – Robertson to Locke in *The Passenger* (Michelangelo Antonioni, 1975)

I have an image of John Sergeant, documentary researcher and creator of the fascinating, ambitious and moving essay-film *The Blue Summer* as a modern-day David
Locke. The troubled journalist of Antonioni's *The Passenger*, Locke worked in TV,
shooting documentaries in trouble-spots. Faced with an insoluble sense of existential
dread, he steps through the screen and takes on another man's life. Bill, Sergeant's
fictional hero – unimaged, an absent voice whose decline into mania is documented
by a series of letters to a woman named Sarah – could be Locke's son. A traveller
with a camera and a need to explain, Bill's disappearance is investigated by another
voice, the film-maker's. This epistolary device is further refracted by it being Sarah
who often reads Bill's letters and the resulting exchange of identities and voices
creates an intimate address that takes in a wide variety of tones. Alternately rhap-
sodic and lamenting, analytical and cerebral, Sergeant gives Bill the voice of an urban
romantic going to pieces in the countryside, sunk in theory, haunted by images of
twentieth century decline and terrified by millennial thoughts. Bill's decline delivers
much along the way, interspersed with an encyclopaedic assault of found-footage
which threads through reports from Bill's country retreat on the border between
England and Wales.

These sequences virtually invent a new genre – new to me anyway – the
'camcorder pastoral'. Domestic video is so thoroughly associated with the intimate
and the interior that to see it used to shoot dramatic landscapes which, at least
initially, are treated with unapologetically Romantic resonance is to be impressed at
the nerve of the film-maker. But the pastoral tone darkens as Bill begins to uncover
details and characters within the rural life around him. 'Psycho Billy' the local butcher
with an offal factory in his home. Johnny Century the local squire, a crystal-planting,
junkie-philanderer. Has Sergeant met these people? Or has Bill invented them? It
becomes hard to tell. Bill, perhaps not unlike Sergeant, has a reporter's sensitivity
to siginifcant minutaie – at the local pub he discovers that the SAS have a training
ground nearby and that the local hunt employs them as beaters. He also learns of
the legend of John of Kent, a local friar who, according to conflicting accounts, was
either an occultist or a man of letters from Chepstow. From paranoia to old myths
and back again, fact feeds fiction in Bill's mind. The strand of digression that are Bill's
letters begins to reveal structure, even as their author unravels. Just as in the use of
his footage Sergeant contrasts and counterpoints, so in his commentary – which is a
real piece of writing, only occasionally sounding like it was written more for the page
than the screen – Sergeant finds stories that comment on one another. The digressive structure also accommodates the sketch-like edge of some of the sequences.
There is a hilarious, hyper-fast commentary on pop-culture's habit of instantly recy-
cling itself. Speed-talking over a lurid Formula One video-game, a breathless Bill com-
mentates as 'the first 90s revival revival, the third 80s revival and the seventeenth

60s revival' all make a photo-finish at the Millennium Raceway.

Sergeant's achievement in *The Blue Summer* is to unite tone with form. The form is that of the essay-film, one which has seen something of a renaissance in British independent film-making in recent years. *The Blue Summer* joins Patrick Keiller's *London* (1994) and *Robinson in Space* (1997), Andrew Kotting's first-person travelogue *Gallivant* (1997), and Chris Petit and Iain Sinclair's *The Falconer* (1997) but for scope, ambition and sheer feeling it eclipses them all. Its tone is a little harder to pin down. As purposefully digressive as any of Keiller's work, its interest lies in how it has taken, extended and deepened what might be termed the 'English Romantic Dystopian' mode. What do I mean by this phrase? It's a way of feeling towards a name for a sensibility that unites figures such as Patrick Keiller, Chris Petit and J. G. Ballard. *The Blue Summer* explores a cosmology of doubt, of the centre no longer holding, of collapse and decay both cultural and personal. In one sequence, Bill writes about images he encountered while in Uganda – a bus station, burnt out and scattered with decomposing vehicles, a wrecked airliner lying a short distance away, nature overtaking both sites. 'For a European' Bill narrates 'a direct encounter with such things can result in a kind of poetic shock from which reverberate profound, half-conscious doubts about the solidity and reality of the concrete future.'

It is a Ballardian landscape and a key motif in the film, one that finds visual echoes elsewhere, particularly in the gradually darkening portrait of the English countryside which Sergeant employs to represent Bill's deepening despair. If the 'Ballardian' can be simplified to such an image of fascinating and troubling technological decreptitude, it is one that reaches back – to Walter Benjamin's reading of Paul Klee's *Angelus Novus*, of every history of culture being simultaneously a history of barbarism, of the fleshy vulnerability at the heart of 'progress'. The Soft Apocalypse. If the 'dystopian' is a vision of technological failure, the 'romantic' is in its being perceived and read as the landscape onto which a contemporary sense of self is projected. Sergeant has worked to extend this visual/literary register to include emotional warmth and in *The Blue Summer* there is an underlying lament that is as old as the English hills, one that sees the hope of some 'human' values as ever-receding in the face of rushing technological progress. But to call Bill, or Sergeant, a humanist would be akin, these days, to spitting in his face.

The most ambitious element of *The Blue Summer* resides in the treatment of its found footage. Sergeant's professional career as an assistant producer and researcher for television documentaries makes him a professional archive-scoper, a viewer and sampler of the image-repertoire of the late-twentieth century. *The Blue Summer* could be seen as a kind of occupational therapy , a personal reckoning with the images of our recent past. When the images we see are those of redundant technology, airliners grounded and decaying, Bill comments that 'modernity's surviving images were carrying a new kind of aura, they were acting as carrier-images of a new kind of collective memory.' And Sergeant approaches these images as carriers. Given that much of his found-footage charts Western visions of technological progress from the end of World War Two onwards, he sees planned obsolescence at work even within the images themselves. Nothing dates as fast as the future, except maybe visions of the future.

'The Sixties were rain on concrete perpendiculars': these were the years of the post-war technocratic elites who created the dominant urban landscapes of western Europe. The ideology of the time, modernism, foundered on its central obsession with a utopian idea of progress. But the technocratic elite has returned, now in the guise of the scientist. Whether as all-purpose populariser (Steve Jones, Richard Dawkins) or as a repository of wisdom on the imminent revolution in bio-genetics, 'the scientist' is, once again, a figure of awe, the impartial imparter of life-transforming wonders that are truly terrifying. The scientist reassures us that our new scientific potentialities do indeed represent 'progress'. But, as Sergeant shows, we've heard these reassurances before. So how to face the radical transformations of technology – digital and bio-genetic – with equanimity when the societies that they will transform are so atomised, unstable and anxious? The portrait that Sergeant constructs is one of a technological utopia turned sour, overarching political ideologies evaporating, the market triumphant, A national decline X-rayed through the infrastructure – aviation, road-building, telecommunications. The Blue Summer is neither a satire nor a mockery of the dream of technological progress, rather it wonders whether the fascination with the decline of faith in this dream was part of the dream in the first place.

Sergeant compiles, sometimes in loose essayistic rhythms, sometimes in tighter montages, an assembly of cultural debris from the Sixties to the present-day. In a virtuoso compilation of rocket disasters, he goes for a troublingly full-on display of multi-million dollar technological malfunction. It's a sequence that's of a part with the fetishisation of catastrophe that informs Johann Grimonprez's Dial H-I-S-T-O-R-Y. If, on one hand, Sergeant comments on technology and the technocratic priesthood, he counters this with a fascinating take on the contemporary British art scene. Or, rather, two takes. At first, Bill considers the while scene as vibrant, exciting, explora-tory and open. Art as the new rock 'n' roll. There's a degree of truth in this. Second time around and the approach is harder, more critical. Where's the poltics, the sense of commitment and outrage in such self-promoting work, Bill demands? In this other perspective, the whole art scene is a racket co-opted by advertising and self-mythologisation. To which any artist would shrug and say 'What's new?' Together, these accounts add up to an entertaining and trenchant mini-essay on the modern economy of what used to be called symbolic values.

From art to the media, Bill narrates the digital future for us: 'Entertainment is a lullaby. Satellites are positioned, cooporations conglomerated. The Emperors know that the entire will of a nation can be shaped by its own view of reality. The imperial impulse marches on.' The future is a mediascape so overloaded as to be excitingly diverse or terrifyingly fragmented. One has the sense these are the thoughts of a man strongly informed by his own experiences in the media. He is aware, having reconstructed an account of history using its own images that 'most of our collec-tive memory is made up of screens'. And he wonders what will become of our 'secret memory'. Whether the most intimate and personal narratives of our lives will become the most reliable indices of reality. Hence the search for Bill's 'secret memory'. Here the film becomes truly ambitious in its structure. The Blue Summer constructs an essayistic rhythm of thought and feeling. 'Leaving our parents behind, we are following our children through the screen and disappearing into wonderland.' An elegy for the future.